WHITETAIL STRATEGIES

A No-Nonsense Approach To
Successful Deer Hunting

by

Peter Fiduccia

Published 2006 by Stoeger Publishing Company
17603 Indian Head Highway, Suite 200
Accokeek, Maryland 20607

BK0329
International Standard Book No: 0-88317-279-8
Library of Congress Control Number: 2003106892

Manufactured in the United States of America.

Distributed to the book trade
and to the
sporting goods trade by:
Stoeger Industries
17603 Indian Head Highway, Suite 200
Accokeek, Maryland 20607
301-283-6300
Fax: 301-283-6986
www.stoegerindustries.com

Cover image: Paul Brown
Back cover images: (left) Mike Searles; (right) Peter Fiduccia
Illustrations and drawings: Frank Sansavera

About the Author

Born in Brooklyn, New York in 1946, Peter's first deer hunt was in a small upstate town in Putnam county, New York during the fall of 1965. He has ardently hunted the white-tailed deer across North America ever since. Peter is a nationally recognized authority on the white-tailed deer and is a regularly featured speaker on the subject of hunting whitetails for the National Rifle Association, Safari Club International and many sportsmen shows across the country.

Peter has written hundreds of how-to articles about tactics for hunting the white-tailed deer for <u>Sports Afield, Petersen's</u> and other outdoor magazines. During his 31 years of hunting whitetails, Peter has taken twelve record-book class animals with bow and gun. But, he strongly believes, "any deer a hunter takes is a trophy -- spike or fourteen pointer. It's each hunt's memories that should be entered in books -- not the size of the deer's antlers."

Peter, his wife, Kate, and their son, Cody, make their home in a quaint mountain hamlet in upstate New York. They also spend "family time" at their mountain retreat in Vail, Colorado. Kate is also a seasoned big game hunter. Their son, Cody, born December 9th, 1988 already has the "deer hunting" embers slowly burning in his being -- with the right guidance and a genuine desire from Cody, Peter & Kate hope to nurture the embers into a brightly burning deer hunting fire of passion.

Contents

Chapter 1 - ANATOMY, BIOLOGY AND BEHAVIOR 15

Chapter 2 - ABOUT THE WHITETAIL 23

Chapter 3 - THE HUNTING GENE 39

Chapter 4 - THE   C + PT X C = CS   THEORY 43

Chapter 5 - WIND AND WHITETAILS 51

Chapter 6 - FOUL WEATHER BUCKS 57

Chapter 7 - THE RUT 72

Chapter 8 - THE REAL DIRT ON SCRAPES AND RUBS 93

Chapter 9 - THE SMELL OF SUCCESS 111

Chapter 10 - BODY LANGUAGE OF DEER 125

Chapter 11 - DEAD DEER TALK 135

Chapter 12 - HOW TO USE DEER CALLS EFFECTIVELY 141

Chapter 13 - RATTLING STRATEGIES 163

Chapter 14 - USING DECOYS TO BAG WHITETAILS 199

Chapter 15 - BACK YARD BUCKS 215

Chapter 16 - WEEKEND DEER HUNTER 223

Chapter 17 - SCORING & FIELD JUDGING ANTLERS 229

Chapter 18 - HOW OLD WAS HE & WHAT DID HE WEIGH? ... 247

Chapter 19 - VENISON FOR THE TABLE 257

Dedication

This book is dedicated to my wife Kate and, to my son Cody. I pray he will enjoy and cherish the outdoor experiences I hope to share with him, especially hunting whitetails. Also, to my parents, Joseph & Lucy Fiduccia and to my father-in-law David Beekman. And, of course, to you -- my readers and viewers -- without whom I would not be able to do what I do for a living. I'm very thankful for all your support over the years.

Acknowledgements

As far back as I can remember, I have always wanted to be a writer. To see my name in print. It has been a perpetual burning desire. I had to work hard at accomplishing the goal I set for myself. I never took a formal course in writing, in fact, I just barely passed English 101!

What I did have were people that cared about helping me. The biggest motivating force in my life both personal and professional is my wife Kate. Her gentle urging in 1983 for me to, "share my knowledge about hunting whitetail deer" by writing an article still remains vivid in my mind and heart. In those days, without her constant editorial assistance, the articles I wrote would not have been as grammatically articulate! Kate's undeviating encouragement, support, patience and guidance is the reason I am where I am today.

Other people who tutored and helped me along the way include Paul Keesler, who published my first article in his magazine -- the <u>New York Sportsman</u>. Tom Halsey, who gave me the opportunity to take a 28-page written proposal about a locally produced outdoor cable television program and turn it into a nationally syndicated television series which has run for eleven years to date. Larry Rickard, Lamar Underwood, Paul Fuller, Vin Sparano, Glenn Sapir and Jay Cassell, a good friend, a talented editor and writer who taught me the value of having professional patience. And, finally to Terry McDonell, who fulfilled a long-held dream of mine by including me on the masthead of the most prestigious of all outdoor magazines -- <u>Sports Afield</u>.

To all these people I owe a debt of gratitude for their unselfishness, their counsel, and the space in which my words were heard, seen or printed in their perspective forms of media. Their efforts are greatly appreciated. I think of them often.

If it weren't for these people, I might have taken to heart the well-meant criticism of my high school teacher and would have not pursued a career in writing. Until today, I distinctly recall the notation written in bright red ink at the top of the first page of an assignment by my 12th grade english teacher, Mr. Callahan. The paper was about what I would like to be doing ten years down the road. I wrote about how I wanted to hunt white-tailed deer and share my experiences and skills by penning articles and books about the subject. The comment written in bold red ink on the paper was short and direct - - "Judging by this, I don't think you'll ever be much of a hunter, and you'll certainly never be a writer." Mr. Callahan was wrong! Desire, persistence, confidence and hard work will overcome most anything.

Author's Introduction

As early as I can remember, I have always been fascinated by wild animals. While growing up in Brooklyn, I traveled to Staten Island (a borough that was far less inhabited than it is today), to see and study the habits of wild animals like pheasants, opossum, ducks and the like in the wilds of Latterett Park and Golf Course.

In high school, I borrowed my dad's car and drove to Sterling Forest in New York to fish, hunt and just observe deer and nature. So this book is a culmination of more than thirty years of experience about observing and hunting white-tailed deer.

I have spent my entire adult life hunting, studying and videotaping whitetail deer at every opportunity. The information I relay in this book is based on those experiences. And, although an overwhelming majority of the information in this book comes from my own experiences, some is compiled from men -- legends in the study of white-tailed deer (Severinghaus, Atkeson, Dawson, Gazin, Matthew, Simpson, Romer and others) who have studied the white-tailed deer their entire lives. I use this biological information gratefully and with admiration.

MID-NOVEMBER

The sun is rising and it's warming rays press softly against my
face.
I've been sitting , looking & listening, but not a whitetail trace.
As the sun rises over the mountain top, the woods begin to stir.
An owl returns to sleep as a chipmunk grooms its fur.
The sun reaches an angle which makes the woods glitter.
And the distracting sounds of squirrels start to make my
patience whither!

I change my position very slow, trying not to cause a sound,
When a black crow cries its warning, "Watch It! There is a
stranger around!"
As I lean my back on the tree during this
day in November,

My mind begins to wander & think of things I love
to remember.
The leaves in all their splendid color have already fallen down.
They're red, yellow, orange and brown as they lie scattered on
the forest's ground.

My ears strain for the slightest sound, my eyes are playing too.
Carefully scanning the forest searching for a give-away clue.
It's mid-November and bitter cold and the sun is just about
risin'.
And I'm in the woods hunting deer which isn't very surprizin.'

Suddenly, a buck appears, holding his rack aloft.
Trying to remain calm, I reach for my bow
breathing ever so soft.

I put the pin on his chest and come to full draw.
The arrow's impact shatters the silent air --
and moments later the buck lies on the forest floor . . .
Not trying to go anywhere.

I approach him cautiously, not really

believing he belongs to me.

Even as I count the points on his rack,

I contemplate the long drag back...

I can't believe I have counted ten --

I'd better relax and count 'em again.

Then I realize I've got eleven months to go -- before it's mid-

November and bitter cold,

And the sun is rising and I am growing old . . . .

P.J.F.

Chapter 1

ANATOMY, BIOLOGY AND BEHAVIOR
OF THE WHITE-TAILED DEER

The modern day whitetail deer got its meager beginnings millions of years ago. Probably, right alongside of man's ancestor — *Australopithecus*. The Tertiary and Quaternary cervids (which scientists depict as having extruded canine teeth) made their slow and deliberate assent up the evolutionary ladder. During that period of its development (the Eocene period) it was grouped in the order of *Artiodactlys* — even-toed ungulates. A mammal whose body weight is maintained by the third and fourth metapodials — or toes.

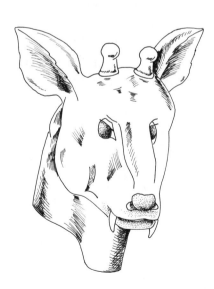

One of the earliest of the deer's ancestors had canine teeth

15

It continued to further evolve during the Miocene Epoch era (Viret 1961) when many of its family group began to become extinct. Other members of the order went on to become breeding stock of today's modern day *artiodactlys* (Pilgram 1941a, Simpson 1945, Romer 1966) which include the *Suina* (pigs, peccaries and hippopotamuses all with four "functional" toes, cannon bones, bunodont molar teeth, canine tusks and simple stomachs) and the *Ruminantia* which contains the cud chewers.

Modern day ruminants most often have two "functional" toes, metapodials melded as cannon bones, complex selenodont molars, upper incisors that are smaller or missing, canines that are inadequate or at best slightly enlarged in males, and compound stomachs.

Today, all families of deer including the whitetail, mule deer, blacktail deer, elk, moose, reindeer, caribou and others are known as *Cervidaes*. They are classified scientifically as phylum Chordata which means they have backbones. They are in the class of Mammalia; because they are warm blooded, have four chambered hearts, have hair on their bodies, give birth to their young alive, and have mammary glands to feed their young.

Since their meager beginnings some 5 million years ago, when deer were no larger than rabbits, they have evolved into an animal that has learned to survive and adapt by being able to run swiftly through thicket or field, to leap without hesitation, effortlessly over an 8-foot obstacle if necessary, and to sneak past a predator (man or animal) without ever alerting the pursuer to their presence.

The earliest deer was no larger than a modern rabbit

16

The entire family of *Cervidae* includes four (4) subfamilies, seventeen (17) genera and about thirty-seven (37) sub-species of deer found world-wide (Ellerman and Morrison-Scott 1951, Cabrera 1961, Koopman 1967). In North and Central America, there are about thirty subspecies of *Odocoileus virginianus*. In the United States and Canada, there are about seventeen sub-species of the white-tailed deer.

The four sub-species of white-tailed deer hunted in the United States include *Odocoileus virginianus* — white-tailed deer, *Odocoileus hemionus columbianus* — the Columbia Blacktail deer, *Odocoileus hemionus sitkensis* — the sitka black-tailed deer, and *Odocoileus virginianus couesi*, the Coues' whitetail deer.

I mention this because today many trophy and non-trophy hunters alike are interested in collecting at least one of each of these deer. In fact, Safari Club International (SCI) and other record keeping organizations each have separate categories under which each of these different sub-families are listed. They also offer awards to hunters who bag one trophy size buck of each sub-family (i.e.: Grand Slam of Deer). Because this interests some whitetail hunters, I am including information about each sub-family, some characteristic information, distribution and exactly what minimum measurements Boone & Crockett and Safari Club International assign to each to consider entry into their record books.

The distribution of these five groups of deer ranges throughout North America. The white-tailed deer, however, is the most widely distributed deer. It is found from the deep south swamps of Florida, north to northern conifer forests of Maine, along the river bottoms of the Rockies, in the shrubs and cactus deserts of Texas, to the frigid northern mountains of Alberta, Canada. And, each year, its range is growing. In fact, whitetails are now quite common in the Rocky Mountain states of Idaho, Montana, Wyoming and Colorado. Where only a decade or so ago, the whitetail's presence in Wyoming and, especially, Colorado was almost unheard of.

It is widely agreed by most that the white-tailed deer is the primary big game animal throughout North America. The whitetail provides millions of deer hunters a challenging recreational opportunity, food and a chance to hang a trophy on the den wall. The white-tailed deer is truly the most versatile big game animal. With little effort, it can make its home almost anywhere. With hardly little more effort — it can even adapt to living (and has) to areas that are inhospitable.

Many Rocky Mountain deer hunting guides in the United States and Canada testify to the fact that over the last few decades the whitetail deer has methodically expanded its range from the thick covered river bottoms and drainages of these states, where they have plenty of food, water and protection from snow and wind, into the less hospitable mountainous regions. One would think the heavy accumulated snow packs of the mountains, which can accumulate to a dozen feet or more in most years, would restrain the whitetail's ability to find enough food, water, and shelter to survive in these harsh conditions. To the contrary, however, the whitetail has not only learned to survive in the mountains of the Rockies, it has adapted so well it is now multiplying and continuing to expand its range even further into the remoteness of the Rocky Mountains — an apparent testimony of how well this Cervidae has evolved in its never ending struggle to reproduce and survive.

No matter where the whitetail calls home, it easily learns to adapt to the conditions and terrain of its range. It has learned how to live within city limits, and how to tolerate and adapt to man's land-use programs (baseball fields, parks and county picnic areas) and man's encroachment with the construction of suburban malls, developments and the like.

In fact, the whitetail actually benefits from this type of human infiltration. As man cuts forests he inadvertently opens them up to second growth, grasslands, pasture and, unknowingly, he creates ideal habitat for the whitetail — who is a creature of the edges and new growth.

In some instances, even clear cutting can be a benefit. In the case of the whitetail, clear cutting of mature forests encourages new growth. The new succulent tender growth is highly sought after by deer. As the new growth develops it provides the landscape with new plants, brush, and second growth trees. All of which increase the carrying capacity for whitetails. So despite how man hunts the whitetail or what man does to alter the deer's environment it seems the white-tailed deer has adapted and gone on to thrive throughout its range in North America.

However, there are some characteristic differences in whitetails that are specific to the deer according to the geographic region in which they live. These differences appear in the color of the deer's hair, the overall body size and weight, the height and length of the deer and its antler size.

This was brought home to me first hand in 1987 when I shot my first south Texas buck, a 14-pointer, in Sarita, Texas. The buck was aged to be 8 1/2 years old. The rack had a Boone & Crockett score of 171 1/8 points. Yet the deer field-dressed at only 98 pounds! Many people who see the head mount of this buck often remark that, "It looks like a rack mounted on a doe!"

The fact is, the buck was killed in the deep south region of Texas — not far from Mexico. Deer of that region are classified as the subspecies *Odocoileus virginianus texanus*, as are Mexico's deer. They are among twelve subspecies of whitetails with the most prominent being *Odocoileus virginianus couesi* and the Key deer, *Odocoileus virginianus clavium*, found in the Florida Keys and are smaller than other whitetails found in North America.

These deer have come to evolve this way for obvious or perhaps not so obvious reasons. Living their lives in an area that is hot and arid for six months of the year, and warm the remaining six months of the year, they have made some necessary adjustments to their bodies via the evolutionary process of survival of the fittest. They are smaller in their overall body size (Keys deer rarely exceed 28 inches at the shoulder and are rarely more than 80 pounds in live weight), the hair on their coats is not as long as other deer, even the ears, face and tails are all smaller than normal size deer. Why?

Adaptation. Deer living in areas where the hot climatic temperatures are often oppressive, like Mexico, the Florida Keys and South Texas, do not need to be as large in body size as their northern cousins who must undergo the ever-changing weather conditions of the four seasons — and, mainly severe winter climates. The "northern" body characteristics would in fact hinder deer that live in these hot, dry areas of the country. A larger body would mean the deer would have to take in more food and, more importantly, water to fuel, nourish and cool itself. Scarce commodities in the hot oppressive heat of South Texas and Mexico and even in some parts of the Florida Keys. In addition, hides with thicker longer hairs would not act as efficiently to keep the deer properly cool — and so on. So, Mother Nature — perfect in her design, has altered these deer over time to live in these arid, torrid regions in order to help them survive better.

This also accounts for why deer living in the inhospitable severe winter climates typical of northern Maine (*Odocoileus virginianus borealis*) or British Columbia (*Odocoileus virginianus ochrourus)* have larger bodies and thicker coats. True, the larger body requires more food, but then it can provide itself with more fat reserve which acts as additional insulation against the cold. Obviously, the thicker coat also helps it through the extreme climates of these regions as well.

The subspecies of deer residing in the northernmost portions or latitudes of the country are mostly *Odocoileus virginianus borealis* and *Odocoileus virginianus dacotensis.* Mother Nature has genetically engineered this subspecies of the whitetail deer to be its largest subspecies — with most specimens standing 40 inches high at the shoulder. In comparison, the whitetails of Texas stand about 34 to 36 inches at the shoulder. In the northern regions of North America, the length of an adult male deer may reach 95 inches from the tip of the nose to the tail. Whitetails found in the central portions of the United States, generally reach a length of 72 inches, with southwestern deer reaching only 55 inches in total length.

Interestingly, the antler size and dimensions of mature whitetail bucks depend mostly on age, diet and genetic inheritance. Although geographic conditions also come into play, too. The largest whitetail buck ever recorded was a Minnesota whitetail taken in 1926. The buck dressed out at 402 pounds and had an estimated live weight of 511 pounds. Another buck taken in the northern tier of neighboring Wisconsin in 1924, had a field dressed weight of 386 pounds, which gave it an estimated live weight of 491 pounds. Additionally, another Wisconsin buck which was taken in 1941, dressed out at 378 pounds which gave it an estimated live weight of 481 pounds. Even today, it is not unusual, especially in Maine, Saskatchewan and the Adirondack Mt. of NY for bucks to have a field dressed weight of 200 to 250 pounds.

Basically, one needs to remember the primary deer found throughout North America is the whitetail deer (*Odocoileus virginianus*). All other names mentioned above are just subspecies and were given their names to describe the locale in which they live and physical characteristic traits of that particular deer.

Present-day *Odocoileus virginianus*

21

Chapter 2

ABOUT THE WHITETAIL

Just the mere mention of the name whitetail leads most to think about one of the deer's most recognizable physical characteristics — its large brown tail with its completely white underside. Many hunters and non-hunters alike have witnessed this graceful animal fleeting across an open field in long graceful bounds as it displayed the white underside of its tail held high in the air swaying from side-to-side as the deer retreated to safety.

As with most animals, specific physical traits are modified through the process of evolution to enhance the survival of the species. It is the external factors that generate changes in its physical evolution. The whitetail is no exception. The whitetail evolved into the graceful, fleet, alert deer that it is, to overcome predation, climatic changes and food source modifications.

The deer also evolved its well-honed sense of eyesight, acute sense of smell, and its superbly camouflaged and thermoregulatory coat to aid in its attempt to survive. Even a buck's antlers have evolved to act as weapons against other competitive bucks, predators (to some degree), and as a form of courtship to aid the buck with the visual attraction of females. All these physical traits aid the deer in its attempt to survive predation (man or animal), climatic changes, and to perpetuate the species.

The three most proclaimed physical characteristics of a deer is its eyes, ears and nose. Each of these sensory organs is used daily by the whitetail for a profusion of reasons including where to find its food sources, to locate and avoid danger and to seek out the opposite sex during the breeding season.

THE EYES

Let's take a closer look at all three of these sensory organs, beginning with the deer's eyes. A whitetail's eyes contain more rods than cones — allowing for better night-time vision. A whitetail's eye only needs 1/8th of the available light a human's eye needs to see in the dark! The white hair which lies directly under the eyes of the whitetail also help it see better at night. The white hair reflects as much light that is available during low light situations. Unbelievably, whitetails can see at least 310 degrees of a full circle (360 degrees) and at least 50 degrees of the 310 degrees can be seen in binocular vision.

Whitetails have evolved to detect motion and depth perception. The eyes of a deer have both monocular vision to each eye and binocular vision to the front, giving the deer a wide field of view (Moen 1982). The design of the orbit (the bony socket in which the eye lies) and the size of the retina (the sensory membrane that lines the eye and is connected to the brain by the optic nerve) allow all ruminant animals (those animals that are cud-chewers and have 3- or 4-chambered complex stomachs) to see back along their flanks and to also detect objects behind them.

Although, for years, it has been said that deer are color blind, recent research now suggests that deer can see shades of color. This research is based on the fact that animals that are predominantly active at night, have eyes that are dominant with light-sensitive rods. To the contrary, animals active during daylight, have eyes principally made up of color-sensitive cones.

In fact, one of the most controversial subjects regarding a deer's eyesight has also revolved around its ability to detect Ultra Violet (UV) light. I strongly believe deer do see shades of color. I have come to that conclusion not from a scientific basis but rather through thirty years of hunting and observing whitetails. I find the UV argument hard to swallow, however. I guess this is a good a time as any in this book to explain to you why I feel this way.

Over the last few years, the subject of Ultra Violet light and how animals see it, has received significant attention within the hunting fraternity. Many hunters are concerned about the effect ultra violet light has on "untreated" hunting clothing under low light conditions. The information about UV light in articles and in other forms of media, is packed with technical-looking information and misleading graphs detailing how animals, and particularly deer, are able to detect hunters when they wear "untreated" hunting garments, including blaze orange and camo clothing.

Although these articles strongly suggest deer do see UV light and colors, exactly how animals interpret UV and the spectrum of colors is very debateable. For instance, in an article I read about UV light, the article began by stating, "Laboratory experiments prove that deer see many things we cannot see, especially ultra-violet light at the blue-white end of the color spectrum." As far as I know, from my involvement in videography and photography, white is not a color and is not on the spectrum!

The question is, are animals, especially deer, able to pinpoint and react negatively to ultra violet light being reflected from hunters' garments?

It is true that most nocturnal animals are able to see as good in the dark as they can during the daylight hours. Because of several factors, they are able to see better in total darkness and, supposedly best, under low light conditions. Firstly, when the sun sets, a game animal's pupil opens wider to admit more light. Unlike humans, who only have cones within the central region of their eyes, deer's eyes contain both rods and cones. The **rods, which are dominant within the deer's eye,** are extremely sensitive to light — moreover dim light. In addition, human eyes have a filter that blocks out UV light, where deer do not have this filter present in their eyes.

But, the question remains, can deer and other game animals detect ENOUGH ultra violet light reflected from camo clothing, worn by hunters from DAWN to DUSK, that will require sportsmen to change their hunting strategies?

Some people think so. Kurt Von Besser is the manufacturer of a product called UV Killer by Atsko/Sno-Seal, Inc. Von Besser was the first to address the issue of UV light and clothing. In his booklet, "How Game Animals See," Von Besser supports his findings of how game animals see through research compiled by a vision scientist at the University of California. According to von Besser, hunters who wear camo clothing manufactured with or which have been enhanced by UV brighteners, are using camo which "has been working against [them]." He feels that the amount of ultra violet light reflected from clothing is detected by game to an extent which gives the hunter away or spooks the game. Thus, with his UV Killer (which is actually another dye to neutralize brighteners in clothing), sportsmen can eliminate UV reflection from their clothing and have fewer game detect them.

If this is the case, where do the ultra violet brighteners come from? They come from standard detergents used to wash clothing. Therefore, if a sportsman washes his clothes in regular detergent, there's a greater chance his detergent has ultra violet brighteners in it. However, for the last 15 to 20 years, much has been written about scent, and how sportsmen should wash their clothing in a non-scented detergent or brown soap. Most of these "hunter's soaps" contain basic cleaning agents — free from ultra violet brighteners. Hunters who use these soaps, therefore, should be wearing camo clothing "safe" from UV brighteners, anyway.

In addition, because of the UV controversy, some leading manufacturers of camouflage clothing have had to take steps to comply with the public awareness of this new "scientific breakthrough." And, although most clothing manufacturers do not agree with theories revolving around the UV rage, they are spending time and money to assure the public their clothing does not contain any UV brighteners. According to the leading manufacturers, most camo clothing fabric houses do not use ultra violet brighteners in their dyes. In a conversation with Bill Jordan, from Spartan-Realtree, he stated, "All cotton fabrics used in Realtree clothing absolutely do not contain any optical brighteners." Jordan is a long-time, whitetail deer hunter. In addition, Jim Crumley, from Trebark told me, "There are no brighteners used in the ink dyes of Trebark fabrics." Crumley has been a successful turkey hunter for many years.

So what are the facts? The ability of deer to detect and react to UV light reflected from clothing, seems to be greatly exaggerated. Leading scientists, who are involved in extensive visionary research, do not support the claims that animals, especially mammals, detect UV light as being brighter than any other light they see. They all agree that since no documented research (using accepted psychophysiological methods specifically for deer) has been performed regarding deer's ability to detect UV light, little can be said to prove they can detect UV reflection from clothes.

John Coulbourn, President of Coulbourn Instruments/Megabucks Trophy

Nutritional Products, who holds a degree in Behavioral Psychology and Zoology, states the following, "The notion that deer see ultraviolet wavelengths with significantly greater sensitivity than other mammals (including humans) is unlikely." Coulbourn feels the pictures displayed in the advertisements and articles are pointless. "No organism with a single lens eye could simultaneously focus on red and green and ultraviolet - [which the pictures portray]. Either it would see an ultraviolet image and a blurred red-green haze or the reverse. Not being able to focus on an image or even detect target movement in this region of the spectrum means evolution would not select for this capability," said Coulbourn. In addition, the graph (by von Besser) depicting how game animals see is, "without labeled vertical axis and supporting data or reference. It is TOTALLY unsupported. Furthermore, the graph seems to have a fabricated curve because its shape implies that there is another unknown photo receptor with its peak at or below 300 millimicron. Such a major discovery would have set the visual research community on its ear!"

Coulbourn Instruments is primarily involved in manufacturing behavioral and physiological test instruments for drug and toxicology research. Having completed extensive studies regarding vision in animals, Coulbourn continued, "Mammals (in fact, most vertebrates) which have color sensitivity, are similar to humans; and any deviations from our green centered sensitivity tend to be to the far red, the opposite end of the spectrum from violet. This is ESPECIALLY true for nocturnally active animals." Coulbourn explained how deer's vision is different from our own, "While we concentrate on image formation and pattern-form discrimination, deer are more responsive to movement or target velocity across the retina. This is a common adaptation in prey animals which are attacked by swiftly moving predators."

Dr. Silas D. White, Professor of Psychology, at Muhlenberg College, finds that the concept of deer being able to detect clear images from ultraviolet reflection difficult to believe. Dr. White explained, "In vertebrate studies performed thus far, in no case does there appear to be much, if any, sensitivity to radiant energy in the U.V. end of the spectrum. This militates strongly against U.V. reflections being perceived as brighter than other wavelengths . . ." Because UV light has such a short wavelength, it is extremely unlikely deer can detect a clearly focused image of UV reflection. "It is unlikely that, if UV were indeed an adequate stimulus, which is doubtful, deer or humans would be capable of perceiving a crisp image resulting from reflections of such disparate wavelengths as those in the typical deer woods background and UV reflections."

In addition to the above, consider Coulbourn's point that nature has evolved all animals that are predated upon with vision that is super sensitive to motion rather than color. For instance, a rabbit who is feeding with eyes focused down, is able to instantly detect a hawk approaching simply by having the hawk's SHADOW trigger an instinctive response. It instantly reacts by hunkering down, pinning its ears back, and darting off. Similarly, a deer reacts much the same way when it sees something that visually suggests a problem. As hunters, we have all had this experience. The deer either stands still and remains motionless or approaches cautiously. With a single movement from the subject, however, the deer flees. **My point is that deer's eyes have not evolved to react to color, but rather, as an animal that is predated upon by man and other animals, their eyes have evolved to detect movement.**

And it is not only scientists outside of the hunting fraternity having doubts about the so-called "revolutionary" findings. Several seasoned outdoor professionals don't think deer can interpret reflections from U.V. light either. Glenn Cole, a Wildlife Manager in Region # 3, for the New York Department of Environmental Conservation, has hunted whitetail deer for over 20 years. He expressed his thoughts about deer detecting UV light reflected from clothing this way, "The hard facts to support what an animal does — or does not see, under low light conditions are just not available. All the scientific literature I have read, says deer see in shades of grey. I have not seen any scientific material to the contrary. I can honestly say that any deer that has spooked from seeing me, reacted to movement or scent — and not because my camo clothing was reflecting UV light."

Game calling expert and avid hunter, Brad Harris, from Lohman Game Call company, said, "I do not feel that I am qualified to say whether 'UV Killer' is a benefit or not. I have heard many discussions for and against this product. I can say that over the past ten years, I have made my living calling game animals and have had many birds and wild game such as deer, elk, predators, turkey and small game within a matter of just a few feet on one or more occasions than I care to count." He attributes getting close to game by knowing the animal's habits and "being properly concealed with a good backdrop to break up my image."

In my personal experience, which includes harvesting 113 whitetail bucks, as well as photographing and videotaping many game animals up close, I can honestly say, to the best of my knowledge, I have never had an animal become frightened or run away because it spotted UV light reflected from my clothing. In fact, I have had, on many occasions, the opposite effects where deer APPROACH me. Over the years, I have done intensive in-field research with whitetails in the wild and at game farms. One such preserve, Davenport Game Farm, is a 250 acre enclosure deer research facility owned and managed by Stephen Novotny. While conducting my research it has been my experience that the overwhelming majority of the deer that I have "spooked" either in the wild or under controlled conditions, occurred from the deer either winding my scent or detecting my movement.

To support this point, think about your own hunting experiences. How many times have you had deer, or other game animals, very close to you while wearing "untreated" hunting clothing? What about the deer who stared you down, trying to decipher what it was looking at, and after many moments of staring, decided that what it saw was not a threat and either began to feed or calmly walked away undisturbed? If it detected a "glowing" would the deer have remained with in the area? My point is, too many hunters have had too many of these exciting close encounters over the years to suggest that deer are frightened from possible problems from UV light being reflected from our clothing.

Other than eliminating human scent, camouflage has been the second most important factor in getting me closer to deer — undetected. I have harvested and videotaped bucks while they were staring directly at me, unable to decipher what they were looking at. Over the years, many of my hunting companions have told me of their experiences of deer coming within touching distance of them while wearing "untreated" camouflage clothing. All this "hard evidence" clearly indicates that the UV issue, related to deer hunting — is primarily designed to sell product.

So, to summarize, many seasoned outdoor professionals, biologists, scientists and plain every day hunters are skeptical about the subject of U.V. light and how it supposedly scares deer. Until there is more viable and conclusive evidence about how deer react to ultra violet light reflected from camo clothing and its affect on our hunting, there can be no emphatic statements made about the subject. The answer lies in trial and error and in docu-mented long-term research conducted with deer.

I intend to continue hunting in "untreated" clothing, not because I want to continue to prove the UV theory wrong, but because I don't want to change my long-time winning formula. Until the time comes when ALL the facts and figures are gathered and carefully analyzed and evaluated, it seems to me and many other folks, that the UV reflection issue is mostly bogus. What is most important to remember is a deer's eye's are designed (because it is an animal that is predated upon) to pick up the slightest movements. Keep that fact uppermost in your mind and you will not have to worry about UV!

THE EARS

That brings us to the next sensory organ, the deer's ears. The whitetail's ears are quite sensitive and respond to unusual sounds immediately. Each ear has about 24 square inches of surface in which sounds are able to glance off of. They use their ears constantly in a radar-like swivel fashion to aid them in determining if anything unfamiliar is occurring in their surroundings and, to monitor the whereabouts and the behavior of other animals that share their domain, especially predators. By closely observing how the whitetail holds its ears you will be able to tell what the deer is thinking and what it is about to do. I will cover this more in Chapter 10 on Body Language.

THE NOSE

Their sense of smell is their number one defense system. Each nostril is lined with epithelium, a membranous cellular tissue which is composed of mucous membranes and sensory nerve endings. Kept moist by the deer's tongue and the internal tissue itself, the epithelium of the nose can pick up odors much better. The nose also aids them in defining exactly who's who - individually - in the deer world. A whitetail also uses its nose not only to locate its food, but also to determine if it is going to be palatable enough to eat. Of course, it used ultimately to detect danger and to locate a receptive doe in estrus. In an upcoming chapter I will cover the deer's sense of smell in more detail.

> **A deer's body temperature is about 104 degrees F.**

I believe - bar nothing - the deer's sense of smell is its key to survival and a hunter's key to success in bagging whitetails consistently. You will hear me repeat throughout this book a couple of phrases — The first and the one you should never forget and that you can "take to the Deer Hunting Bank," is this, "In order to be a consistently successful deer hunter, bust the bucks ability to use its nose against you, and you will bust the buck."

The amount of membranous cellular tissue which lines the nostrils found in man is about 1/8,000 of the skin's total surface. And, about 1/80 of the skin's total surface in deer which is the same as found in a dog. Obviously, because deer's nose has more epithelium membrane tissue than a human's (in proportion to total skin surface), it is much more capable of sensing the slightest of odors. Although deer can detect odors from as far away as 3/4 of a mile or more, by the time the olfactory sensory organs pick up the scent, it is dispersed enough not to make a significant impact on the deer. Many biologists agree that a whitetail has to be no more than about 50 to 100 yards away from the source of a scent to react one way or the other. Of course, these figures are altered by wind currents to some degree.

THE STOMACH

As I have mentioned, the whitetail is a ruminant, which simply means it has a four-chambered stomach. Each of these chambers are shaped differently and have different linings. In addition, each compartment is capable of only holding a certain amount of food and serves a different and a specific function. The large paunch or compartment, which lies on top of the intestines, is the *rumen*. Its primary function is to store the deer's unchewed food. It holds about two gallons of material. The rumen allows the deer to quickly swallow the food it eats in large chunks. When a deer is eating it's head is down which does not allow for the deer to see as well. In this particular feeding position the deer is more vulnerable to predators. But being a ruminant, the deer can gather its food quickly and retreat to a safe area of cover. A useful and practical gift of the evolutionary process from Mother Nature. Once in a secure area the deer brings the food back up into its mouth again and chews it more thoroughly. This is known as cud-chewing. The rumen is a digestive or fermentation compartment of the stomach unique to ruminants. It acts as a holding area for unchewed food. Fatty acids then ferment the food which the deer regurgitates to chew and then re-swallows. The rumen consists of small papillae varying from 3/8 to 1/2 inch in length. Papillae look very similar to small lengths of spaghetti; there are 1600 papillae to the square inch.

The second compartment of the deer's stomach is known as the *reticulum*. It looks very similar to a honey comb. The reticulum forces liquid into the rumen deferring small food particles which are carried back to this compartment and then on to the third chamber called the *omasum*. The reticulum is about the size of a large orange.

The omasum primarily serves as a dehydrator. It removes excess water from the food. This section has about 45 to 50 flaps of different sizes which strain the food as it passes through. This is the compartment where digestion really begins to take place before moving on to the fourth compartment called the *abomasum*.

The abomasum secretes digestive enzymes and is the final area where digestion takes place for the deer. The abomasum is similar to the stomach of non-ruminants in that it is smooth and sleek. With about sixty to seventy feet of intestines. This is where all non-absorbed foods are then prepared to be passed out in the form of excrement — or deer dung. The entire digestive process can take about 24 to 36 hours for food to be eaten and then passed out as dung in an adult deer.

OTHER BODY INFORMATION

This chapter would not be complete without the following statistical information and biological facts about the white-tailed deer that every dedicated deer hunter should know.

THE TAIL

On a Northern whitetail the overall tail length is about 12 inches from its rump to the end of its tail. When spread, the white hairs on the underside of the tail can reach 10 to 12 inches wide. When a doe holds her tail straight out and off to one side, she is visually signaling that she is now "ready" to accept the advances of an accompanying buck. Hunters who observe does exhibiting this type of tail flagging behavior should keep a keen eye open for a trailing buck. Seldom will a doe showing this "ready" tail signal have a buck far behind her! I use this behavior as a decoy tactic which I will explain more about in the decoy chapter.

THE HOOVES

The deer's feet are actually two extended toenails. The whitetail's prehistoric ancestors had five toes on each foot. Over time this proved to be disadvantageous for the deer. It hindered the deer's ability to run fast enough to escape their enemies. So once again, Mother Nature stepped in and through the process of evolution the other three toes changed. The first toe completely vanished. The other two slowly began to regress or atrophy. Today we see them as dewclaws. The two remaining toes have slowly developed into the two main toenails or hoofs that we see on the modern deer of today.

The whitetail's hoof has also evolved into a highly efficient "foot" for the firm type surfaces of woods, fields and the like. However, it is not very functional at all on ice surfaces like a frozen lake or pond. Once a deer falls on ice it may never be able to regain its footing. In fact, many deer have died from exhaustion after falling on ice and not being able to recover their balance quickly.

The deer's hoof is also used as a protective weapon. Both bucks and does use their hoofs to fend off predators. The deer stands on its hind legs and in an aggressive manner flails out its forelegs and strikes the intruder. The blow is powerful enough to crush the skull of a wolf, coyote or domestic dog. If the deer fails to connect with the head, just a glancing blow to the body could inflict a tearing deep wound to the flesh of its adversary. Does usually use this form of antagonistic behavior with other deer only when all other types of aggressive body language and vocalizations and the more docile foreleg kick have failed to get the desired results.

Much has been written and said about the deer's hooves. Some argue that a hunter can tell the difference between a buck and a doe by the size of it's hooves, by it's tracks, or by the distance between each track.

When it comes to trying to identify a buck from a doe by the how deep the track is in the ground, the track's size and shape, or the distance left between tracks, remember this — information left by deer tracks is all relative! There are no absolutes or positives about what a hunter can or cannot tell from tracks. Not unless you see the deer who is in the tracks at the time. Here are some basic facts about hooves and the tracks they leave.

A deer's front hooves are usually larger than the rear hooves. Deer are also knock-kneed. This fact accounts for why the outside of the hoof is most often larger than the inside of the hoof on each foot. Deer are inclined to walk on the inside "lobe" or toenail" more often, accounting for the unique angle we see when we look at tracks left by deer.

Much has also been written and argued about the size of a deer's tracks. Old timers as well as some so called "experts" emphatically state that a hunter can identify the sex of a deer by its tracks alone. I have never seen either prove their abilities to me about this subject with any consistent success. They go on to say that a buck will leave deeper, wider tracks, that the buck track will have a rounded hoof, and that the angle of the track also is specific to whether it was left by a buck or doe. At the risk of sounding righteous, this is pure nonsense. The only absolute way — notice I said absolute — to determine whether a buck or doe left a particular track is to see the deer standing in the track itself. Take that fact to the Deer Hunting Bank!

Many mature older does can attain large body weights, especially in states where does are protected during hunting season. These old females leave deep tracks with rounded lobes that are often associated with buck tracks. Remember, throughout the country, most bucks, a majority in fact, are shot before they reach 2 1/2 years of age. Most does are much older than that before they are shot — if they are even hunted at all. In my home state of New York, does that reside within the Northern Region of our state are protected from hunting because the population density in this region has been traditionally lower than the western or southern portions of the state. Does of the Northern region often reach live weights of 140 to 170 pounds.

It is "OK" to speculate about a track belonging to a buck as long as you are practical about it and remember that it is only a conjecture at best. That way after you have followed a "buck" track for miles over hill and dill for 8 hours and it turns out when you catch up with the deer as its making the tracks you are following, it turns out to be a doe — you are more than ready to accept the misjudgment you made without frustration.

One of the only half-way reliable track indications that I know of is usually visible after a light snowfall of one to two inches. In this instance, the buck's hoof tracks are accompanied by a drag mark of several inches. Traditionally, a doe will pick up its feet clear of the snow and leave just the hoof track itself. A point to remember, especially for novices — button bucks, spikes, and mature bucks all leave drag marks. Size of the track becomes an important factor here. If you follow a track with a drag mark, thinking you have definitely found an antlered buck, you may discover you've been following a button buck or a yearling spike — which may not be the buck you hoped he was going to be regarding the size of his antlers.

After hunting whitetails for 31 years I can tell you that if you absolutely depend on a track to indicate the sex of the deer that left it — you're making your deer hunting more difficult than it has to be. And, you are not hunting with good ol' common sense on your side. Common sense is a major relevant factor to consistent deer hunting success!

One other fact about this subject. A whitetail's walking stride which is calculated at a steady walk of about 3 1/2 to 4 miles per hour (which is just a little faster than man's) is 18 to 19 inches. Their trotting gait which is a speed of about 10 to 12 m.p.h. is 30 to 36 inches.

THE COAT

A whitetail's coat comes in many different shades and in a few instances even different color phases. Different shades of the coat are mostly dependent upon in what section of the country the whitetail lives. Changes in their primary color such as **melanism** (all black), **piebalds** (patches of white and brown or all-white with brown eyes), or **albinism** (all white with pink eyes) are hereditary. In general, the overall color of the a deer's average coat is made up of black, a few different shades of brown and white hairs.

The deer's coat is an evolutionary thermoregulatory marvel. In summer the whitetail's coat is reddish in color and is made up of solid, straight, thin hairs with no undercoat. Although the thin coat helps to keep the deer cool during the heat of summer, the downside is the thinness of the coat offers little protection from insects allowing the pests to easily bite through it. Interestingly, however, the summer coat of a whitetail is compiled with more hairs per square inch than a winter coat.

To the contrary, the hair of the winter undercoat is soft, thin and kinky. The upper coat is hollow, longer and thicker, with each hollow hair filled with air cells. Offering the whitetail two layers of superb insulation. Confirmation of just how good the winter coat insulates the deer can be found by watching a deer during a snow storm or on a frosty morning. In each case the deer's coat will not melt the frost or snow that has accumulated on its back. Verifying how little body heat the whitetail actually loses through the top of its coat.

Any hunter who has ever seen where a deer has previously bedded down in the snow can attest to the fact the snow in the bed has melted. It does so because any heat that has escaped is trapped by the snow beneath the animal and the earth. However, snow falling on any other part of the upper body will not melt as long as the deer keeps the hair standing on end. When the hair is laid flat against the body, snow will melt rapidly on the deer. Interestingly, the hair on the front of the chest (brisket) points forward while all other hair on a whitetail is directed back or down.

It is also important for hunters to know that on different sections of the whitetail's body, the hair is of different color and texture. I have used this hair color and texture information many times in determining exactly where I shot a whitetail that ran off — especially when I am bowhunting.

The color, or colors of the hair will give insight to what part of the body it came from. For instance, hair falling from the lung area will be coarse, brown and it will not have black tips. Hair from around the kidney area will be long, dark and brown, and sometime it will have black tips. Knowing how to identify what hairs comes from what portions of a deer's body is critical when tracking wounded deer.

Through hair identification, you can determine more accurately just about where on the body you hit the deer. This will also give you a clue to what type of blood trail to expect and how long to wait — or not to wait — before going after the animal. It should also give you a good idea about how far the deer should travel before expiring from its wound. All very important information in the recovery of deer which run off after being shot — especially for archers.

> *Use common sense when hunting deer. The most successful whitetail hunters constantly apply heavy doses of good ol' common sense about deer to their deer hunting strategies.*

A buck at the alert position, using his eyes, ears and nose to sense danger.

CHAPTER 3

THE HUNTING GENE

Why is it a person like me, born and raised in a non-hunting family in Brooklyn, New York, developed such an overwhelming desire to hunt? Let me try to explain why I think I became a hunter and what it is that divides people into one of the following groups -- anti-hunter, non-hunter or hunter.

As man developed from a primate to the walking, talking and thinking animal he is today, he accumulated certain genetic characteristics which enabled him to survive and advance to his present state. During this time, as his survival and environmental needs changed, these genetic characteristics were either abandoned, altered or enhanced. I believe, one of these genetic traits was the gene to hunt. It has been well documented that man evolved from the surviving *Australopithecus africanus*, the first man-like ape to walk erect. There was a second Australopithecus species (*A. robustus*) about the same time which was the heavy-jawed vegetarian offshoot of the hominid family which finally went extinct about one million years ago (ref. The Ape That Spoke by John McCrone). *A. Africanus* was our original ancestor and was predominantly a vegetarian who also developed into a gatherer, scavenger and hunter some five million years ago. Two to three million years ago, *Homo habilis* developed tools, but still was not considered a true hunter, but rather a gatherer. As recently as only one million years ago, *Homo erectus* discovered fire and hunting.

From that point, *Homo erectus* survived predominantly as a hunter. However, as most of us know, during man's evolution, the need to hunt wild game in order to survive decreased as man evolved to the early *Homo sapiens* who farmed, gathered and hunted and then went on to evolve into the more present day *Homo sapiens* who still farms and gathers, but no longer has to hunt to survive.

Although his inherit ability and desire to hunt has been environmentally and economically repressed over a period of thousands of years, man still carries the gene to hunt within him. This gene, however, is either dominant, nonpartisan or recessive to several degrees, depending on the family tree from which it was passed and current environmental and social conditions placed upon each individual.

Let's take my case for an example. I am from a large Italian family of aunts, uncles and cousins (on my father's side there were three brothers and three sisters and on my mothers side there were nine sisters and one brother all of whom had a gazillion children). No one other than me and my two cousins, Ralph and Leo Somma, whom I introduced to hunting by taking them with me on small game hunting trips starting at the age of ten, became hunters. Not only in our immediate family, but also in the extended family as well. The point is, there was no external influence on me to hunt. Only an internal desire that built within me as I matured.

But where then did this desire come from? In the late 80s, my mother's mother passed away. My grandmother's husband was my mother's stepfather and had raised my mother from the time she was an infant. He was a non-hunter. Before my grandmother passed away, she told my mother all about her biological father. It seemed that the whole essence of the story was wrapped around my biological grandfather's love of HUNTING! My mother enjoyed telling me how her mother told her that his house was filled with big game trophies and how he loved to fish and go crabbing and clamming. At last I knew why I hunted. **The gene to hunt was passed on to me via my biological grandfather** -- who obviously carried a dominant hunting gene, while the rest of my parents' families carried the dormant hunting trait.

My theory explains why some people hunt and some don't. And why some are so anti-hunting that they become extreme in their views about the subject. People with dormant hunting genes, have feelings about hunting that are neither pro or con. And they go through life, perhaps not understanding the need to hunt, or hunters, but this group does not make a big issue out of the matter.

People who receive a recessive hunting gene, depending on how recessive that gene is, have an inherent apprehension about hunting. Depending on how recessive the gene is, which is based on the lineage from which it was passed, this group will experience various degrees of disdain and even a hatred for hunting. Even to the extent of becoming overly emotional about the subject (i.e. the radical anti-hunter).

This is why I believe some people hunt and some don't. More importantly, it also accounts for why some hunters seem to have an uncanny ability to be successful while other hunters have to work harder at their sport.

Hunters who receive dominant genes from ancestors who excelled as hunters, will have a natural instinctive ability to hunt game. These hunters are often referred to as the "lucky" ones by their friends because of their consistent success. Others who receive a less dominant hunting gene have to work harder at their sport. However, all have a hidden characteristic regarding hunting whether they realize it or not. This hidden trait only needs to be nurtured by confidence in order for it to emerge and blossom. It is the inherited urge, desire or whatever you want to call it to be a hunter. Remember all of us who hunt have inherited this hunting gene and this trait. By having the confidence that you are in fact a hunter, you will develop a higher skill level and better success ratio.

My son, Cody, and I posing with four bucks shot in the northeast during the 1994 hunting season.

CHAPTER 4

THE C + PT X C = CS THEORY

<u>CONCENTRATION + POSITIVE THINKING X CONFIDENCE = CONSISTENT SUCCESS</u>

Until this point, the information which I have shared with you, though important, isn't too strategic or unique in its makeup. From here on, however, it will be. So, in order for this book to help you become a more consistently successful deer hunter, you must not only believe in the information I am sharing with you, but more important, **you must believe in yourself as a deer hunter to be most effective when hunting whitetails.**

You must commit to making both a conscious (whisper to yourself, "I know I am going to see deer") and subconscious effort (think only about deer and seeing them) while you're deer hunting. These deliberate pep-talks will be one of the most helpful tactics of your hunting strategies -- at least I hope you will feel so by the end of this chapter.

As with anything one does in life, having confidence in what you do and how you do it -- automatically produces more success. The confidence and positive thinking theory also applies to sports. Your sport happens to be deer hunting. Therefore, starting right now -- before reading another page of this book -- make an unconditional pact with yourself to develop an unwavering positive attitude about your deer hunting capability.

TAKE THE PACT -- AND BELIEVE!

I am a good deer hunter.

I am confident that I make sound decisions about the hunting strategies I use.

I know my quarry's strengths and weaknesses.

From this moment on, when I think about deer hunting I will do so with **confidence and a positive attitude.**

When I am in the field, I will **totally concentrate on the hunt.**

I promise myself that I will not let any other matters interfere with my thoughts when I am deer hunting.

I WILL MAINTAIN A POSITIVE AND CONFIDENT ATTITUDE EVEN WHEN I DON'T SEE DEER DURING A HUNT.

I will **trust my judgment** about the location and tactics I have chosen to use.

Most importantly, from this day on, I will remind myself that I am as good a deer hunter as any one else -- and will hunt that way.

The philosophies of the powers of positive thinking have been written and talked about in many subjects by numerous people including L. Ron Hubbard, Tony Roberts and, yes, even our own, Gene Wensel. It is simply learning how to exploit the powers of positive thinking -- and using this force to its maximum for your own benefit.

I can guarantee you that if you are sitting in the woods, thinking about bills, family problems, your job, or worse of all, not seeing deer, you won't see deer! Why? You ask. It's easily explained -- especially when it comes to hunting big bucks. Most bucks sneak along taking advantage of all the available cover rather than nonchalantly walking in the open. It doesn't take a buck more than 10 or 15 seconds to quietly slip by a hunter who isn't paying attention to his surroundings. I have seen this happen time and time again.

At least 50% of the time, I would not have seen a buck or, sometimes, bucks, skulk by my stand if I wasn't constantly in tune to the hunt and looking around in all directions **expecting to see a buck moving by my stand**. Typically, I have turned to see an antler or a hind quarter moving through a patch of cedar or undergrowth only moments before not seeing the buck at all. By having confidence and a positive attitude, I sit in my stand expecting the above scenario to develop.

Hunters with negative attitudes get lost in their thoughts and often don't realize they are not paying meticulous attention to what's happening in the woodlands around them. This often leads to bucks getting past hunters totally unnoticed. Trust me when I tell you that this one simple lapse in concentration can make the difference between going in the woods and seeing deer or getting skunked! Often, lack of concentration sets a hunter up for having a lack of confidence and positive attitude in his buck hunting abilities. It's what separates what some hunters call the "lucky hunter" who consistently shoots a buck year in and year out from the guy who is always complaining about not seeing or shooting deer -- especially more elusive bucks.

To see more bucks, you must devote yourself to CONCENTRATING at the job at hand. Seeing more bucks isn't a matter of luck. It's a combination of skill, positive attitude, woodsmanship, positive attitude, concentration and more positive attitude . . . **all of which develop a tremendous amount of confidence which translates into seeing and shooting bucks.**

Never underestimate your ability as a deer hunter. None of us, including the so-called "experts," are any better than any of our hunting comrades. Some are just able to develop their deer hunting skills better than others. As I said in the previous chapter, I believe all deer hunters have an inherent ability to hunt. As all hunters have inherited what I referred to in Chapter 3 as the dominant hunting gene.

What I'm about to say now, should be read several times, because this will definitely maximize your time afield, the number of deer you see, your outlook about yourself as a skilled deer hunter and, most importantly, your success ratio as a buck hunter.

We all know of a hunter who, although he doesn't make any special effort at deer hunting, is successful year in and year out. This hunter's success been called "luck" by many. I feel this "luck" is really a higher developed instinct to hunt via the hunting gene. In other words, some hunters are "lucky" to have hunting genes that are more evolved than others. As he becomes more productive at deer hunting, the gene allows his brain to develop his abilities even further. Accordingly, this hunter develops greater instinctive capabilities that increase his confidence and, therefore, his consistent success.

This is the hunter I referred to above. He sits in his stand and maintains a constant and fine tuned awareness of what is happening in the hunting grounds around him. Nothing in the field slips by him unnoticed. If blue jays start chirping an alarm for no apparent reason, this type of hunter focuses all his senses immediately to try to analyze the reason of the blue jays' disturbance. Should he hear a faint snap of a twig, see a turkey fly by, or even hear the woods suddenly become unusually quiet, he reacts immediately and emphatically by assuming all the above were caused by an approaching deer. I call this the "Assume everything and anything is a buck, until absolutely identified as something else" concept.

Now, here's the part to burn in your memory. While most of the above scenarios usually are nothing other than blue jays reacting to crows, a turkey escaping in flight from a hunter, a twig being snapped from wind, and so forth, this type of hunter isn't bothered by the fact whatever got his attention originally didn't turn out to be a buck. He realizes with each passing incident, the odds increase that the next time he responds, it will be a buck. This expectant attitude is a result of a high level of confidence and a positive attitude.

Take this to the Deer Hunting Bank. A consistently successful hunter assumes every noise he hears is the result of an approaching buck, every deer he sees (even before he can identify what it is) is a buck and every tactic every strategy he plans will work. By assuming these things, you will always be ready and never caught flatfooted when a buck, especially Mr. Big, finally walks in. Having a positive attitude increases your success dramatically.

I am no better deer hunter than you. I have been fortunate enough to have taken 113 whitetails under "fair chase" conditions, 13 large enough to be listed in the archery record books of Pope & Young and one even scoring high enough to be entered in the prestigious Boone and Crockett record books. But the numbers of bucks that I have taken along with my record book trophy achievements **don't make me a better hunter than you.** I have a lot of time to spend hunting and have the unique opportunity to hunt several different states and provinces each year. In addition, I take off from work for the entire New York deer season to hunt whitetails. Why I am I telling you this? Not to brag -- but to help you understand that part of being a successful deer hunter also boils down to having the opportunity to spend a lot of time in the woods. This doesn't mean you can't maximize your time in the woods to be successful (even if it is only for a few days or a week).

Over my thirty odd years of deer hunting, I have gathered a lot of experience. Much of my knowledge came from making mistakes during my earlier years and some from my successes. All of the learning experiences lead to me attaining more confidence in my capability as a deer hunter and giving me the all-important positive attitude. Once a hunter develops this higher level of confidence in his or her deer hunting ability, consistent success in scoring on bucks won't be far behind.

Over the years, I have hunted with many friends and relatives who for no other reason other than an obvious lack of confidence in their deer hunting skills have proved to be less than productive deer hunters. This 'lack of confidence' syndrome becomes compounded each time an unsuccessful hunt takes place. It can be compared to a ball player who sinks into a batting slump. Each time he steps up to the plate and doesn't get a hit -- he becomes more apprehensive about his next time up. Until he concentrates on getting his confidence back, consistent hitting is out of the question. Lack of confidence will make any problem get worse and worsen as the confidence level continues to drop.

A hunting companion, I'll call Ed, is a classic example of how frustrating it must be to be a hunter without confidence. Ed never knows just where he wants to sit along a deer trail. When he does find a location, he's sure there's a better spot just around the next bend or over the next ridge. He spends whatever time he's at the stand questioning himself about how effective his location is.

As Ed sits there arguing with himself, he unconsciously becomes fidgety. He's constantly moving around trying to get comfortable. When Ed finally settles down, he's sure not even one deer will pass him and acts that way by not paying attention to the job at hand! Many times the result is that Ed falls asleep (literally or, at least, figuratively) when he's deer hunting. The pure stress of 'second guessing' all his hunting decisions is just too much for the brain to handle and it actually shuts down regarding the deer hunt. It forces a hunter like Ed to begin thinking about anything else other than deer hunting.

Mother Nature uses this maneuver to subconsciously decoy the body into relieving the prevailing high levels of stress it is dealing with at the moment. Therefore, Ed literally falls short during the hunt. He never sees or hears a buck as it quietly and carefully makes its way past Ed's stand and, most likely, was totally unaware of Ed's presence. Perhaps this scenario now helps you to understand why some hunters may not take a buck every year or why other hunting buddies do.

Always remember the 'second guessing' syndrome is the Number One enemy of any deer hunter. It eliminates all possibilities of ever attaining a high level of confidence. Second guessing -- without reservation -- results in a deer hunter seeing and bagging fewer deer. Hopefully, before you read another page, you have decided at this point that you must make the decision to make a pact with yourself to have a positive attitude and greater confidence about your deer hunting capabilities.

Now that you are almost finished reading this chapter, you should be absolutely convinced how important a formula like $C + PT \times C = CS$ is. Without question, this formula (Concentration plus Positive Thinking multiplied by Confidence equals Consistent Success) is the key to your future of successful deer hunting. After all is said and done, you're not an average deer hunter -- reading this book proves that. A deer hunter who takes the initiative to study more about deer and deer hunting strategies has already decided to be a more informed hunter -- which is the first step to adhering to the $C + PT \times C = CS$ axiom and becoming more confident about this sport.

The very next time you are deer hunting, use your common sense (most successful deer hunters use a healthy dose of common sense in their hunting strategies) and, above all, trust your gut feelings about your decisions and you'll experience a new type of hunting. I promise you you'll write me a letter telling me about how this chapter changed your deer hunting for the better and forever!

Bucks like this can be taken more regularly as soon as you start applying the C+PTxC=CS Theory

CHAPTER 5

WIND AND WHITETAILS

Although every chapter in this book offers good advice about deer and how to hunt them -- the following sentences are MOMENTOUS to consistently successful buck hunting. The number one factor to shooting a buck each fall (other than C+PTxC=CS) is to pay attention to the direction of air currents. Know and understand these currents, thermals, convections and prevailing breezes generally known as wind. There is no other hunting strategy that equals the importance of knowing wind and how it carries human scent and other odors to whitetails.

White-tailed deer, especially bucks, survive predominantly through using their primary sense of smell. As deer hunters, we all have witnessed a buck questioning what he sees. He may doubt a message sent to him through his brain from his ears; but, as most hunters have also witnessed, he will never, under any circumstance, doubt the messages sent to him via his sense of smell. Deer use wind direction constantly as an aid to their movement, always allowing it to detect the relative safety of the paths they are traveling. Therefore, as hunters we must be enlightened about currents of wind to be the best hunters (predators) we can be.

There are several components associated with wind. Meteorologists define wind as air in horizontal motion relative to the surface of the earth. This atmospheric motion called wind is better identified as ascending or descending currents -- and not wind at all. As a hunter, you should always know from which direction the wind is coming because this will tell you whether the wind is cooler, warmer, drier or more moist than the air you are currently encountering. Along with the direction, the makeup of the wind should be noted. Is it beginning to shift or holding steady out of a certain direction? A change of direction in the wind could very well be a sign that a high pressure system is about to move north or south of your location. If you can pick up this sign, then you can use this information to better plan your hunting strategy.

Wind normally picks up during the day with an increase in the air's temperature and it slows in the late afternoon around sunset. If the wind does not slow down come sunset, the barometric pressure is going to change. Deer movement always increases with changes in barometric pressure. If the wind does not decrease or there is very little change in the wind speed throughout the day, then the current weather condition will not be changing. In this case, deer will not be spurred to more than their normal activity and you may want to try more active deer hunting tactics like calling or rattling.

Wind currents include prevailing, convection and thermal currents. Each can help or hurt a hunter depending upon the hunter's knowledge of each condition.

PREVAILING WIND

Every state or region has what is called a prevailing wind. You should pay meticulous attention to the prevailing wind during the hunting season. Throughout much of the United States, it is the wind that emanates from the slightly south of west to north of west. This prevailing wind direction is crucial to you when planning a stand's location. This is especially true when you are deciding whether to post in a field, bottle neck or ravine. By not paying attention to the prevailing wind currents, your scent could unknowingly be carried to deer who are not yet in eyeor ear range. The result is that you could spend hours on a stand without ever seeing a single deer simply because your scent was carried to them by a current of air you did not pay attention to. Prevailing winds are easy to determine in any area you hunt and, bar some unusual circumstance, you can count on these air currents blowing in the same direction day in and day out.

CONVECTION

Convection currents are nothing more than just another type of distinct circulation of air currents. What makes a convection current different from a prevailing wind is that a convection current is specifically indigenous to a particular section of terrain. Despite the prevailing wind, convection currents do their own thing, often blowing in an entirely different direction or directions than the existing prevailing breeze. Convection currents can be a real burr under your saddle if you don't know or understand what they can do.

I first learned about convection currents many years ago. Knowing what direction the prevailing breeze came from most of the time within a certain area I hunted, I set up on a ridge-top overlooking a steep draw so that my scent was carried away from the direction from which I knew the deer would come. After sitting in my stand for about an hour or so, I heard the distinct sound of crunching of leaves as deer approached. "Excellent," I thought, "the wind is blowing perfectly. They'll never know I'm here." Moments later, I saw two small bucks approach my stand. Unconcerned, they steadily moved down the trail. About 50 yards from my stand, both bucks jammed on their brakes and without an instant's hesitation, they whirled and disappeared back from where they came. I was dumbfounded and watched them run away as the wind gently blew against my face. I hadn't walked anywhere in the area from which they approached and, unless another hunter had, I just couldn't understand what went wrong.

That evening, I was speaking to a friend about what happened. Coincidentally, this fellow was a high school science teacher. And, although he didn't hunt, he had an immediate explanation for what might have happened to spook the deer the way I described. "You understand that although you positioned yourself with the prevailing wind in your favor, that wind could have been upset or changed as it continued down toward you by some specific feature or features of the terrain at the exact location of your stand, don't you?" "No," I bashfully replied. "Oh, yeah. They're called convection currents." He went on to explain to me what a convection current was and how it can be directly OPPOSITE of a prevailing current.

Basically, a convection current can develop as prevailing air currents are carried along their general direction by a large rock, an upsurge in land, a rock wall or any other solid object with enough mass to deflect a current of air. These objects generally cause the prevailing wind "fits" by swirling them around in different directions before sending what's left on its way. Hence, convection currents take place vertically and, therefore, can carry your scent both up and down. "So, although the prevailing wind was blowing in my face, the large rock ledge behind me caused the current to change direction and blow back toward the two oncoming bucks?" I asked. "That's right," he said.

I never forgot that lesson. Now whenever I setup to post in an area, I hang a large strand of black sewing thread from a branch or my gun or bow and watch to see how it blows in contrast to the prevailing wind direction. Sometimes I am amazed to see it flagging off in every direction but the direction of the prevailing wind. Other times, it will conform to the direction of the prevailing wind current. However, whatever it does -- because I am now aware of convection currents -- I can adjust or even change my location to compensate.

To be absolutely sure of how a wind current is blowing, however, use an unscented powder. Several companies package them. Primos has one called "Wind Checker," Pete Rickard makes one called,"Wind Tracker." These spray powder devices, simple as they are, have been VITAL to my hunting success. Many hunters say they are not important to use on windy days when it's easy to detect wind direction. These hunters, like I once was, are not in tune to convection currents that, despite a prevailing wind, may be different. The unscented powder will definitely tell you which way your scent is blowing. These handy little devices are extremely helpful, however, when there is hardly a breeze at all. When there isn't a detectable wind - use a wind checking device - you won't regret it.

 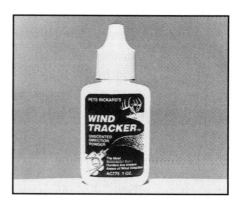

To be absolutely sure what direction your scent is moving, especially on days without a noticeable breeze, always use a spray powder device.

Another easy method of understanding currents is to make entries into a log book. After sitting in a certain stand for several days, take note of the air currents that prevail, despite the general direction of the wind. Log them and take advantage of the information for future hunts. Air that is being cooled off can also be a cause of a convection current. But this is a less common cause of a convection current than the other reason described above.

THERMAL CURRENT

The final air current that hunters should understand and know how to use a thermal current. A thermal current has specific characteristics. All hunters should pay attention to this phenomenon especially when hunting in the early morning and late afternoon, when thermal currents are most active. At dawn, as temperatures usually begin to rise, the thermal current direction or flow is upward. As evening approaches, however, and the temperatures begin to cool off, thermal currents begin to fall. A hunter who takes a stand at dawn should position himself above the area where he expects to see deer. By doing so, his scent will rise skyward. However, the same stand should be avoided in the evening, because his scent will be carried downhill.

You can overcome the phenomenon created by thermal currents by acting the same way a buck would. All bucks have alternate runways leading to and from bedding areas. A buck, who has survived just a couple of seasons, has learned how to keep the prevailing winds blowing in his face. The seasoned hunter should have alternate stands and should use these alternate stands in direct relationship to conflicting thermal, convection or prevailing wind currents.

By keeping wind uppermost in your mind, you will substantially increase your chances for success. Wind is the common enemy of all hunters as it is the overall force responsible for carrying human scent and dispensing it throughout the woods. Inevitably, there isn't a hunter who can escape the fact that, as humans, we smell. No matter how hard we try, the very fact of the matter is, human odor cannot be totally eliminated. We can, however, control and minimize it and therein lies an additional aid to success.

CHAPTER 6

FOUL WEATHER BUCKS

Contrary to what most of us are told and believe, hunting deer in bad weather can be productive. Yes, there are times to stay in bed when the weather turns sour. But, generally, deer hunting in the rain or snow can put a buck on the wall and meat in your freezer.

I became enlightened to the benefit of foul weather hunting early on in my deer hunting career. Let me share with you, over the next few pages, some experiences that should help those who, for whatever reasons, have convinced themselves to stay home when the weather gets bad.

The doorbell rang just as I placed another log into the fireplace. "The door's open, Felix. Come on in," I said as the hot burning embers instantly ignited the bark of the new log. "Guess you've decided it's raining too hard to go deer hunting," said Felix. "No. Quite to the contrary. We're going. I just want a good warm fire to dry us off and warm us up when we get back," I said.

I could see by the expression on Felix's face that he thought I was either kidding or trying to be macho. He couldn't believe that I was about to take him to "The Buck Tree" during a heavy rainstorm. While driving to the stand he kept reminding me that deer, "aren't supposed to move during rain - especially in downpours like this."

I glanced at him and with as serious a face as I could gather said, "If you want to shoot your first racked buck, don't worry about the rain, just post by the Buck Tree today. I don't think you'll be there too long before you see the racked buck I've been telling you about."

This story took place in the early 80s. The reason I began this chapter with it is that most deer hunters are too frequently talked out of using sound hunting strategies by well meaning but, less knowledgeable hunting companions who want to be the most successful of the group. Even if your hunting tactics are a bit off-the-wall -- use them and use them confidently. As you will read later in this chapter, Felix, was a semi-successful deer hunter, taking a small buck almost every year. However, he never killed a racked buck. That soon changed on this one rainy afternoon. To this day, I remember him saying how surprised he was to see the big buck walking toward him in the pouring rain only several minutes after posting at his stand.

Take a moment to pause here. Think about what might not have happened if I didn't insist that Felix and I go hunting that afternoon. As you reflect, think about how many times, foul weather has stopped you from going deer hunting. Many of us have read and heard that foul weather puts deer down. And while some severe inclement weather stops deer from moving temporarily, all but the worst of weather conditions will put deer down for any long time. I can promise that as long as you have the motivation to hunt in inclement weather, you will score on big bucks. This is another chapter you can deposit in the Deer Hunting Savings Bank Book -- to enhance its balance!

Interestingly, after evaluating my **foul weather** deer hunting statistics that I keep regularly each year on my Deer Diary Stat Cards, I have discovered that deer, especially bucks, move normally during nasty weather. Foul weather, as far as deer are concerned, encompasses rain, wind, ice, snow, fog, extreme cold, mist and even unusual, hot, arid conditions. Each of these conditions triggers a different type of activity response from whitetails. If you discover how to capitalize on each of the above conditions and learn how to hunt deer under these circumstances, you'll be amazed at the success you'll enjoy.

I can clearly recall an old timer (at the time he was in his 70s) I hunted with in Colorado named Shorty. He would sit in camp for several days while everyone else went out to hunt deer. Each day, we would ask him if he was going to hunt. Each day he'd say, "Conditions just ain't right yet, boys."

Since Shorty was the best hunter of the group (having killed several very large bucks over the years), we trusted his wisdom. I'd have to admit we did occasionally scoff at his seemingly lackadaisical attitude. But, somewhere in our hearts, despite his overwhelming success each year, we thought luck probably played a role in his good fortune. Traditionally, the first day of any type of SERIOUS foul weather, Shorty would be up and gone long before we took our first sips of coffee. And, as usual, he'd be back in camp that night with a magnificent buck. The only thing he would say was, "Foul weather is the key to killin' big bucks, boys!"

Bucks use specific areas (terrain) more frequently during nasty weather than during good weather. For instance, I have several stands that I post in only during foul weather. If it's a bluebird day, I don't bother wasting my time at these locations. I have learned that the bucks in my area only frequent these areas when the wind is howling out of the north or when other types of bad weather move in. Evidently, because of the terrain and cover, deer find certain areas more attractive in foul weather than in good weather.

Perhaps a certain area protects them better from the chill of high winds because a unique formation of the landscape blocks the heavy gusts. Maybe a certain low-lying area is slightly warmer due to thermals. Or, it could be that during foul weather, certain areas simply make the deer feel more comfortable as they move through a particular area. For whatever reasons, deer definitely have a preference to using certain areas in foul weather.

The trick to hunting successfully during foul weather is to employ my second formula for buck hunting success: $D + P \times S + C = S$ -- **Determination plus Patience times Stamina plus Comfort equals Success.** Without these fundamental components - foul weather hunting is an exercise in futility. That bears repeating. If you leave out any of the above factors, the potential for your success drops accordingly. Leave out more than one of any of these factors and the possibility of success is almost nonexistent.

As we all know, deer hunting under fair weather conditions is a challenge within itself. Intensify those demands tenfold when it comes to hunting whitetails during inclement weather. Although there are foul weather hunting strategies that will help you score, there are strategies at least equally important for the hunter to consider before stepping from the truck and entering the woods. These non-hunting strategies are the fundamental roots to foul weather hunting success. Ignore them and no hunting strategy that I can offer you will work to its greatest potential. Hunting under difficult weather conditions takes this challenge to new heights.

To be a successful foul weather deer hunter, one must motivate himself to going hunting on a snowy or rainy day - even during a torrential rainstorm. Without this determination, the battle is lost before it has begun.

Once you have convinced yourself to hunt in this type of weather you must be prepared to be in the woods as long as you would if you were hunting on a clear day. Hunting in foul weather demands this type of determination. It will regularly pay off in big dividends.

In all but the most severe and extreme weather conditions (i.e., 48-hour snow storms, gale force winds, ice storms and a 3-inch torrential rain storm over a 12-hour period), deer generally are **unable to remain bedded when the weather turns nasty** -- not for long anyway. They instinctively know they must feed even if it means at heightened levels of awareness. They must do so in spite of a steady rain, windy day, or snowy afternoon. These types of weather conditions give some of "the edge" back to the hunter. For instance, besides taking some big bucks during rain storms, I have used a day with gusty winds, to sneak up undetected on a buck bedded in laurels or on ledges, or nervously feeding in a woodlot or field.

A classic example of the success you can have when hunting during windy conditions is underscored by a hunting companion, Don Sampson. Sampson owns a few hundred acres in upstate New York. A few years ago, Sampson's property was logged and he intentionally left the tops of trees to create a myriad of blow downs for cover. Whenever it gets very windy, Sampson quietly and slowly stalks through the blow downs with the wind in his face. Often, bucks never hear or smell his approach because the wind muffles his steps and quickly dissipates his scent. One year, Sampson shot one of his biggest bucks using this foul weather tactic. Once, Sampson used a heavy snow storm to bag another big buck.

Hunter Don Sampson shot this buck while stalking through blow downs during high winds after a heavy snow storm.

Every night during the deer season, I pay meticulous attention to the local weather report. Then, I record wind direction and speed, barometer reading, humidity and other pertinent weather factors onto my Deer Diary Stat cards. This information is used in preparation for my next day's hunt. I also compare the activity I saw during the day to the weather statistics I record that evening.

During high winds, a deer's senses are dramatically reduced. It is why you will see deer, especially bucks, behaving nervously in windy conditions. The stronger the wind, the more jittery deer become. Although all their senses are altered somewhat, their sense of hearing is most affected.

Unfortunately, especially during a prolonged period of windy days, deer must eat and they venture out of the security of their beds to do so. Remember that wind is an ally to a hunter, especially those who are skillful at stalking. Wind puts a hunter on a more equal playing field with bucks. By using the wind to conceal your scent, noise, and to some degree the sight of your approach (with everything in the woods blowing in the wind, it's harder for deer to detect your movement), you can sneak up on a buck that otherwise would have spotted you during a calm day.

During snow storms, you can quietly track deer into their bedding and feeding locations. You can also patiently position yourself on known trails. During a snow storm, deer traditionally move a few times along trails to feed and bed down again -- even if they're not traveling far from their bedding areas. Waiting along these trails during a continuing snow storm can pay off handsomely. In addition, there will be a flurry of activity after the storm ends. At first, the movement is concentrated close to the bedding areas and it eventually disperses (within 24 hours) to normal feeding areas. Knowing what the deer were feeding on prior to the storm and waiting there after the storm, will result in a successful buck hunt.

Next, and probably the most important factor in successful foul weather hunting, is protecting your body and equipment from the elements. If you don't dress right - you'll never be able to stay on stand long. If you neglect your equipment by not protecting it properly, I can almost guarantee the result will be equipment failure and a bad experience as far as foul weather hunting goes.

CLOTHING

Foul weather deer hunting requires some special preparation and planning for both your tactics and equipment. By thinking ahead and employing some unusual strategies, you can brave all but the most hostile of weather conditions and come out successful. The first step in foul weather preparedness must start long before you leave for your favorite hunting ground. If you're prepared for the worst weather, you can remain comfortable and stay in the woods long after other hunters have given up and headed back to camp.

Dressing in layers, wearing quiet rain gear, bringing a dry change of clothes, and using hand warmers are some important points to remember. Over the years, I have found that wool clothing offers great protection from the elements as well as being quiet. It is what I use over a layer of long underwear. On top of the wool, I wear a quality set of rainproof jacket and pants. Wearing the right hat (one that diverts rain way from your eyes and the back of your neck), gloves and socks is also important to successful foul weather hunting. Outfitted with quality clothing, you can put your first strategy into play. Staying warm and dry assures that you will remain on stand much longer, no matter how foul the weather conditions turn. The longer you are on post, the more you increase the possibilities of seeing and taking a buck. If you're a still hunter, quiet outerwear and warm wool undergarments will enable you to walk through the woods quietly while remaining comfortable and dry. Remember, if you are stalking game in inclement weather and you begin to perspire because of the amount of clothes you have on, you are stalking too fast. Slow your pace down by at least two-thirds.

FOOTWEAR

The next strategy is to keep your feet DRY AND WARM. Waiting for or stalking a buck in a cold rain can play havoc on your feet, especially when they are wet and cold. There is no compromising on this matter. A quality pair of warm, comfortable, waterproof boots is an absolute necessity. If you don't heed this advice about using quality footwear, your hunting will be over before it starts!

A quality boot will keep you warm, comfortable and dry in the woods after other hunters are long gone -- giving you the opportunity to see and score on more bucks.

EQUIPMENT

Besides protecting yourself against the elements, it is equally important to protect your equipment. If you're using optics, make sure it is a quality waterproof optic that has either flip-up or other style of lens covers to keep the lenses dry and clear. I always carry a soft, absorbent cloth to occasionally wipe water or snow off my optics, if need be. It's a good idea to carry several packets of lens cleaning paper to repeatedly clean optic lenses, too. A camera lens cleaning brush is included in my pack to wipe off debris and a small gun cleaning rod in the event I fall accidentally and my muzzle clogs with mud or snow. In other words, when hunting in foul weather, I am totally prepared to stay out as long as possible to hunt.

If you're using a rifle in sub-freezing weather be sure you've disassembled the bolt and de-greased it. Bolts can and do freeze in weather as warm as twenty degrees. Reassemble the bolt and lubricate it sparingly with a lightweight gun oil. Heavy grease may cause the bolt to freeze solid or, just as bad, the primer may strike so lightly it won't ignite the round.

It's also a good idea to put a light coating of car wax on your gun's barrel. It makes rain and snow slip off the barrel just like it does from the hood of your car or truck. This will help protect it from dampness and allow you to keep your mind on the activity at hand -- hunting -- not rust! Use an odorless wax. Once you've learned how successful you can be when hunting during foul weather, you may eventually want to purchase an all-weather rifle with a synthetic stock.

FOOD

Lastly, in this category, a strategy that pays for itself over and over again is to never go afield in foul weather without a thermos of hot liquid (soup or broth) and some food items. Nothing helps to persuade you out of the woods faster than a hungry stomach or a chill that cuts to the bone. It's amazing how a thermos of hot soup and some food can turn a miserable day into one that's at least tolerable.

SURVIVAL

Although most of my foul weather hunting is done on a daily basis and most likely, yours will be too, accidents can and do happen -- especially in inclement weather when the ground is slippery. Therefore, I always carry a small survival pack in my backpack that includes a space blanket, waterproof matches, flashlight, batteries and other survival essentials. By carrying this equipment, I hunt without worry about getting hurt or lost and having to stay out in inclement weather.

HUNTING STRATEGIES

Now let's examine some unusual traits white-tailed deer may exhibit in foul weather and then discuss the tactics to successfully take them under such adverse conditions.

At the start of most types of extreme bad weather, deer usually "hold up" in the heavy brush or dense stands of evergreen trees like cedar. Deer become nervous in strong winds. However, it takes gale force-type conditions to put deer down and keep them there. This is often evidenced when winds reach conditions referred to by meteorologists as Fresh or Strong Gale force speeds. This is primarily attributed to the fact that two of their most relied upon senses -- hearing and smell -- are significantly reduced during these conditions. Deer try to make up for this deficiency by relying on their other prime sense of sight. To do so, they must stay on the move and always scan their surroundings for activity and danger. Even this becomes difficult when everything in the deer's environment is moving from the blowing wind. Contrary to popular belief, even when high winds are blowing up to 40 m.p.h., deer will continue to move and feed. Taking a stand on the fringe of heavy cover often proves to be a very productive method.

Another unusual behavioral trait brought on by bad weather is deer activity at odd times of day. Generally nocturnal, especially in heavily hunted areas, the whitetail may spend a large part of the day moving just before or after a storm. This activity often intensifies as the storm begins or ends. Dramatic drops or increases in temperature or barometric pressure will also increase deer activity before, during and after a storm. This is especially true if extreme bad weather conditions have held them stationary for a long time.

Stand and still hunting remain the best tactics for foul weather deer hunting -- but with one serious twist. Instead of a little moment here or there, it will be a feast or famine situation. If the deer are moving, they will move continually. Unfortunately, if they're not traveling, it will take additional effort, of a hunting strategy like stalking, to sneak up on them. Learning how to recognize the varying conditions that govern these different patterns is the key to deciding which hunting technique you will employ.

If the wind is above 38 m.p.h., and the storm has been in the area more than a few hours, chances are the deer will bed down and stay that way until the storm breaks or their hunger becomes such that they are forced to look for food. Under conditions such as these still hunting can be deadly. Hunt any place that affords more secure cover to deer than they normally require. In these type of weather conditions, bucks won't be bedded where they normally bed. Instead, they will seek out the thickest and, what they feel, is the most impenetrable cover they can find. This type of cover is usually found in a very thick stand of evergreen trees or in large shoulder-high patches of inaccessible laurels that are void of the snapping branches of hardwood trees in open woods.

When using these tactics, I can't stress enough how important it is to take your time and move slowly. Still hunting in standing corn during conditions like this can also be a "good thing." During heavy winds and rain, deer, especially mature bucks, often head for standing corn swales and other timber-free hiding places. I have found that bucks frequent standing corn on misty, foggy mornings. But, I don't know exactly why, either.

Primary variables besides wind, precipitation and temperature include: food availability, time of year, and stage of the rut. The closer it is to the full rut, the more the chances are that bucks will be moving despite the severity of all but the foulest of weather conditions.

Taking this into consideration means you can employ a rut-hunting strategy during foul weather, too. Use an estrus scent in a drip dispenser (like a CoverTrak) or on the bottom of a boot pad as you are walking to your stand. Often, a buck on the move will pick the scent up and move into your area. During heavy rain, I often hang a boot pad saturated with estrus scent in a couple of different locations to help attract a buck moving in the rain. It is the only time I hang more than one boot pad and use excess scent. Rain holds odor down substantially, and, therefore, using more scent and pads is necessary for the strategy to work. However, although I'm using a few pads with more scent than normal on them, I do not soak them to excess.

Two other key factors to consider during bad weather hunting are the distance you'll be shooting at and your shot placement. Chances are your vision will be slightly impaired at best. At worst, it can be cut by half or more. Think about this and shorten up your self-imposed maximum shooting distance. Also, be even more careful than usual about shot placement. In the rain or during a continually heavy snowfall that obliterates any sign in minutes, all sign left by a wounded animalwill be more difficult to read mere minutes after it's made. Therefore, you're looking to place one clean shot that will kill the animal if possible -- in its tracks.

This is especially true when bow hunting. Because of this, I rarely bow hunt in the rain, unless it begins to rain while I am on stand and there is a buck underneath me that offers a perfect kill shot (if such a thing really exists). Then and only then will I shoot a buck. Too many wounded bucks are lost by hunters that lose the animal's trail because of heavy rain or falling snow washing away or covering all sign. If you decide to bow hunt in the rain because of the good hunting opportunities rain offers, resign yourself to the fact that you may lose a buck even with a perfect kill shot. For instance, a heart or lung bowshot deer could run 100 or more yards. In a heavy rain storm, most, if not all blood signs could be eliminated. To help alleviate this dilemma, reduce your effective range in half and only shoot when you think your arrow placement will be perfect.

Due to the elimination of sign under foul weather you should start tracking a wounded animal immediately. Yes, you stand a chance of spooking a wounded animal and causing it to run farther after it's hit, but you also stand a much better chance of finding the animal than you will if all sign is washed away or lost under new snow.

Remember that all types of climatic conditions including relative humidity, air temperature, wind, snow depth, precipitation, barometric pressure, cloud cover, and, according to some, moon phase always play an important role in deer behavior and activity movement. Learning what consequences each specific weather pattern has on deer movement, will make you a much better hunter whether you are hunting in fair or foul weather - as each of these conditions can be applied to both fair and foul weather hunting strategies.

Only the most severe weather conditions will dramatically change deer movement. Snow depth of 18 inches or more will immediately put deer into the yarding behavior and they will congregate in soft wood wintering areas. Strong gale force winds (47-54 mph), when large tree branches are snapped and trees are bent in the wind and uprooted, send deer seeking the thickets and most inaccessible cover they can find. Rain storms that drop several inches of rain in a couple of hours will deter deer from moving. Extreme frigid conditions over extended periods will also put deer down. Other than these **extreme** types of conditions, you can count on white-tailed deer moving about during foul weather. Simply, they are not that affected by the forces of foul weather. Physically, it doesn't bother them enough to deter movement. Remember this, and you may dress out a good buck.

Here's another example of how good hunting opportunities can be lost when a hunter either falsely assumes that hunting in foul weather is unproductive or when he can't motivate himself enough to hunt in foul weather. Last year, a hunting companion, who will remain nameless, lost the opportunity to shoot a buck because he didn't want to hunt in a heavy rainstorm that moved in one afternoon. This took place on one of the most productive days of the entire season -- opening day of firearms season in New York. According to NYS DEC officials, opening day accounts for 80% of the doe and buck-take for the entire deer season.

It began with a cloudy and dank morning. By two p.m., the skies opened and it began to rain heavily. My companion said with a disgusted frustrated look on his face, "It's raining like hell. I think I'll go home." "It's not raining hell" I said, "It's raining deer." His response was negative, "Do you mean to tell me you're going out in this and that you actually expect to see a buck?" "Yup. I am and I do," I confidently replied.

In any event, I couldn't talk him into staying to hunt that afternoon. Now, take into consideration he doesn't shoot a buck every year. Yet, he continually complains about his hard luck. Still, even after all my encouragement, he was sure I was crazy and that no buck in its right mind would move in this type of heavy downpour. By 3:00 p.m. my wife and I left for our stands. By 3:30 p.m. I was dressing out my buck on the stand at which I was going to leave my hunting companion. Katie also saw several deer including two small bucks that she let pass. The bottom line -- deer, including bucks, move during rain storms -- even when it is raining heavily. Had my companion trusted this information, he would have ended his season on opening day and would have shot his first buck in a few years.

It amazes me how some of my closest hunting companions refuse to accept my advice even after they see both Katie and me taking good bucks year-in and year-out. I find it even more curious that these same hunting companions ask me dozens of questions about deer and hunting tactics over the course of the year. Still, when it gets right down to it, they hunt very differently than I do. It just seems that they refuse to believe what their ears hear and what their eyes see. I was always told, you can't argue with success. Therefore, I would think that ALL my hunting buddies would use my hunting strategies. Sadly, some, for whatever reason, don't. Instead, they follow a very predictable pattern of applying very routine tactics during deer season and do just what most hunters do -- hunt without believing in themselves -- an obvious lack of hunting confidence. Don't fall into thiscategory. Remember, I am no better deer hunter than you. My success comes from confidence and being flexible enough to try different tactics.

When you get good advice, use it confidently. Taking the advice of this last sentence is what started me on the road to deer hunting success. I took the advice of a very consistently successful deer hunter whose theories were mocked at by traditional hunters, despite the fact this man took trophy bucks year after year. Today, he's regarded as one of the most knowledgeable and successful deer hunters in the nation and I'll bet he still has some hunting friends who refuse to believe his tactics work. Be open-minded; learn to accept new hunting ideas and use them. You have nothing to lose.

Felix also discovered how good foul weather hunting can be on the day I mentioned in the beginning of this chapter. I placed him by the Buck Tree at 3:15 p.m. and told him from where I thought the buck would come and when. I explained to him that the buck regularly traveled through the area between 4:00 and 4:30 p.m. I cautioned him, however, that tonight, because of the heavy rain, he might come through earlier. As Felix settled in, I walked to my spot about 100 yards away. As I was tying my gun to the string to hoist it into my treestand, I heard the shot. When I got to Felix, all he could say was, "I can't believe how casually this buck was walking and feeding on acorns in such a heavy rain storm. He never knew I was there [25 yards] when I shot him." Felix's 8-point buck had an 18-inch spread and dressed out at 160 pounds. His first racked whitetail was a dandy -- even though it was shot on a lousy(?), rainy day. Hunting in all types of foul weather including rain -- even heavy rain can and will pay off in big buck dividends despite anything you may have heard or read to the contrary!

Although hunting is not recommended or likely to be successful, this chart is provided to give you a clear comparison of wind speeds, designations and descriptions.

The Beaufort Scale

Wind Speed (m.p.h.)	Designation	Description
13 - 18	Moderate breeze	Small branches move
19 - 24	Fresh breeze	Small trees sway
25 - 31	Strong breeze	Large branches move Wind whistles in wires
32 - 38	Moderate gale	whole trees move; walking slightly affected
39 - 46	Fresh gale	twigs break off trees; walking slightly difficult
47 - 54	Strong gale	slight structural damage; high waves; branches break
55 - 63	Whole gale	trees uprooted; considerable structural damage; v. high waves with crest
64 - 74	Storm	Widespread damage; extremely high waves;
75 +	Hurricane	severe and extensive damage; sea visibility greatly reduced

Source: The Audubon Society's Field Guide to North American Weather.

When the weather turns sour, get out and hunt to score on bucks like this.

CHAPTER 7

THE RUT

This is the chapter most of you probably opened to read first. It is a subject that 99.9 percent of all deer hunters want to learn and understand more about. The rut requires constant study and examination by biologists in order for them to provide us, the hunters, with accurate and useful information. Unfortunately, it is not a topic that draws large research funds. So, information about the subject over the last few decades has been slow in coming. Most of the data gathered has been compiled by biologists who are hunters and, therefore, write their papers about the mating habits and rituals of whitetails. Without these dedicated and enthusiastic professionals, we would be living -- when it comes to understanding the white-tail's rut -- in the proverbial dark ages.

Lately, researchers have developed a greater interest to shed more light on the rut -- especially over the last few years. By doing so, they have helped to eliminate much of the misinformation and falsities that have circulated among hunters for years.

This is understandable, because for most sportsmen across the nation, what they know about deer and deer hunting, has for the most part, been hunting information and techniques passed down to them by their fathers, grandfathers and friends. Although some of what they have learned is based on solid, hard-core knowledge and experience, some of it is also information taken from a generous portion of old wives' tales and misnomers.

The simple facts are hunters of today are lucky to have a lot more facts about deer available to them from both the scientific and hunting aspect than any other group of hunters has ever known before. Today's well-read hunter knows a deer has thirty-two teeth, knows how to manage a deer herd, understands a deer's body language and cannot only name all the deer's external glands but tell you how each functions as well!

Yes, indeed, today's deer hunter is well read and therefore more well informed than ever before. No longer do we depend solely on the advice or information that the "old timers" passed on to us -- we want the facts -- and we want them in plain English!

As I said in the beginning of this chapter, for most deer hunters, the most anticipated, and least understood part of deer season, is the rut. A most frequently asked deer hunting question of the "deer hunting authorities" is "Exactly, when is the rut?" If I had a dollar for every time I have heard a hunter ask that question, I would be a rich man -- spending my money deer hunting across North America during one of the three distinct periods of the rut!

For instance, we've all been told, at one time or another, that the rut is totally dependent on "cold weather," that there are vast differences in the dates the rut occurs throughout the country, and that whitetails breed during a two to three week period in November. Understandably, most of us are confused. After all, we have had this erroneous information drilled into our minds by our deer hunting fathers, relatives and friends. For years, they have enforced word-of-mouth information over and over even though the information amounts to nothing more than an old wive's tale.

In studies performed at several universities and by state game departments, deer biologists have uncovered some very interesting and stunning information about the rut -- information most hunters will find hard to believe! Worse yet, they won't know how to use it effectively to score on bucks.

Let's take a closer look at what the rut is really all about and after we do - it should riddle these old wives-tale theories full with factual holes. When it comes to deer hunting, as you've read earlier, I apply several philosophies and axioms to my hunting. Basically, I address most of my deer hunting with a lot of common sense, even when hunting for big bucks. Deer hunting simply isn't as difficult as some would like us to believe. That bears repeating -- deer hunting isn't as difficult as we'd like to believe! Deer do not have the power of reason. They can't think things through, and, they do not have the ability to plan a **detailed** escape. Instead, they are creatures of habit that mostly act and react instinctively to their environment, and that includes predators -- man or beast. Tune in on those actions and reactions and you have immediately increased your odds of scoring on white-tails, even big bucks.

One of the most persistent old wives tales about the breeding season is that the rut is extremely dependent on cold weather. After all, everything I heard and read as a young hunter emphasized that the best hunting for bucks would be when the cold weather brought on the rut. In fact, throughout my early hunting years, I often planned my strategy to pursue bucks that coincided with colder weather. To do this, I decided to hunt in the northern regions of my home state where cold weather came early and stayed late. Many of these hunts took place in the small town of Childwold, New York nestled in the foothills between Tupper Lake and Cranberry Lake in the Adirondack mountains. There, I hunted a large tract of land owned by International Paper Company that was open to hunters in the early 60s.

I took my vacation in late November where I thought the rut was "on" because of the cold weather. It wasn't until the mid-70s that through sheer experience I discovered there was a flaw in this philosophy. I saw the same amount of breeding activity, whether it was warm or cold. And it didn't matter whether I was is in the southern or northern part of the state. It was like I was hit on top of the head with a ball-peen hammer -- and a light came on.

Although cold weather stimulates diurnal (daytime) activity during the rut, it is not responsible for the onset, or even the intensity, of the white-tail's breeding cycle. Mother Nature, perfect in her design, just can't rely on weather to carry on the species -- plain common sense would tell you that. Where cold weather does come into play is that it spurs deer to move about more throughout the day. In other words, it simply generates more daytime buck/doe activity levels. Bucks are motivated by the crisp temperatures to seek out does and, in extreme conditions, their daytime movement aids them to stay warmer. During a warm rutting period, deer become lethargic and tend to bed down throughout the day. Bucks breed mostly at night when the air becomes cooler and they feel more motivated to seek the does out. A good comparison is to ask yourself, when are you more motivated to participate in love making? During a 95-degree day with high humidity or in the evening when the humidity is lower and the temperature has dropped 20 degrees? These type of weather factors are what motivate deer to move throughout the day during a cool or cold rut as opposed to staying bedded and moving to seek out does during the night and at dusk and dawn.

This also holds true for sign left by bucks like scrapes, licking branches and rubs. Warm rut -- less sign. Bucks are not as motivated to paw out as many scrape sites or rub as many trees. The plain and simple truth is they're just more lazy. However, as the weather turns cooler bucks leave much more sign -- they move about not only seeking out does, but also making many more scrapes and rubs than they would in warmer weather.

Unfortunately, when a hunter doesn't see a lot of rubs, scrapes or bucks chasing does during the day, the analysis invariably leads him to the errone-ous conclusion -- a conclusion that is too often shared and believed by all too many buck hunters -- the rut is late, or worse yet, it's over! Shockingly, be-cause of this assumption, many hunters unknowingly wind up hunting either the early or late sides of the peak of the rut. Warm fall or cold fall, the peak of the rut, as with the entire rut itself, will take place one way or the other. You can take that to the DEER HUNTING BANK and deposit it for a future withdrawal.

Mother Nature **must** rely on a **much more dependable stimulus mecha-nism** to set the breeding cycle into motion. Light, or more correctly stated, photoperiodism (except near the equator) is what Mother Nature depends upon to initiate the breeding cycle of the white-tailed deer. As fall approaches, there is a "decreasing ratio of daylight to darkness that triggers the start of the reproductive cycle in whitetails." (Halls, White-tail Deer). This has been documented with deer moved from one hemisphere to another. These deer adjust their breeding cycle to the current photoperiod in which they are liv-ing. (Marshall 1937) This clearly shows how the rut can begin as early as October in some northern latitudes, and as late as January in some southern ranges. Let me be a bit clearer here. If you live in a northern latitude that covers southern Canada and northern United States, where the temperatures are colder stimulating activity, you can bet the rut will seem to start in early

November and peak around the 10th. In somewhat more southern ranges, New York, Missouri, etc., it will peak around the 10th to 15th; while in the southern most ranges, the peak of the primary rut usually takes place late November and early December. In fact, in the deep south, because of latitude changes, the primary rut may often occur in early January. However, generally, you will be very secure in knowing that throughout most of the country, other than the most extreme southern and northern latitudes, the peak of the primary rut falls within the dates mentioned above.

In laymen's terms, this simply means the breeding cycle of a white-tailed deer, no matter where it lives in North America, generally lasts about four months. However, there are high and low points to this four-month long breeding cycle. For instance, the breeding period of white-tails from the northern mid-West to the northern East Coast is approximately three months in duration. Because of photoperiodism, it occurs like clockwork within specific periods throughout the latitudes encompassing these states. However, many variables come into play and there is documented evidence of bucks breeding does as early as September and as late as March! The bottom line is whitetails will mate over long periods if the opportunity presents itself despite weather conditions. If a doe comes into heat and a buck has antlers on his head, he'll breed her no matter what time of the year it is or how warm it might get. Hunters who understand this will immediately be rewarded with more success.

So far, this chapter has covered an overview on the entire breeding sequence. Now, let's more closely examine the three different stages of the breeding cycle. The first stage is the most overlooked and, therefore, least capitalized on by hunters -- the highly productive first rut -- which is also often called the preliminary rut, false rut or pre-rut.

PRE-RUT

Generally, the false rut occurs in early October. Just prior to this period, bucks of the same age class hang out together in small groups called bachelor herds. And, although they can breed soon after they shed their velvet, which can occur as early as the end of August, but mostly in early September, their primary concern in September and into early October is still food.

However, archers hunting this time of year can relate to and confirm what I am about to say. As archers, you know that you can be hunting in an area that really doesn't exhibit much sign in the way of buck rutting activity. You know what I mean. For several days you're hunting and you see an occasional rub and not much else. Then, one day, out of the blue, you find not only one scrape, but several that weren't there just 24 hours ago. And these aren't old scrapes. They are pawed bare to the ground, muddy and have a strong musky odor. What just happened? You have just observed a yearly phenomenon regarding the rut. What happens to cause this obvious intense breeding activity in bucks? Mother Nature - perfect in her design, has just initiated the first of three stages of the rut called the <u>false rut</u>.

Basically, as a bachelor group of bucks leaves their beds to go feed, they aren't thinking of anything else but gathering food. They casually walk through the woods eating acorns as they plan on heading to the apple orchard. Then, out of nowhere, they're met by the pheromones of a mature estrus doe. Wham-o! It's like a cold slap in the face and the next thing you know, there is a flurry of intense activity by bucks to locate the first possibility of sex for the year. I believe they are somewhat confused and their immediate instinctive behavior to the estrus pheromone is to react by making scrapes. Mother Nature uses the pre-rut to intentionally knock the buck over the head (so to speak) to alert him to the onset of the breeding season. From this point on, the bucks will think more about mating and less about food.

As stated above, biologists recently acknowledged the evidence that the white-tail's breeding period can last as long as six months, with periods of high and low breeding activity. More interestingly, they have made reference to a brief estrus cycle (18 to 24 hours), which occurs early in October. This brief estrus cycle is brought on by mature white-tail does that are part of every herd (4 1/2 to 5 1/2 year old) that come into their first reliable and predictable estrus period for the year. Contrary to popular belief, it is not the bucks in a herd that initiate the rut. As I mentioned earlier, a buck can breed soon after he sheds his velvet. However, it is several weeks from that time before most of the does begin to come into estrus. It is the doe population, therefore, which determines the onset of the rut and, to some degree, its intensity.

It's just like a woman in her prime -- her menstrual cycle is predictable and reliable. As a younger woman, it's less so and she may even skip a cycle here and there. As an older woman, her period will definitely become less calculated and stable and lead into menopause. You can relate what happens to female deer to this scenario. Or, if you're still not convinced, relate it to what happens to a female dog. Young female dogs experience erratic estrus cycles. Mature bitches, in their prime, cycle reliably twice a year and as the female dog grows older, her cycle becomes erratic again and inevitably stops all together.

Once bucks discover estrus pheromone permeating their range, they forsake eating and everything else other than frantically searching out estrus does. This is the dramatic increase in scrape and rub activity that archers get to witness during this false rut cycle of mid-October (usually around Oct. 15 to Oct. 20).

Only a few lucky bucks who quickly locate these hot does will get to service them. The rest are destined to be frustrated. This false rut plays a role in quickly breaking up the bachelor herds. Troubled bucks are no longer tolerant of each other and become more belligerent toward each other every day. They will often engage in immediate aggressive behavior and spar upon meeting any other buck. In addition, because of the building tension and continuing decrease in daylight, they will also take out their anxieties on the nearest sapling or tree -- nature's way of helping to strengthen their neck muscles. Venting their frustrations also helps to get them physically and mentally prepared for the inevitable and more serious battles that are sure to come over the next several weeks.

The pre-rut also accounts for a sharp increase in buck activity. During this time, hunters often report a two to four day period when bucks are running around during the middle of the day. These are bucks who have been aroused by the pheromones of the mature estrus does.

This activity also accounts for the fact that archers, who have not seen a single scrape, suddenly see several fresh scrapes appear within 24 hours. What is more important, many archers are confounded by what happens next. Just 24 to 48 hours after this spurt of activity, there is a lull in the brief, but excited, breeding behavior. It begins with the scrapes that were pawed bare to the ground and moist with urine one day, drying up and becoming dormant from lack of attention by bucks almost the next day. What accounts for this phenomenon is that Mother Nature - perfect in her design, only stimulates these mature does into a very brief however potent (scent-wise) estrus period. Over the next 24 to 48 hours, each of these mature does is attended to by a few lucky bucks. Then, it's over. Loss of estrus scent now has the buck paying less attention to breeding behavior and, to a certain degree, more attention to his normal routine.

It is during this "false rut" period that hunters can incorporate a variety of different types of hunting strategies to bag a good buck. Non-aggressive rattling and calling are two excellent techniques this time of year. Just remember not to be over aggressive. Bucks are just not fired up enough to respond aggressively now. Creating mock scrapes, rub grunting and shaking brush and saplings will also dramatically increase your odds of success during this first period of the rut.

Subdued rattling for bucks during these two to three days will usually create immediate response from bucks who are frustrated from not finding a willing doe to breed. And now, they are looking for trouble. I have had bucks respond, sometimes several bucks, with every rattling sequence as long as I kept the rattling toned down. In addition, mature does undergoing this brief estrus cycle are eager to respond to this hunting technique as well. There is no better lure than rattling in a hot doe. She will inevitably attract a horny buck.

I have kept detailed records on my stat cards of strange encounters I have had with bucks during the false rut, all of which have helped prove how productive this early rut can be. I specifically remember making an entry about rattling in several good bucks one day during the false rut in New York State. The entry was made Oct. 10. I was slowly putting up my portable tree stand and now and then it made some noise that, when I thought about it, could have sounded like two bucks in a pushing and shoving match. After a few minutes, I heard a deer crash down the mountainside toward me. I stopped climbing mid-tree and waited to see what was about to unfold. Within moments, I could see a large racked buck trotting toward me. I could hear him grunting as he got within 15 yards. His eyes were bulging from his head. Within seconds, he saw me. To my surprise, the buck totally ignored me and paced defiantly around the tree several times. He then walked off several yards, pawed up a scrape and left -- all the while continually grunting. My only regret is that I couldn't get to my bow that still laid at the base of my tree stand.

The buck probably thought there were two other bucks fighting over one of the few does that were in estrus at the time. Throwing caution to the wind, he came in ready and willing to meet the challenge head on. When he left, I thought my opportunity had disappeared along with him. Once I got set up, however, I rattled the determined buck back in only 30 minutes later. This time, he never got close enough for a shot. Over the next few hours I rattled in three more bucks.

This buck responded to an estrus grunt on Thanksgiving afternoon.

Another testimony to the success a hunter can have during the early rut happened on October 13, 1989. It was 1 p.m. and I had just finished my first grunting sequence when I heard a twig snap. I watched a really big buck recklessly walk through a patch of second-growth just out of range from my tree stand. Grunting and drooling from the corner of his mouth, he walked around the area several times before departing. I waited a few minutes and tried grunting him back. When he didn't respond, I became a bit depressed.

As I began to feel sorry for myself, I heard the soft grunting of a deer behind me. A small six-point emerged directly under my stand and paced nervously several minutes before leaving. Again, I waited a few minutes and grunted. Within a few minutes, ANOTHER buck responded -- an eight-pointer this time. As I drew on the buck, he looked at me, turned inside out, and bolted away as my arrow sailed harmlessly over his back.

Not believing the intense activity of the day, I blew one more grunt, not thinking for a moment that I would attract yet another buck. I did. This time, however, it was slightly different. After grunting very softly for several minutes, a doe stepped out, looked around, urinated and walked off. Moments behind her, another eight-pointer appeared and, with a purposeful walk, slowly followed the trail of the doe. He never saw me stand, draw and release the arrow as all his attention was focused on the hot doe's trail. Remarkably, as the buck ran off before surrendering to his fatal injury, two more bucks walked past my stand! A testament to the unimaginable success the falserut can generate for a hunter who knows when to expect it.

By acknowledging that the rut is three to four months long, you can prevent yourself from falling into the routine of believing that there is only a short period of time to hunt the breeding period. By understanding that there are three peak periods of rutting behavior during these months, you can capitalize accordingly. The next time you are hunting in October and you discover a lot of scrapes that seem to magically appear over night, you are about to become involved with the false rut for the next 24 to 36 hours.

PRIMARY RUT

If you count 28 days forward from this period, you will have the prime time of the "primary rut." During the primary rut, which has its peak activity for about two weeks, most of the does in any herd come into estrus. In most of the northern half of the United States, this primary rut occurs from Nov. 10 through the 15 (give or take a few days on either side). These dates are generally regarded as the peak period of the primary rut. In addition, the mature does who came into estrus 28 days earlier who were not bred, also come into estrus again during this period. As proof, ask any guide worth his salt when you should come to hunt, and he will tell you mid-November -- no matter whether he guides in Canada, Colorado, Maine or New York.

I have talked with Justin B. Henry, owner of a hunting lodge in Sherwood Park, Alberta about this several times. Henry is noted for having guided many of his clients to take some of the largest-racked and heaviest white-tail bucks in North America. During one conversation, I asked Henry when he thought I should hunt at his lodge. Henry said, "I'd be a fool if I had you here any other time than the peak of the primary rut. A good time would be any time during the second or third week of November." In case you missed it earlier, Henry's lodge is in Alberta, Canada, where it's cold, and snowy and the peak of the primary rut is the same as the peak of the primary rut in the east: mid-November!

If you still need more convincing, a peer and friend, Gene Wensel has often told me that in his state of Montana, "Our doe deer normally come into heat about Nov. 16 through Nov. 18 on an annual basis. This peak lasts for a week or so at a fever pitch." That's Montana, folks. And, it's very close to the exact dates I suggest are the peaks of the rut throughout New England and the rest of the country for that matter.

A week to ten days before the primary rut is the peak time of aggressive activity. Bucks are frustrated and are more than just jousting for position prior to this second phase of the rut. At this time of the year, they mean business. All encounters with other bucks are serious encounters because they are playing for all the marbles now. Aggressive types of hunting strategies bring maximum results. If you are a rattler, you can rattle aggressively and have success.

However, this is an appropriate time to say that I am not a believer in over aggressive hunting strategies. Despite what you might have read or heard from other experts, I can assure you from the standpoint of sheer common sense and my own experience, that even when bucks are at their most aggressive behavior, they will fail to respond to over aggressive tactics. No buck, no matter how big or how sexually frustrated he is, wants to have a physical encounter with another buck that may wind up kicking his ass.

A comparison of this can be made by simply remembering your high school days. Remember? Did you ever or did you know anyone whoever picked a fight with someone who was **OBVIOUSLY** physically stronger, taller or heavier? As a buck can easily detect by sight the larger antlers and body size of another buck, the chances are overwhelming that the answer to that question is a resounding -- No. Even if you were one of the toughest guys in school, odds are when you had a fight it was with someone who was of similar or lesser size, strength and weight.

Mother Nature is no different. Within the male whitetails' society, the pecking order is established mostly by body language during the spring and summer months when the bucks are in velvet (which is explained in further detail in Chapter 12). By the time a buck sheds his velvet, he is aware of his rank within the male herd. He knows who is superiors are, his equals, and his subordinates -- only testing (fighting) his status with his equals during the mating season.

If you decide to rattle too aggressively and even if a buck is so frustrated that he decides to respond, he does so very cautiously and at a distance. I cover this subject more thoroughly in the chapters on calling and rattling. Let it suffice to say, you will be a lonely hunter if you think using over aggressive calling or rattling tactics are going to work best.

Making your calls or your rattling techniques sound submissive will draw the attention and aggression of all size bucks -- especially big so-called dominant bucks as they realize most the time all they have to do to scare off a submissive buck is exhibit aggressive body language. This only changes when a physically stronger buck with a rack of equal or slightly smaller size, who hasn't had as many fights, temporarily overpowers the number one, larger racked, and momentarily exhausted buck from his position.

I shot this love-crazed buck while he was busy sniffing a Love Potion #9 mock estrus trail.

LATE RUT

Now, getting back to the rut. Count 28 days from the primary rut date, and you have the prime time of the "late rut" which is the third phase of the white-tails' breeding cycle. During the late rut, most of the immature (or latest born) does, and any other doe that was not successfully bred or skipped a cycle during the last period, come into estrus to be bred during this period. It is Mother Nature's way of ensuring the perpetuation of the species. Many hunters have relayed stories to me that during the late rut, they have had much success with rattling and calling. This doesn't surprise me. Rattling and calling can even be effective into January and February. That's because some does are still experiencing estrus cycles in December with a few cycling as late as January and February.

An innovative hunter firmly believes and understands the rut can last a quarter of the year. More important, he uses this information to plan a lethal whitetail strategy. Some of these strategies include patterning bucks. Although all, but a very few, "knot-head" bucks are **truly** "patternable," especially in the heavily hunted areas of the Northeast, bucks become even less patternable during the post-rut because they must substantially extend their roamings throughout their range to locate late-season does that have come into estrus. Therefore, deer hunting strategies that pay off in big dividends during this period are those that imitate bucks seeking out does in estrus. Once a buck thinks he hears, smells or "sees" bucks that are after a doe in estrus, he is sure to investigate it in hopes of getting the doe himself.

Other late-rut strategies include rattling, calling, mock scrape making, using decoys (both male and female), laying mock urine trails, and using new techniques such as "Shake, Rattle N' Roll." These methods are covered in detail in their appropriate chapters. In addition, some traditional tactics can pay dividends. These methods include posting near well-used runways along secluded swamps and ridges, watching and waiting along agricultural field edges, and ambushing deer in social areas.

During the third phase of the rut, just a single doe in estrus can attract several bucks. This means a hunter could see a few different bucks over a period of time following the trail of one estrus doe. Having patience during this last phase of the rut can yield a hunter a trophy buck. Often, I have passed up lesser bucks who were obviously using their noses to trail one of these late-bloomer does. I specifically recall one such incident while hunting on the ridge behind my home.

It was December 19, and I was hunting during the black powder season that starts the day after regular firearm season ends. Two days earlier, I had noticed a flurry of rut-type behavior activity. This was after not seeing a buck in this area for several days. Knowing that the post rut was due (keep in mind that the post rut is similar to the first or false rut in that it is relatively short compared to the primary rut), I immediately anticipated the activity I saw was because the bucks were scenting the pheromones left by an estrus doe. I decided to hunt the area for the next two days from a tree stand that over-looked a social area. On the last day of the season, I saw four different bucks walk up the trail and continue up the mountain without ever lifting their noses from the ground. The first two bucks were small four and six pointers. By the time the third buck had passed, the rack size increased as he was a decent eight-pointer. I was contemplating shooting him when I spotted yet another buck about 100 yards away making his way up the same trail. As he slowly trotted past my stand with his nose firmly held to the ground, the big 10-pointer never suspected I was there as one clean shot ended his pursuit of this estrus doe.

It doesn't take a rocket scientist to learn how to identify and capitalize on methods to take good bucks during the late rut. During this time of year, throughout most of the whitetail's range, except in the south, there is usually snow cover on the ground. This is an ideal opportunity for hunters to narrow down their search of a doe in estrus. Obviously, if you can locate a "hot" doe, it won't be long before you will also locate the bucks that will be searching her out. Very often, hunters see pink or red droppings left by an estrus doe as she urinates in the snow. Because there are not many does in estrus during the post rut, it doesn't take long for the pheromones from this scent to per-meate the woods and attract a lot of interested bucks from great distances.

Once I have located this type of sign, I try to figure out the route the doe is traveling. Keep in mind, as with bucks, does are also difficult to pattern, especially in highly hunted areas, as they, too, have increased their overall range in search of mates. However, what is unique with does as opposed to bucks during the post rut, is that there are far more bucks ready to service an estrus doe than there are during the primary rut. During the primary rut, an estrus doe has a substantial amount of competition from many other estrus does.

During the post-rut, an estrus doe simply has to follow her normal travel routes and amorous bucks will enthusiastically seek her out. By keeping track of her travels, you will inevitably find yourself at the right place at the right time.

The late rut often offers this type of opportunity to hunters as the few does that come into estrus often attract several bucks to themselves. Unless the very first buck is the one you want to take, patience pays off by waiting to see what other buck has picked up the does' estrus trail and makes its way by your stand. Getting to see several bucks chase after one doe is one of the most exciting aspects of hunting the post rut.

Although the false and primary ruts get much attention, the post rut continues to be a stepchild by being mostly ignored by hunters. Perhaps, as I said earlier, it is because most hunters are led to believe that the rut is long over or perhaps they grow tired by the end of the rutting season and fail to effectively interpret rutting behavior and sign and turn this information into a harvested buck. This season, if you find yourself still looking to score on a buck when the post-rut arrives, chin up.

PHASE #4

Finally, this is a phase of the rut that many hunters are not aware of. It occurs under certain extenuating conditions, most times relating to extreme weather conditions occurring during the normal phases of the primary and post-rut stages of the whitetail's breeding cycle. It normally occurs during the months of January and February. Only a few does experience this late, late phase of estrus, but the few who do quickly attract bucks to their sides. Biologists are beginning to understand this breeding phenomenon more and they should be providing interesting and exciting documentation over the next few years regarding this "extra" late phase of the rut.

FRENZY PERIOD

Now that we have examined the phases of the rut, here is some additional information you probably haven't heard before. This is the meat and potatoes of this chapter. While most hunters assume that the best time to try and take a buck is during the peak phase of the primary rut, and to a large degree, this is true, it is also misleading. While it is certainly true that bucks are looking for does during the peak of the primary rut, and keep the words PRIMARY AND PEAK in mind during this paragraph, bucks who are high on the status ladder, are most likely to already be hooked up with a doe in estrus. This buck is the one so often heard about who mindlessly and, almost like a robot, follows a doe in estrus through the woods and is inevitably intercepted and shot by a hunter. While the peak of the rut certainly presents these type of opportunities, if you really want to be successful while hunting the PRIMARY phase of the rut, always prepare yourself to hunt several days prior to when you think the actual peak of the breeding will take place.

By hunting just a few days prior to this peak period during the primary rut, you increase your chances of seeing many more bucks and taking a really big bruiser -- tenfold. I call this the "frenzy" period of the PRIMARY RUT. And, unlike the other phases of the breeding cycle that Mother Nature has designed to be shorter, this phase has a definite and obvious frenzy demeanor to it. It's when most of the does begin to come into estrus and begin to emit the estrus pheromone.

Although does are discharging an estrus pheromone, they are not ready to breed. Basically, it is fore-play by the doe to excite as many bucks as possible. As more does come into heat, the pheromone begins to dominate the whitetail bucks' world. These does unknowingly accomplish their goal to excite any and all males within their range. Now, bucks become extremely aggressive toward each other and will no longer tolerate other males' presence. While the pheromone puts the buck in an excited sexual state of mind, he is destined to stay frustrated until the estrus cycle reaches the point where does actually accept a buck's advances to mount and breed her. Actual copulation is quick and can happen often over a 24 to 48 hour period.

However, before this acceptance takes place, bucks are so excited by the pheromone they will, at times (like bull elk), masturbate from frustration of not having a doe accept their advances. As the odor of the pheromone gets stronger and stronger, bucks literally go haywire. They chase every single doe they see to stick their nose between their legs to check their current estrus status. If they can't visually locate a doe, they run hell-bent (we've all seen this happen) through the woods, fields and mountainsides searching out does who are leaving these tantalizing pheromones scattered throughout their range.

For 30 years, I have kept 80 different detailed statistics on my Stat Cards and, year-in and year-out, a majority of the time, this frenzy period falls between Nov. 10 through Nov. 13. Some years, my records show it was from the 7th to the 10th and other years it was from the 12th through the 15th of November. Generally, the frenzy period lasts 36 to 48 hours and during warm falls, 24 to 48 hours. It is unmistakable to identify. If you are driving to work during any period from Nov. 1 on, and you happen to see a big racked buck zigzagging through an open field, call in sick. The frenzy period is on! Other indicators that the frenzy period is on include bucks running along fence lines in the middle of the day, bucks darting from woodlines into fields and back again, and just more abnormal buck activity, especially midday. Besides this, if a buck acts atypical by being defiant, you surely can bet the frenzy is on.

Let me explain what I mean by defiant bucks. Often while calling or rattling, I have encountered bucks that, for one reason or another, actually see me. Most times, these bucks turn themselves inside out (a few because of their general belligerent nature stand their ground; but, this is the exception rather than the rule this time of the year) and hightail it back into cover. However, as the primary rut gets closer and the estrus pheromones become more widespread, the general attitude of bucks changes. During the frenzy period, I have called, rattled, walked up on, and accidentally bumped into bucks while hunting. I immediately know the frenzy period has begun when these bucks exhibit very unusual behavior in relation to man. Bucks have stared me down as if they were saying, "Yeah, What do you want?" Others, which were only a few yards from me and clearly identified me as a man, continued to casually walk past me almost as if I didn't exist. Obviously, a buck showing this type of behavior is smelling something so sweet that he ignores the danger nearby. Still other times, I have seen bucks with their eyes bugged out, come zigzagging past my stand and disappear into the brush as quickly as they appeared. Only to reappear moments later and repeat the process again and again, sometimes for many minutes. This kind of behavior is a definite indication that these bucks have forsaken their normal fear of man and are preoccupied with only one thought: sex. Understandably so. I guess I'd be preoccupied, too, if I had to wait a year between my sexual encounters. Come to think of it, if I had to chase my wife around for several days before she'd accept me, I might ignore even a Tyrannosaurus Rex standing between her and me when the time was right!

Hunting this frenzy period will be like no other type of hunting you have ever experienced. No matter where you live, every primary rut phase is preceded by this 24 to 48 and sometimes 36 hour frenzy period of sexual activity. I REGULARLY RECOMMEND TO HUNTERS TO PLAN VACATIONS AROUND THIS PERIOD. IT IS THE BEST 2 TO 3 DAYS OF HUNTING THE ENTIRE SEASON. IT BEATS HUNTING DURING THE OPENING WEEK OF FIREARMS SEASON! No matter where you live, with a little investigation that will take a year or two to fine tune, you can narrow the frenzy period down and plan to hunt it. Throughout New England, you can bet it will fall between November 10 and November 15 (give or take a few days either way) each year. One of the best ways to determine if the frenzy period has begun is to read the police accident report section of your local newspaper a few days before Halloween. If you live in the city, have someone start mailing you a local paper from the area you hunt about the same time. Each week, you will see a definite increase in the number of car/deer accidents reported. As the number of accidents climbs, you can bet it's because bucks are seeking out does as they are emitting more estrus pheromones. It is no surprise that most buck/car accidents occur during the dates I gave you above.

With the new-found information, strategies, and confidence formulas you are building up as you're reading this book, you are creating the foundation that will have you putting your crosshairs on the biggest buck of your lifetime this season. Remember that there will always be controversy among hunters about the rut and when it occurs throughout North America. Don't let that dissuade you from confidently believing in and applying what you have just read. To sum it up, you can take the above information about the rut to the Deer Hunting Bank.

PRE-RUT
Generally begins about Oct. 13 and has a high activity level for 24 to 48 hours, extending an additional day or two depending on variable factors. Then it abruptly ends.

PRIMARY RUT
Starts with the frenzy period around November 10 to the 15 -- give or take a few days either way. It then continues into the period where both bucks and does are matched up for a week and then experiences a slight decline in breeding activity around November 22 or 23.

LATE RUT
Approximately December 13 or so, sexual activity rises again with bucks going into an excited state for two or three days and declines until around the 25th of the month. Generally, if a hunter counts 28 days between peaks of sexual activity, he will discover the heart of the frenzy period during each of the three phases.

CHAPTER 8

THE REAL DIRT ON SCRAPES AND RUBS

Without a doubt -- more bucks -- especially big bucks have been shot by hunters watching over scrape sites than any other hunting strategy used. However, since I have been hunting deer, I can say that the subject of scrape hunting has generated more controversy, disappointment, apprehension and misinformation among buck hunters than any other of the hunting methods combined.

Right up front, the information I'm sharing with you about scrape hunting is functional, common sense based information I have learned the hard way -- through trial and error. Over the years, I have been just as confused about scrapes as you. By making a lot of mistakes while hunting over scrapes and having more than my fair share of success, I have formulated certain ideas and theories about this subject. I can state unequivocally, that scrape hunting is more successful when you apply a healthy dose of common sense to this tactic.

Let me also say, I have learned the success you encounter when hunting over scrapes is positively related to the balance of the deer herd in the area you hunt (buck to doe ratio). In areas where there is a one-sided ratio of bucks to does, the purpose of the scrape is no longer as consequential to the buck. Bucks living within any given area where the doe population is greater than the buck population, may simply, out of instinct, paw out several scrape sights and briefly attend them. But, when most of the does begin to enter their primary estrus cycle, these bucks no longer have an interest or the time to make new scrapes or tend established ones. There are simply too many estrus does roaming the woods willing to give the buck all the amorous attention he is seeking. Therefore, he has no need to hang out at one of his scrape locations waiting to meet a doe and accomplish his lifelong goal -- to mate with as many does as possible.

This is why those who hunt in wilderness areas that don't have a high population of deer, but have a buck and doe population equitably balanced, have better success when hunting over scrapes. Areas like the remote regions of northern Maine, the Adirondack Mts. of New York and a province like New Brunswick in Canada are classic examples. In these remote areas the scrape site plays a critically important role as a convenient meeting site for deer. It is the most practical place for a horny buck to meet a hot doe.

Want a comparison? When you were in your teens did you go to the library to meet a girl? Or, did you go to a dance club, bar, or the beach. I'll bet the latter. You knew where the odds were best for you to meet someone from the opposite sex who was looking to enjoy a night out. The same holds true for a buck. Instinctively, he knows the best and quickest place to meet a hot doe is over a scrape. Therefore, it's important to keep in mind these factors as we discuss scrapes. Not only do they work best in areas where the ratio balance and age structure of both sexes of the deer herd is ideal, but also in remote places where there are so few deer (again equally balanced) that the quickest and easiest way to locate each other is at a scrape site. These factors will determine how often scrapes are used by resident bucks. It's also important to understand that although one buck may make a scrape (does also make scrapes), other bucks and does may use this scrape. Most of the time this is related to the pecking order established in July and August.

According to some biologists and experts, the optimum sex ratio of one buck to every three deer creates terrific scrape hunting conditions, providing all the other factors related to scrape hunting are favorable. The best sex ratio for any deer herd is ideally a herd managed with a ratio of 1:1. At this point, I know you're asking what are the other factors. In talking with several biologists while writing this book, they analyze the following components when figuring out if an area will have optimum scrape making and activity levels.
* Buck-to-doe ratio
* Numbers of mature bucks within the herd
* Number of mature does within the herd

       * Age structure of both sexes

and

       * General health of the herd

In addition, there are hunting factors to also consider when determining how successful scrape hunting will be.

       * Time of year
       * Wind patterns in the area hunted
       * Weather conditions
       * How far the deer move between bedding, social and feeding areas

And, my favorite, because I think it's the most important factor when it comes to everything related to deer hunting, whether you are hunting **disturbed or undisturbed deer**:

       * **Hunting pressure** -- Are you hunting deer that are relaxed or spooky?

Getting back to optimum sex ratios, as the sex ratio increases, which means the balance becomes less than one buck for every three does, scrape making and activity and the results from hunting over them, decreases appropriately. For most of you reading this book, the real hard truth is that you probably don't live in an area with an ideal sex ratio. You probably hunt in an area that is heavily hunted. Therefore, you are probably hunting deer that are disturbed. So, can scrape hunting be an effective hunting strategy for you -- you bet! It will just take a common sense approach and plan for hunting scrapes to make you a successful scrape hunter.

First, try to locate areas that don't receive much hunting pressure. Some of my best success with scrape hunting has been in populated suburban areas while chasing bucks I call Backyard Bucks (by the way, I dedicated a whole chapter to this adaptable buck). By just simply doing a little research -- **by yourself and without making any fanfare to your hunting companions about what you're doing**, you can find ideal out-of-the way places to hunt scrapes. Remember whenever you locate a good scrape or discover a big buck, keep it to yourself. It doesn't take but the slightest bit of pressure -- and that could mean just one other hunter entering this buck's bailiwick -- to alert him to the fact that he is being hunted. The result will be the buck will become more cagey and hunting him will become much more difficult. Hunting pressure is a hunter's second worse enemy (with wind being the first).

Ideal places to search out secluded scrape areas include small islands in rivers, small patches of brush or wood lots, private estates (the smaller the better), lands owned by corporations, military bases, manufacturing plants, church properties, land surrounding suburban reservoirs, golf courses, country hospitals, small outlying strip malls, rural airports and one of my favorite, prisons. All these areas usually get overlooked by hunters who are afraid to ask for permission to hunt from these property owners. Or, simply because hunters don't believe these small pieces of land can offer great deer hunting. I could tell you here and now it is worth your effort to carefully check these places out. If you can't hunt within the areas I mentioned, hunt as close to the property borders as possible.

If none of these type of places are available to you and you hunt on public lands that are heavily hunted, here is the key to successful scrape hunting on public land. Get off the beaten track. I normally don't recommend a hunter must go "way back in" to score on a good buck. However, when it comes to using a scrape hunting strategy on public land, it's better to hunt further in. Besides getting yourself away from the crowd, you are likely to discover some remote swamp or cedar patch that will be alive with fresh primary scrapes. The bucks in these areas are usually bigger and there are usually more of them. When you find an area with undisturbed bucks, especially mature bucks, you have found a scrape hunting hot spot. The competition between mature bucks not undergoing heavy hunting pressure is intense and this is the single most desirable factor when scrape hunting.

For years, I have listened to disappointed hunters explain to me how they have had little success when hunting scrapes. Their reasons are wide and varied, "The primary scrape I was watching was abandoned by the buck" or "The buck is only checking the scrape nocturnally" or "I don't know how to tell the difference between a primary scrape and any other scrape" and the one I used relate to, "I watched a primary scrape for days without ever seeing a buck."

Not only have I heard them all, but I've lived them all, as well. That is until 15 years ago when I decided to figure out how to successfully identify and hunt active scrapes. **Scrape hunting isn't easy despite what anyone including the experts may tell you. If scrape hunting was so foolproof, hunters wouldn't need any other tactic and all of us would be killing big bucks every year.**

Some hunters and most experts say it's important to classify scrapes. Hunters must know whether the scrape they are hunting over is a primary or secondary scrape and so on. To this, I simply reply, "Bull dinky!" Not necessary. In fact, it can lead to more confusion about the subject. Through experience, I've learned that in some areas, there might not even be a single primary scrape to be found. Instead of wasting a lot of time looking for PRIMARY or SECONDARY scrapes, remember, just find a fairly large scrape (3' x 3' or larger) and you'll have found as good a scrape to hunt over as any other. The scrape you're hunting should be:

* moist, or at least damp
* fresh and dark-looking
* pawed cleanly to the bare earth
* almost free of debris (no branches, leaves, etc.)
* **and has an overhanging branch, (esp. if bitten in two)**

If the additional following conditions exist, the scrape is even better than the one described above:

* is surrounded by rubs
* has a strong musky or urine odor
* has visible droplets of blood (from the estrus doe, most visible in scrapes made in the snow)
* tracks in and around the scrape (the bigger the better)
* lots of droppings (look for clumped dung from bucks)

If you find a scrape showing most or all of the above, worrying about whether it's a primary or secondary scrape is ridiculous. Stop and please read that sentence again. Instead, stop worrying about trying to find primary or secondary scrapes. Look for a scrape like I described above. Then go down wind and set up. Just hunt the darn thing -- confidently.

With that said, for the sake of providing you with the information to be a more informed deer hunter, here is how you can simply and quickly identify primary and secondary scrapes. Primary scrapes are usually 4' x 4' and are often larger. They are usually churned up, muddy from buck urine and are free of debris. They will ALWAYS be accompanied by an overhanging branch. This branch, more often than not, will show signs of having been chewed and frayed by the buck as he deposits scents from his mouth, eyes and forehead while he refreshes his scrapes by urinating down his legs, over his tarsals and into the scrape. Most times, the buck leaves a hoof print somewhere near the center of the scrape. Primary scrapes are made in areas off the beaten trail. They are still placed where the buck has learned he will receive the most attention by passing does. A buck does not make many primary scrapes.

Secondary scrapes are made with much more frequency than primary scrapes and receive much less attention by a buck. They are usually much smaller (3' x 3' and less) and are not given the meticulous construction attention a buck pays to creating his primary scrape. Secondary scrapes are often erratic in shape and contain a small amount of debris (leaves, twigs, etc.). They are generally made close together and often form a line of direction. This collection of scrapes is often called a "scrape line" and, although they attract both bucks and does, they are not as productive as primary scrapes.

Remember that scrapes can be abandoned by bucks for a variety of reasons. In the pre-rut, as you read in the Rut chapter, scrapes are abandoned almost as soon as they are made because the bucks are too busy chasing mature does who came into a brief estrus cycle. During the primary rut, scrapes are abandoned for many reasons. Most often, however, it is when many does (in a herd with an unbalanced sex ratio) all come into estrus simultaneously. Remember what I said above, in this situation, a buck doesn't need scrapes.

Some hunters sit over abandoned scrapes not realizing another hunter may have already killed the buck that made the scrape. Or, estrus doe activity levels may be altered and the bucks moved to another area with a higher concentration of estrus does. One of the most common reasons for abandonment, at least daytime abandonment, is hunting pressure . . . and so on.

Bucks use these single scrapes as meeting places for does. They create scrape lines to "lure" does in. These scrapes are often left in areas where does frequent, such as fence lines, edges of fields and brush lines. A scrape line is designed to encourage does to follow these smaller scrapes. Resembling the trail of bread left by Gretel (in the fairy tale Hansel & Gretel), this scrape line is used not as a rescue effort, but rather to lead the hot doe to a secure place where the horny buck is waiting.

Many hunters ask me how long should they hunt over an active scrape before giving up. This is probably one of the most difficult questions to answer. A realistic answer depends on a myriad of factors. To be quite candid, I'd have to see the hunting area, figure out the pressure from other hunters and look at the actual scrape to give an educated answer. However, generally, if the area you are hunting has a buck to doe ratio of about one buck to every four does, you'll see enough buck activity at active scrape sights that should last right through the peak of the primary rut. If the ratio is higher than 1:6 when the peak begins to fall off, I recommend abandoning the scrape and, instead, concentrating your efforts on locating does.

As many of you have often heard me say, "I am not a buck hunter, I am a doe hunter." **What I mean by that is I always concentrate my efforts during the frenzy and rut phases on locating does. If you locate the does during this time of year, you'll locate the bucks.** I only abandon this theory in the early part of October during the archery season when hunting the more secluded areas I think the bucks are using this time of year.

I have found most scrapes left by bucks are left in areas most frequented by does in late October. Look for scrapes where you find heavy doe activity during that time of the year. When you find a scrape opened up in November, you can rest assured it will be more active than any of the October scrapes described above.

So, now let's get down to it. Now that you understand scrapes, how can you hunt them successfully? There are several methods to increase your scrape hunting success. Some require some imagination;and others just require standard hunting tactics -- both work. I have had much more success by getting creative. I cover these in the chapter called Unorthodox Tactics. I'll touch briefly on them here.

First, let's look at the more traditional strategies you can use. The over-all goal in hunting over scrapes should be to attract the buck to you, rather than waiting for the buck to come in to check the scrape on his own. Many of my hunting strategies are directed to this end. I believe big bucks are like spiders in a web. They can hang out all day without ever moving, unless they are INSTINCTIVELY MOTIVATED to do otherwise. By using these moti-vating tactics, you eliminate having to wait on a buck who may or may not make his way past your stand.

By using these active strategies, you are no longer a passive hunter. You are a hunter who has now taken much more control of his deer hunting destiny -- and success.

The most common error made when hunting over scrapes occurs when hunters investigate the scrape too closely. Don't walk right up to it, walk around it, poke at it, or handle the overhead branch. Obviously, all you ac-complish is forewarning the buck via his most effective sense - his nose - that trouble has arrived! If the buck isn't immediately alerted to your presence after such a close investigation, he's certain to pick it up when he checks it out after you have left. If the human odor left behind is too strong when he arrives at the scrape, the buck may even abandon the scrape for a few days.

So, **Scrape Hunting Rule #1** is to investigate all scrapes from a dis-tance of several yards. If you want to investigate a scrape more closely, make sure the soles of your boots, whether they are rubber or leather, are washed clean with a non-scented cleanser. I wash the bottom of my hunting boots at least every other day. Also, carry surgeons' gloves and use them if you think you have to poke around (or plan to create a mock scrape) and touch any-thing in and around the scrape. Next, even if you take all the precautions above, don't stay at the scrape longer than necessary.

Scrape Hunting Rule #2 - The next thing to avoid is setting up too close to the scrape. For bow hunters, I recommend setting up no closer than 15 yards no farther than 30 yards. Getting within 15 to 20 yards is a "roll of the dice" as any buck approaching a scrape usually checks out his surround-ing before he comes in. When I get this close, I make sure I am thoroughly concealed. For firearm hunters, I recommend never getting closer than 30 yards and, most times, I suggest setting up 50 to 75 yards away, depending upon how thick the cover is. **Always set up down wind of the scrape.**

If you've ever been at one of my seminars, you've heard me say this again, the problem with hunting scrapes is that most bucks have learned to check their scrapes downwind and from the safety of cover. They only venture forth when the wind currents tell him that a hot doe has come into the scrape or when he smells the urine or tarsal gland of a competitive buck. In either case, he'll come in to investigate. It is this type of behavior response that has enabled me to create several unusual tactics that can provide you with some amazing results.

SPIDER SYNDROME

I discovered this when a hunter at one of my seminars related the following story to me. At the end of my seminar he said, "Peter, I was hunting a big primary scrape when I was in Maine. Every morning when I went back to the stand, I saw that the buck used the scrape the night before. After spending several days watching the scrape all day long without ever seeing a buck, I decided on the last day to leave early and slowly stalk along a logging road on my way back to the lodge. I thought I would get lucky and jump a buck and not go back home empty handed."

Without taking a breath, the discouraged hunter went on to say, "When I decided to get up, I grabbed my wool day pack. When I swung it around my shoulder to put it on my back, the strap got caught in the brush behind me and it made noise when I pulled it free. Then, I grabbed my rifle and, as sure as heck, the sling got hung up in the brush and made more noise when I pulled it free. At this point I was thoroughly pissed off. So, when I took a few steps, I snapped a branch. Now, I was really mad. So, I kicked the branch as hard as I could I was so angry. Once the branch stopped skidding along the leaves, I heard branches breaking and leaves crunching. Almost instantly there was a big racked buck standing less than 10 yards from me! Before I could get my gun off my shoulder, he made me, whirled and was gone."

Before I could say a word, the hunter turned and melted off into the crowd. That night in the hotel, I thought about what he said. It was so obvious that I couldn't believe I never thought of it before then. This hunter motivated the buck into responding. He was probably sitting within 100 yards of this buck the entire week he was hunting the scrape. For whatever reason, perhaps the wind was carrying his human odor toward the buck, the buck never approached his scrape while the hunter was there. Perhaps the buck had been hunted hard by other hunters before this hunter arrived anddecided the best time to check the scrape was nocturnally.

In any event, the buck acted like a spider in a web. If you look at a spider, she'll stay in the same spot all day long until something shakes the web. It could be an insect, or an eraser from a pencil. Whether it's a food source or a foreign object, the spider is motivated by the vibrations to run down the web to investigate. This is exactly what happened with this hunter.

The sounds he made unintentionally imitated the natural sounds another buck or doe might have made as it approached his scrape. Both bucks and does can be very possessive about a scrape even if they didn't make it themselves. These natural sounds sparked the buck's interest enough to have him abandon his caution and run in and check out whether a hot doe had moved in or to see if it was a competitive buck scent-marking his scrape. Had the hunter been ready, his hunt would have ended successfully. Noise is not nearly as bad as we have been lead to believe, especially if the noise you make is made with a healthy dose of good ol' common sense.

Proof that some foreign noises attract deer is brought home each year by hunters I talk to. Often, I've been told about how a buck ran in as a hunter was climbing a tree with his portable tree stand. Obviously, the buck responded to the sounds of the stand scraping against the bark of the tree. Others have told me about bucks running in after snapping off branches to clear shooting lanes. Still others, have related stories how bucks have come in while they sawed or chopped saplings. Many times, as I am raking a trail free of leaves and debris to my stand, I have had bucks and does trot in to investigate the noise. All these types of natural noises can trigger an instinctive reaction by bucks to investigate what they may perceive to be a competitive buck or hot doe.

Other than seeing a big buck frequenting your hunting area, the first big scrapes will confirm that a mature buck is present. Big mature bucks start making NON-ACTIVE scrapes as early as September. These are scrapes are made, I believe, through instinct rather than being initiated by any onset of the rut. I firmly believe immature bucks don't start scraping until mid to late-October.

The best time to hunt scrapes is not during the actual peak of the primary rut, but, as I mentioned in the chapter about the Rut, rather a week earlier during the frenzy period. By being informed and knowing how to take advantage of hunting scrapes, you will capitalize on this interesting and challenging facet of deer hunting.

Try using antlers to rub a nearby sapling -- the noise often attracts other bucks!

Other than finding a fresh scrape, discovering a rub irrefutably gets the adrenalin flowing in deer hunters. Without actually seeing the buck, we know he passed this way. It gives us momentum. We become confident that we are hunting in an area with bucks.

Like scrapes, however, rubs have also been a source of controversy and misinformation, creating a quagmire of confusion about the subject. Determining why a buck makes a rub and when and where he makes it has been the preoccupation of many biologists and deer hunters alike. Unfortunately, the information gathered about rubs for the most part, has only created more questions than answers.

The trick with rubs is to separate fact from misinformation. Rubs have important implications for deer hunters. To begin with, bucks do not make rubs solely for the purpose of removing velvet from their antlers. Bucks remove their velvet on bushes, saplings and with their rear hooves. In fact, many bucks even tear off loose velvet with their teeth and eat it. On occasion, they remove small pieces of stubborn velvet by rubbing their antlers on a tree.

However, the primary reason bucks make rubs is to first establish a visual and olfactory (scent) sign post to other bucks and even does. **RUBS ARE PART OF THEIR COMPLEX SYSTEM OF COMMUNICATION.** Understanding this single fact can help you sort out all the other important implications of rub making by bucks.

Bucks don't rub a tree just to rub it or solely to strengthen their neck muscles. They rub tress to establish their position in the herd, to warn off inferior bucks, to attract does and to release frustration. But, the behavior of rubbing goes much farther. As a buck rubs a tree he releases scent from his forehead gland. This pheromone, or scent, also acts as a sexual stimulant to does. Some biologists believe the scent left after a buck has rubbed a tree can actually stimulate does into their estrous cycle. It is something similar to how horse breeders use a stallion as a teaser to get mares primed to breed. Does interpret rubs as sexual sign posts. The more they see and smell, the more primed they become.

I once read that some biologists believe that these pheromones act as biological stimulants which can induce early ovulation in does. Instinctively, bucks realize this and, even before the rut begins in earnest for the does, bucks begin to make rubs. Made lethargically at first, these are the rubs you see in September and early October. Then as the buck's own testosterone levels increase, his instinct to make and deposit scent on more and more rubs becomes a preoccupation with him accounting for the dramatic increase in rub sightings by hunters in late October and early November.

Some biologists go as far as saying that the more bucks rub in a given area, the more likely an early estrus will take place among does! The bottom line here is that if you are hunting in an area with an exceptional amount of buck rubs you may experience rutting behavior earlier than normal -- a fact that would be overlooked if you weren't aware of the consequences of excess rubbing activity.

Rubs indicate a lot more, too. Many of us have heard that small rubs are made by bucks with small racks and big rubs are made by bucks with large racks. While this is generally true, it is not written in stone. In order to better determine if a rub was made by a yearling or by a mature buck, examine each rub very carefully -- even if it was made on a small sapling tree. Big bucks leave a couple of tell-tale signs on their rubs. Inevitably, a mature buck will leave small gouges (from the points on his antlers) in the tree. In addition, a lot of times rubs made by mature bucks will be longer than a normal rub, starting almost at the base of the tree and going up higher than a normal rub. Also, the tree will usually have some broken branches or may even have its trunk bent or broken.

Like this 8-point is doing, a buck always licks and sniffs a tree after rubbing his forehead and antlers on it.

Rubs can also indicate a travel pattern. During my early days of deer hunting, I found a single rub entering the woods from a corn field. As I examined it, I discovered several more rubs in somewhat of a line heading deeper into the woods. Obviously, a buck came from the field where he was eating or attending does and on his way back to his bedding area made or added to the rubs I had discovered.

As I continued into the woods looking over the rubs I glanced back toward the field. To my surprise I saw another line of rubs -- about fifty yards away from the rubs I was looking at. Interestingly they were made on the opposite side of the trees I was looking over. Clearly, the buck made this line of rubs as he exited the woods and made his way to the field. Most bucks will take a morning route that is different then their evening route. At any rate, after finding several small gouges in the rubbed trees I determined the buck had some points on his antlers. I decided to hunt the area that evening.

I posted along the line of rubs that made their way into the field. At 4:30 PM an 8-point buck made his way through the woods heading to the field. As he stopped to rub a small sapling tree directly in line with the other rubs I had examined earlier in the day -- I shot him. I have used rubs to determine the general direction or travel patterns of bucks ever since -- and so can you!

I've also used rubs to help me determine the core area of bucks. When you discover an area of rubs that are clumped in close proximity of one another and are in a semi-circle, you've more than likely discovered the very heart of a larger buck's core area. Often, but not always, these spots are off the beaten trail. They are frequently very close to a buck's preferred bedding spot. A spot big buck will go to when he seeks solitude from hunting pressure.

I use this tactic on a mountain I hunt in my home town. Early in the season, I search out a spot that has the kind of rubs I described above. From that point on, I leave the area alone until hunting pressure sends the bigger bucks sulking for cover. When the pressure is on, I hunt the area. Over the years, I have taken several trophy size bucks using this tactic. The most recent being a 12-point buck that I shot after posting in a spot with an excess of rubs in a semi-circle. The buck scored 149 7/8 Boone & Crockett points. Bucks this size often revert to using these types of areas after the firearms season gets underway.

I also like to look for rubs that are concentrated next to beds, droppings and in and along thick cover. When I find rubs with this type of additional sign and terrain, I have found a hot spot. If, however, after a diligent search, I have not discovered a normal amount of rubs in my area, its time for me to think about hunting elsewhere. A lack of rubs in a given area could be a good clue to a low buck population. A lack of substantial size rubs could indicate a lack of mature bucks. In either event, I look for another spot to hunt. The only exception to this rule according to some biologists, is that there will be less bucks rubbing activity when the acorn crop is low. I have never been able to prove or disprove that theory.

Another interesting point about rubs takes place during the frenzy period of the rut. That's when buck rubs take on a completely different look. They begin to make much larger rubs during this time. These "frenzy period rut-rubs" can be seen for quite a distance by other deer. The bucks even change the types of trees they rub on during this period using sumac, cedars, pines and other aromatic type trees. The more mature bucks will make lots of rubs now and hunters will begin seeing a lot more scarred trees in their hunting area.

Finally, I strongly believe that aggressive mature bucks within a herd will make different types of rubs than the lesser or subordinate bucks do. These rubs tend to be VERY LARGE and are made on big cedar trees. These individual trees are often revisited by the same buck year after year. These types of rubs also attract other large bucks. However, they are not left all over the woods. They are few in number in heavily hunted areas -- but they are there. In fact, I have noticed this behavior more in areas that are specifically managed for trophy bucks.

I once found such a rub a few years back. It was on a cedar tree that measured 10 inches around! In fact, I have never found one on any other type tree other than a cedar. I think that's because cedar trees are the only trees that can withstand the onslaught of this type of rub. After a long three day vigil of hunting the area, I shot a twelve point buck as he was walking toward the exact tree. Until this day I am not sure if he was the buck who made the original rub, or, if he was just another dominant-type buck who was coming in to check the large rub out and refreshen it with his own scent.

The simple fact is, big rubs attract BIG bucks. A few big bucks may even use the same tree to rub! I mentioned this behavior in the chapter on decoys. It's also why I strongly recommend that hunters make big false rubs to attract big bucks. These visual sign posts are hardly ever ignored by big bucks. They instinctively HAVE to check the rub out. They want to identify through scent deposited on the tree by the last buck if that buck was more dominant (aggressive) than them or not.

Rubs are too often ignored for nothing more than an indication of a buck being in an area. They shouldn't be. Look them over carefully to determine what they mean. They can and will provide you with several important clues. When you become proficient at reading rubs, you will be able to identify the size of the buck that made the rub, a direction he was traveling, whether or not it was his core area, and even the time of day it was made (i.e. morning or afternoon route).

Keeping in mind everything I've said above, here's a hunting strategy that I named several years ago which I named, "Shake and Break." Simply put, bucks sometimes react to sounds that they think are being made by other bucks. A buck that hears branches being snapped, leaves shuffling, or the grating sound of a tree trunk being rubbed, can be fooled or, more precisely,instinctively motivated into believing these noises are being made by a competitive buck or bucks.

Many times, especially during what I call the "Big Chase" (the 48 to 72 hour period when bucks are frantically chasing after estrous does), bucks respond to these fraudulent natural sounds by throwing caution to the wind and enthusiastically running in to check out what they believe to be a racket being made by another buck. Bucks have even responded when I took small saplings and brush and shook them violently for several minutes. Other times, bucks have reacted to the sounds when I took a single antler and rubbed it up and down a small tree. I intentionally look for trees with loose bark and rub high enough so that the bark can fall to the leaves below. The added noise of the bark landing on the leaves acts as an additional motivational stimulus. As you will discover when using this tactic, however, you must be ready to shoot quickly. Most bucks that respond to these noises often race in, look around briefly, and then leave in as big a hurry as when they arrived. Be creative when deer hunting; don't be afraid to make noises that imitate natural sounds made by rutting bucks.

Here a hunter checks out a large rub made by a mature buck.

CHAPTER 9

THE SMELL OF SUCCESS

Scent and whitetails go hand in hand. Without question, the whitetail's sense of smell is its key to survival and your key to hunting success. Disregard a deer's ability to scent man, predator, a food source, or a mate, and you begin your hunting behind the proverbial eightball. No other sense in the whitetail's survival arsenal is more relied on or more effective than its sense of smell.

As I mention in Chapter 5 (Wind and Whitetails), you must keep wind direction uppermost in your mind. Hunting with the wind in your favor is critical to consistent success whether you use scents or not. In addition, it's critical to keep your body as clean as possible and your equipment and clothing free of foreign odors. To help reduce human and foreign odors, you can use a variety of commercially made attracting, masking, and food scents in addition to non-scented soaps.

Some experts believe that scents are just hype and swear they are not effective. Others are more practical in their opinion about commercially made scent. And then, there are the zealous ones who make outrageous claims about the effectiveness of commercially made deer scents.

My view on scents is more realistic and is based solely on common sense -- forgive the pun. I believe using commercially made scents to mask human odor or to attract a buck requires a lot of common sense. I can guarantee you no matter what type of scent you use, you will have more success using it SPARINGLY than by following the directions that recommend using large doses of scent throughout the woods. Too much natural deer scent (doe estrus, buck urine, tarsal,interdigital, etc.,), will spook a buck almost as quickly as human odor. However, I have found that using commercially made scent WISELY has helped my deer hunting and not hindered it.

Remember this saying for the rest of your deer hunting days, "**Bust a buck's nose and you've busted the buck**." Please read that sentence again. **Learning how to fool a buck's nose is the key to your deer hunting success**. All this means is if you block or impede a buck's ability to pick up your human odor, the battle is better than halfway won. In addition, if you can fool him into believing there is a hot doe or a preferred food source nearby, you will increase your chances of seeing and shooting more bucks.

In this chapter, I'll talk about how to use glandular scents from deer, commercially made attracting and food scents, and how to substantially re-duce human odor when hunting. If you would like to have the most exciting and challenging deer season you've had in a long time, read this chapter carefully. First, let's look at how you can capitalize on attracting and fooling bucks by using scents from deer glands.

DEER GLANDULAR SCENTS

You can create a variety of responses from deer, by using — or avoiding — different gland scents. In creating these responses, you can attract or stir deer even when other hunters are having a hard time seeing game.

White-tailed deer have several external glands that play a significant part in their communication and behavior. These glands include the tarsal, interdigital, metatarsal, orbital/forehead and preorbital. Pheromones created by these glands are received and interpreted by deer. These olfactory mes-sages act to alert, calm, attract, frighten, identify and even help in establishing a deer's rank within the herd.

Recently, however, more is being written about other newly researched glands. One such researcher is Dr. Karl Miller at the University of Georgia, a leading expert on the physiology of whitetails. The **nasal gland** is found inside the nostrils of a deer's nose. The gland consists of two almond shaped organs that scientists are not sure whether it produces a scent or only lubri-cates the lining of the nose. They have speculated, however, that it does play a role in marking overhead branches when making a scrape.

Another recently discovered gland is the **preputial gland** located on the inside of the buck's penal sheath. Research so far suggests that this gland doesn't play a significant role regarding the rutting odor of a buck during the breeding season.

According to Dr. Miller and other leading deer experts, "so far we know that deer have seven different glandular regions. How many more will we find? Who knows? But, I think it's a safe bet that we will find more."

The "**forehead gland**" is comprised of sebaceous and aprocine hairs. During the rut, these hairs swell up and produce a scent that the buck deposits on trees as he is rubbing. Both bucks and does use this gland as a scent marker. In the 10 years I have videotaped deer, I have taped dozens of bucks rubbing their antlers on trees. To the buck, they all exhibited the same behavior while rubbing. First, they approach the tree or sapling, smell it, and then begin to vigorously rub their antlers against the trunk. After rubbing their antlers up and down several times, they pause, step back, smell the trunk and then lick it. Then, if the mood strikes them, they repeat the process over again. Obviously, this behavior is not a random act, but rather a specific behavioral routine bucks seem to stick to when making a rub. The rubbed area often carries an odor for days.

TARSAL

The tarsal gland, a true external gland, is on the inside of the hind legs of all deer. This tan gland turns almost black as bucks continually urinate on it throughout the rut. Deer use tarsal gland pheromones (which are mostly made up of lactones) several ways, as a visual and olfactory signal of a mature buck, as an alarm, to identify individual deer, and in mature deer, it becomes involved with breeding behavior during the rut. When excited, the hairs on the tarsal gland stand erect and can be seen for quite a distance by other deer. All deer urinate on their tarsal glands and this contributes to their pungent odor.

To obtain optimum response from tarsal scent during the rut, put several drops of commercially-made scent in a drip boot dispenser, rag or pad and hang it from a branch close by. Its scent will permeate the area and act as an attracting or agitating smell. Don't place it on your clothing. You don't want the deer's attention to be zeroing in on you. Instead, focus his attention or aggression ten to twenty yards from you. More about why I recommend this at the end of the chapter.

Although the scent from tarsal glands of harvested does attracts bucks, many hunters have had equal success attracting bucks with commercially made tarsal scent. Often, this scent lures in a belligerentbuck who thinks another buck is working his area. AT TIMES (not always), the odor of tarsal agitates bucks so much they respond within a short period of time after putting out the scent.

When creating a mock scrape or hunting over a natural scrape, I use tarsal scent. I also use it when I am hunting with deer decoys. Placing a few drops on the inside of a buck decoy's legs adds to the flavor of realism. Remember the key phrase of this book, "Always try to create the ENTIRE illusion." In addition, I use tarsal with estrus scents when I am hunting during the rut.

Tarsal scent agitates bucks during the rut.

Several years ago, my wife, Kate, began using tarsal scent. That year, she placed several drops of tarsal in a drip dispenser and on rags tied around her thighs. She left a tarsal scent trail on the ground and on foliage a few feet off the ground. Her stand was a few hundred yards from where she began laying down the scent trail. About 30 minutes after settling into her stand, she saw several young bucks walking up the tarsal-scent trail she left. In once instance, two bucks were approaching one behind the other. Once the bucks reached the end of the scent-marked trail, they became confused and belligerent. These two small bucks waited at the base of Kate's treestand for about 20 minutes. Deciding to pass up the small bucks, she watched them spar with each other before they walked away.

Tarsal is a pungent odor. Use it only during the peak rut and then only sparingly. Using tarsal at the wrong time of year and too much of it will be ineffective. The key to all these glandular scents is to try to use them in conjunction with the times of year that deer are accustomed to naturally associating their smells in the woods.

INTERDIGITAL

Interdigital is a potent scent that attracts all deer when used sparingly.

The interdigital gland is located between the deer's hooves. It is a yellow waxy substance that emits a secretion with an offensive potent odor. Interdigital scent is like a human fingerprint, individual to each deer. Although

115

I don't know of documented evidence suggesting the interdigital odor from bucks and does is different, I would speculate the interdigital scent from mature bucks and does is more potent than the scent from immature deer.

Hunters can use interdigital scent two ways. Used sparingly, it acts as an attracting scent. All deer leave minute amounts of interdigital scent as they walk. Other deer follow trails marked with a normal amount of interdigital scent. Use only one or two drops of a commercially-made scent on a boot pad. When you are within fifteen yards of your stand, remove the pad, hang it on a bush, and wait for deer to come and investigate the odor.

Deer also use interdigital scent as a warning to other deer. When a deer stomps its hooves, it's warning other deer of danger through sight, sound, and scent. Deer that smell excess interdigital scent often refuse to continue further down the trail. They will mill about nervously for several moments, walk around the scent or retreat the way they came, while instinctively heeding the pheromone warning left earlier by another deer. Hunters who use interdigital scent incorrectly (in excess of a few drops) will definitely spook rather than attract deer.

Here's my favorite way to make deer move out of heavy cover. When I was a guide, I placed clients on known buck escape routes. I moved about 100 yards away, spread excess interdigital scent (about 10 drops), stomped my feet and blew an alarm-distress snort. This imitation of a deer sending out an alarm — through both audible and olfactory scent messages — sent bucks and doessneaking down the posted escape routes while trying to flee the danger signals their ears and noses were receiving. Of course, you would not want to use this ploy too often or in more than one or two locations in the woods you are hunting. It could have the tendency to genuinely motivate deer to become reluctant to use the area.

To convince you of the potency of this scent, simply spread the toes of the next deer you kill, and, with the tip of a knife, dig between the toes. *Caution:* Don't be naive enough to place the knife tip directly up under your nose. You'll regret it for the rest of the day. The odor is so foul it can make you nauseous. I use a commercially made interdigital scent (Pete Rickard) rather than collecting it from dead deer.

PREORBITAL

The preorbital gland is located just below the corner of the eye. Its main function is to serve as a tear duct. However, deer continually rub this gland (together with the gland on their forehead) on bushes, branches, and tree limbs, especially during the rut. Biologists speculate deer use this gland to deposit a specific pheromone to mark certain areas and to help identify individual deer to each other.

I know an avid bow hunter who regularly removes the preorbital gland, along with the gland from under the forehead, from the hides he capes from deer -- preferably bucks. Once he has caped the hide, he turns it inside out and cuts the entire eye section free including the tear duct (which is the preorbital gland). Then he removes the section of the forehead containing the forehead gland. With rubber surgeons' gloves, he rubs the tear duct and forehead gland on branches that are in shooting lanes around his tree stand.

"Over the years," he has told me, "I have watched deer moving through my area, stop and raise their noses trying to locate the odor. They slowly approach a branch I rubbed the scent on and begin to mouth and rub their eyes and forehead on it. It has often given me the opportunity to shoot at a buck who isn't paying attention to me or that might have walked past my stand without ever stopping."

I do not know of a manufacturer making a synthetic preorbital or forehead gland scent. If you want to try these scents, you'll have to gather them from harvested deer. This is a job, however, which may prove to involve a considerable amount of effort and work.

The first time I tried these scents was during the 1994 season. I had limited success -- which didn't surprise me. Whenever you are using natural scents, there is a period of trial and error in the testing. I probably used too much although I know enough to use all scents sparingly. I intend to try using these glands again during the 1995 season. In any event, the limited success I had in attracting two bucks while using these scents encourages me to continue to use them.

METATARSAL

The metatarsal gland is a controversial gland. It is within a white tuft of hair located on the outside hind legs just above the dew claws. Some naturalists and biologists believe the gland is atrophying (getting smaller through evolution because deer no longer need it), and therefore, has no real purpose. Others believe the gland omits a pheromone, and is used by deer for identification and as a warning signal. In any event, this gland is not well understood. When using metatarsal scent, be ready for anything to happen. You may be fortunate enough to attract deer, or unfortunate and spook game when using metatarsal scent.

Some old timers swear by metatarsal scent. They tie the gland to a boot and drag it through the woods. Many claim they have attracted deer to their stands using this gland and method. For now, the jury is still out on the effectiveness metatarsal scent has while deer hunting. My suggestion coincides with my philosophy about deer hunting: be innovative. Give metatarsal a try and experiment with it this fall.

Over the last dozen years, I have used metatarsal in the way described above. Although both bucks and does walked down a trail where the scent was deposited, they did not seem to follow the scent trail. Interestingly, both bucks and does appear to walk along the trail when I use this scent. However, I remain confused, or at least unconvinced, that they were attracted by the metatarsal scent. The first time I see a deer walking down a trail of metatarsal with its nose held to the ground, is when I will be absolutely convinced of its effectiveness.

When using scents, especially gland scents, be careful not to mix conflicting pheromones. For example, don't use excess interdigital with attracting scents. Excess interdigital scent is meant to warn deer of danger, not attract them. You can, however, use one or two drops of interdigital with an estrus scent, as both are attracting scents.

Another caution. If you use gland scents collected from recently harvested deer, be careful not to use too much. The concentration of scent from bagged game is more potent than commercially-made scent. Scent glands or even the urine from bladders can be overused and lead to problems. I stick to glandular scents made by reliable scent manufacturers. This is important. Each year, a dozen new scent companies hit the market. To become profitable, many newcomers water down their scents or use chemicals that act negatively to deer. To have confidence in the scents you use, stick with scents made by the longstanding manufacturers. Most commercial brand scents provide reliability and a lot less work for you.

SEXUAL LURES

The most overused deer scent is doe-in-estrus. Although estrus scent works, do not use this scent throughout the entire deer season. Estrus works best for a few days prior to each peak period of the three phases of the rut and is most effective when it is used sparingly.

I use doe estrus every year. However, I use it with an open mind and a lot of common sense. There isn't a buck in the woods who confuses the estrus scent from a hot doe with a commercially-made deer scent. When used correctly, big bucks have come in to investigate an estrus-laden boot pad or scent wick hung near my stand. I think estrus scent works best PRIOR to the actual peak periods of each phase of the rut. In other words, I have had most success using estrus scents before bucks pair up with does. The best periods of success with estrus scent have been October 5 - 10, November 10 - 15, and December 10 - 15 -- throughout North America. This is the time of the chase when bucks are scurrying all over the woods in search of estrus does. Commercially made estrus scent works best during these periods and not when bucks are matched up with does.

One of my favorite sex attracting scents is made by longtime scent manufacturer, Pete Rickard. In case you're wondering, yes, this is an endorsement of the Pete Rickard Scent Company that has been in business for over 60 years. The scent is Love Potion #9™. I developed the concept and application and then field tested Love Potion #9 for several years before Rickard agreed to include it in his line of scents.

Love Potion #9 is an interesting combination of scents with a realistic application. It is specifically mixed to combine the natural pheromones of a submissive buck with the urine of a mature doe-in-estrus. Love Potion #9 was formulated to create the illusion of a scent trail to naturally attract bucks and does. It fools mature bucks into thinking a submissive buck is following the trail of a hot doe. This unique combination of scents instinctively triggers an aggressive urge from bucks to immediately seek out what they think is a submissive and competitive buck closing in on "their" doe. This competition factor is what generates response when other sexual scents won't.

Love Potion #9 scent is a lethal mixture of doe-in-estrus and young buck urine.

To lay down a mock young buck and doe-in-estrus urine trail, simply apply several drops of scent to a boot pad or COVERTRACK ™ and walk to your hunting location. Remove the scent pad and hang it on a branch 10 to 30 yards from where you will post. As the odor of Love Potion #9 spreads -- deer will approach the area with their guard down. Often, bucks are reluctant to leave the area until they have checked out the source of the scent. Most other sexual scents (doe-in-estrus) can be used similarly. Although I have had unusual success with Love Potion #9, there are other manufacturers who make reliable estrus scents. Unfortunately, to find a company that makes quality scents, it's all trial and error. As with all other sexual scents, don't use a lot. Instead, opt for using less and you'll benefit more.

FOOD SCENTS

One of my favorite types of lures to use are food scents. Use food scents with an open mind. I have heard some so-called experts recommend you can't use food scents that are not native in the area you are hunting. If there is one point of deer hunting hype that annoys me -- this is it. It is my pet peeve when it comes to deer hunting. There are those who say you can't use apple scent in a hardwood forest because deer will "know" that apples are NOT growing there. They are wrong at the least and are bull crap artists at the worst. Trust me. When used correctly, food type lures are highly effective whether they are native to the area you are hunting or not! And you can take that fact to the Deer Hunting Bank!

If you don't believe apple scent (or any other type of food lure for that matter) attracts deer where wild apples don't grow, you're missing out on a productive hunting strategy. Try this. Before hunting season, take either a couple of real apples or a scent pad soaked in commercially made apple scent (food scents are the only scent you don't have to worry about using too much). Place the lure or fruit in an area you are absolutely sure has no wild apples. As deer move through the area they will smell the food source and investigate it -- whether it is natural to the area or not. I promise.

Common sense would tell you deer instinctively check out odors from potential food sources. If they didn't, they would have a lot less food available to them. Deer have no way of figuring out if a scent pad laden with apple scent is a lure left by a hunter and not an actual food item. There isn't a buck alive that would make his way through a hardwood forest free of natural wild apples and pick up the odor of the apple lure and say, " A-HAH, THERE ARE NO APPLES HERE. THAT'S SCENT FROM A FAKE APPLE LURE! I'VE BEEN HAD." And then run off.

Apple scent is my favorite covering & attracting scent -- I use it throughout the season, especially in areas where there are no apples.

Apple scent not only acts as a food attracting scent, but is also excellent as a cover scent to help mask your human odor. I often place several drops on my cap to help keep my human odor down. You can use acorn in the same way and use it in areas where there are no natural acorns. Like when I'm hunting in evergreen forests. Guess what? Many deer have walked through the pines, wind the acorn scent pad and walk over to check it out. This is additional evidence that you don't have to use food scents indigenous to the area you're hunting.

Quite the contrary. It's a simple matter of common sense. If you put out apple scent in an apple orchard or acorn scent in a hardwood forest filled with acorns or corn scent in the middle of a corn field, the only thing you would accomplish is to help mask your human odor. The natural food will attract the deer long before the imitation food scent will. My advice is to use natural food scents in areas where they are NOT NATURALLY PRESENT.

Natural woodland fragrances like hemlock, pine, spruce, cedar, earth and the like can be worn on clothing without risk of attracting a deer's attention to the hunter. I treat food scents (like acorn, apple, corn, wild grape and vanilla), exactly the way I treat attracting lures. I hang them ten to twenty yards from my stand. All except apple scent. While I hang apple scent away from me, I also use it on my cap to reduce human odor, as mentioned above.

REMEMBER - THERE IS NO WAY TO TOTALLY ELIMINATE YOUR HUMAN ODOR. You can reduce it significantly, however, by following some important guidelines. Keep yourself as clean as possible before each hunt. If you can shower between hunts, do so. Use unscented deodorants. During deer season, always use non-scented sportsmen's soaps to clean your body, hair and clothing. Scrub the soles of your boots (which you should never wear anywhere else but in the woods) every couple of days with a finger nail brush and unscented sportsmen's soap. In addition, wash your hunting clothes at least every other day. If you can, dry them outdoors. If not, hang them outdoors for a few minutes to remove the odor from the dryer before putting them on.

Don't fill your car's gas tank while wearing hunting clothes. Avoid camp odors like cigarette smoke and cooking odors as if they were the plague. Also, never get dressed and then take your morning constitutional. Instead, wait until after you have relieved yourself to put on your hunting clothes. This next suggestion maybe a bit tacky, but my obligation is to pass this information to you. A savvy deer hunter always washes himself thoroughly after making Number 2.

Deer pick up scents mostly from the foreign odors collected on the soles of your boots. Avoid wearing your hunting boots ANYWHERE ELSE other than the woods. If you are driving to a hunting area, leave your boots in a small cardboard box filled with pine branches, leaves and earth. When you arrive at your hunting location, remove your sneakers or shoes, put on your boots and head into the woods. When you return, immediately remove your boots and put them back in the box. By following these suggestions, you will keep your boots totally free of any foreign odors. I still wash the soles of my boots every few days to remove any human odor that may have permeated into the sole. By taking these scent suggestions seriously, you will eliminate as much human odor as possible and gain back the edge you would have otherwise lost.

Scientists and hunters have just begun to understand the entire scent phenomenon. New glandular information is constantly being researched. I believe over the next few years hunters will become more educated about the physical and internal characteristics of their quarry; and in doing so, will enjoy the experience of hunting much more.

Pheromones, from external glands, are natural everyday, olfactory odors in the deer woods. Used properly, they will add to your total deer hunting experience. They will create deer hunting opportunities that you may never have had otherwise. In addition, you will have opportunities to witness the amusing and interesting reactions of raccoons, coyotes, foxes, bears, and elk have when they stop, smell, and react to scents laid out for deer. By using all the other suggestions within this chapter, you will not only gain an edge, but you will also have an interesting and exciting season watching and learning how does and bucks respond positively to scents when used correctly.

CHAPTER 10

BODY LANGUAGE OF DEER

UNMASKING THE THOUGHTS OF WHITETAILS THROUGH BODY LANGUAGE

To hone your skills as a deer hunter, no - as a predator -- you must learn to interpret signals your quarry sends you via its body. By learning to decode these subtle indications, you'll add yet another valuable strategy to your bag of deer hunting tricks.

Have you ever wondered why you can walk past a buck after deer season is over and he'll just stand and watch you? Why will a herd of zebra feed within yards of a pride of resting lions? Or, why do some dogs bark aggressively at some people and not at others? It all has to do with body language.

In the instance of the buck, your body language, while it may indicate interest, does not exhibit aggressive posture, as it would when you're stalking game. With the zebras, they can tell by the lion's resting posture and fat bellies, that they have already fed and are not ready to hunt. The dog interprets fearful body language from some as a signal for it to establish its dominance, therefore the aggressive barking. Body language is an art all hunters should learn more about.

Over the last two decades, there have been many biological findings filled with new information about the fascinating world of body language and the messages this means of communication delivers to all forms of life --

including deer. These visual, physical signals display what is subconsciously on and in one's mind. Most people are not aware of the powerful visual messages that can and are regularly interpreted by others around us.

A friend of mine, who, along with me, became fascinated with the study of body language in the 1970s. He saved himself from an embarrassing situation with his company by reading body language. "Although I had become a bit complacent lately, I felt it was time to ask for a raise. During a subsequent conversation with my boss, he began to shower me with accolades, telling me I was doing 'a great job' and my 'motivation was high' and I 'contributed a lot to my position.' However, all during the conversation he shook his head from side-to-side. I interpreted his body language as a form of subconscious denial of his compliments to me. I immediately decided to change my strategy and, instead of asking for a raise, I asked what I could do to further improve my productivity."

The above scenario is an example of how body language and being able to read its messages can play a crucial role in our day-to-day existence. Through body language, you telegraph your thoughts by the way you fold your arms, cross your legs, walk, stand, move your eyes, lick your lips, or touch certain parts of your body. Through body language, animals can display attachment, fear, aggression, disgust, pleasure, or exhibit threatening postures meant to fend off possible dangers. Without the ability to display body language, these feelings would begin to fester. Soon, the simple matter of being at a social gathering or, in the case of a buck, coming face-to-face with another buck, could provoke a discharge of responses that may not be appropriate or necessary for the moment at hand. More important, the ability to quickly read and interpret body language signals tangibly increases your ability to digest and correctly react to all types of situations.

Reading and interpreting body language exhibited by game animals instantly increases your awareness of the game you are hunting. This not only allows you to consistently harvest more deer, but also helps you score on larger racked bucks.

While on a bow hunt during the primary rut, I grunted in an 8-point buck that I was going to take. As the buck approached my stand, I decided when I would take my shot. Seconds before drawing my bow, I noticed the buck's hair on the back of his neck was standing straight up. For a few moments, it confused me. I wasn't grunting aggressively, but, perhaps because the buck was only an average size eight-pointer, even my subtle grunt could have sparked this aggressive body language. I decided to look over the buck more carefully before I shot.

As I studied him, I could see that although his head was pointed directly to my left, his eyes were looking directly behind him to my right. Then, the hair fell flat on his neck and he tightly tucked his tail between his legs. Slowly, but with a deliberate, purposeful demeanor, the buck started walking sidewards, away from me and opposite the direction his eyes were looking. It instantly clicked! The buck seemed to be reacting to an obviously more aggressive and larger racked buck in the woods behind him and to my right.

I continued to glance at the eight-pointer to stay in tune with his body language, while desperately straining my eyes to pick up any movement of another buck. Then, the guessing was over. In a confident and assertive manner, another buck walked under my stand. Now I knew why the first buck was concerned! This second buck was obviously more aggressive and held a higher rank in their pecking order. Although their rack sizes were comparable, the second buck had 10 points and a slightly wider spread. He was also much larger in body size than the first buck.

As the second buck walked toward the eight-point buck, he arched his back, laid his ears back flat along side his head, and started to lower his head as if he was preparing to lock antlers. He never got the chance. I released my arrow as he got closer to the first buck. I wish I could say I wound up killing him -- but I didn't. My arrow sailed harmlessly over his back and landed smack dab between him and the other buck. The larger buck turned, and without hesitation, disappeared. I watched the smaller buck take this as a sign of his superiority and he began to strut his stuff under my stand. Each time I look at his mounted head on my wall, I chuckle to myself. I wonder what the hell he thought happened when the arrow hit him. Maybe he thought the bigger buck had extendable antlers and gored him from a distance!

If didn't interpret the body language of the first buck, I would have never had the chance to shoot at the larger buck. Just seeing the two bucks together under my stand was worth not shooting at first. As things turned out, other than having the satisfaction of knowing there was another buck close by, I could have shot the first buck 15 minutes earlier.

On another occasion, I was posted in a ground blind and a doe approached my stand. Coincidentally, I was going to shoot her on video as part of a deer management piece we were taping. As I drew back my arrow, the doe flagged her tail from side-to-side. It wasn't a nervous twitch. Her tail deliberately flagged from one side to the other. It was a body language signal I was well familiar with. I put my bow down and waited. Moments later, a nice 8-point buck walked into the woodlot with his nose held to the ground. He trotted up to the doe and, as he was sticking his nose under her legs, I drew back and arrowed him.

The slow, purposeful flagging of the doe's tail should have been a clear and unmistakable message to anyone who understands deer body language. This type of slow tail flagging by does is an indication that they are in estrus and are ready to allow bucks to mount them for breeding. Knowing this, I opted to forego shooting the doe for the management piece until another day!

Although deer exhibit a profusion of body language gestures, here are some more easily recognizable signals that, when interpreted quickly and correctly, will dramatically change your whitetail hunting strategies.

BUCK PRANCING

(A BUCK WALKING WITH ITS HEAD HELD HIGH AND TAIL HELD HALF-WAY OUT)

This form of body language is a threatening posture. It suggests the buck may be looking at another buck a hunter can't see . . . yet. Through his body language, the buck is announcing to the "other" buck that he is the more aggressive or dominant animal. He is saying, "Stay where you are, if you know what is good for you." A perceptive hunter makes the immediate decision to either take the buck exhibiting the body language or carefully waits and inspects the surrounding brush before shooting. It may conceal an even larger buck.

A DOE WITH HER TAIL HELD STRAIGHT OUT AND SLIGHTLY OFF TO ONE SIDE

This is a crucial deer body language signal. Hunters who are unable to interpret this signal often decide to harvest the doe or a smaller buck, because they do not know how to interpret what they are looking at. **A doe exhibiting this type of body language is in full estrus and is accepting bucks. Almost assuredly, she is being followed by a mature buck** with subordinate bucks trailing along the fringes. When a doe crosses a vulnerable area, a mature buck usually hesitates long enough to ensure the passage is safe, allowing the subordinate bucks to catch up with the doe. Hunters who are aware of this fact have the opportunity to harvest the doe or the first buck that is trailing her. Their second option is to wait and see if a larger buck is about to appear. By reading this body language message, you can allow smaller bucks to pass and still remain relatively confident that you will have the opportunity for a shot at a larger buck who will almost certainly pick up the does' trail.

A BUCK HOLDING HIS HEAD HIGH AND TILTED BACK WITH HIS UPPER LIP CURLED EXPOSING THE GUMS

(HE'S EXHIBITING THE FLEHMAN POSTURE ALSO KNOWN AS LIP CURLING)

This is an important message. It is made by deer trying to find the source of a pleasurable scent -- especially estrus. When you see a buck exhibiting a lip curl, it might be wise to immediately harvest the deer before the scent he is smelling and following lures him off in a different direction. If the buck doesn't offer an opportunity for a shot before he is out of range, lay down a commercially-made estrus scent to try and get that buck to return or attract a different buck all together.

A DEER FLICKING ITS TAIL SIDE-TO-SIDE

(THE TAIL LOOSELY HANGS IN THE NORMAL DOWNWARD POSITION AND OFF TO ONE SIDE THEN THE OTHER)

There are several signals a deer sends through motions of its tail. This is, however, one of the more important tail signals you should pay particular attention to. Often, when a hunter spots a deer standing still and concentrating on its surroundings, he is lured into a false complacency that the deer is not alarmed. However, deer often stand still to gather more information before proceeding along a trail. You can be sure the deer will remain relatively still as long as it does not flick its tail from side-to-side. Once the deer exhibits this body language, it is about to move. If you think about taking the animal, do not hesitate a moment longer after seeing this signal.

HEAD FAKES/HEAD-BOBBING

Hunters can be tricked by this maneuver and usually think a deer has not spotted them and they unconsciously give themselves away to the cagey animal. Deer, who suspect something is wrong but cannot immediately identify the problem, will extend their heads forward to get a better look. When a hunter doesn't move, the deer tries to trick the perceived danger into giving itself away by pretending it doesn't see or care about what it is looking at. The deer pretends it is relaxed, begins feeding and then puts its head down. At this point, a hunter thinks it's usually OK to move. Then, he is surprised as the deer never really intended to feed at all. It quickly lifts its head to check out the suspicious object. A hunter is usually caught off-guard by not interpreting this body language properly. When a deer extends its head and looks at you and then puts its head down, don't move. That head will be up in a moment as the deer was only trying to fake you into giving yourself away!

FOOT STOMPING

Deer stomp their hooves for many reasons. Usually, however, it is a warning or a way to goad movement from a possible threat. The animal also sends visual and aural warnings to other deer within seeing and hearing range. Most important, the deer is also leaving a chemical message for others who are not close enough to see or hear the warning. The chemical message is from a gland between the deer's toes, called the interdigital gland. This excess scent is meant to warn other whitetails traveling down the trail that another deer encountered danger at this point. If you see deer stomping or you alarm them into repeated stomping, you should consider relocating your stand. Unfortunately, the odds of a deer coming past an area permeated with excess interdigital scent are low. You will see more deer by changing your location.

A DOE WITH ONE EAR CUPPED FORWARD AND ONE EAR CUPPED BACKWARD

When you see a doe walking down a trail and she stops to listen for potential danger before proceeding, pay particular to the direction her ears point. If they are both cupped in one direction, she is probably alone. However, if one ear is forward and the other ear suddenly rotates toward her backtrail, she is listening to either her fawns or yearlings approaching. More important, especially during the rut, a buck could be following her. Try not to alarm this deer. The chances of seeing what is coming up behind her will be greater.

FLAGGING OR TAIL WAVING

One of the most familiar deer body language signs is tail flagging. Deer use tail flagging as they run off to warn other deer. Does flag much more frequently than bucks. They give a visual reference to the smaller yearlings and fawns about the direction she is running. Should you jump or perhaps see deer driven past you that are on the run with their tails held high, you should be on the lookout for other deer running with their tails down or tucked between their legs. Since tail waving is an action more related to does than bucks, a deer running in a group with its tail down is likely to be a buck. Focus all your attention on this animal and you will have most likely picked out the only buck in the group by correctly interpreting this form of body language.

A BUCK WITH HIS EARS LAYING ALL THE WAY BACK ON HIS SHOULDERS, HIS BACK ARCHED AND HIS NECK HAIRS STANDING UP

This form of body language is reflected from a nervous or extremely agitated buck. He is displaying every form of non-combative aggression he can muster. Most often, although not always, he is displaying this form of body language to a much larger deer. By appearing so aggressive and hostile, the buck hopes to fend off his rival with a bluff and avoid actual physical combat. When you see a buck displaying this type of body language and you do not see a second buck, you should use binoculars to carefully check the surrounding area. Look in the direction the aggressive buck is watching and chances are you will find another buck. Or, as in the example I gave above, just sit tight and wait to see what develops as long as the first buck remains in range.

A BUCK PAWING A PATCH OF GROUND

Bucks paw the ground for several reasons: to search for acorns and other food, to warn off other deer and to prepare or freshen scrapes. When searching for food, his body language is relaxed. Ears are slightly forward, the tail hangs straight down between his legs, hair lays straight down on his back and his muscles are relaxed. This deer is content with his surroundings and is unaware of the hunter. A deer pawing the ground aggressively is on full alert. It may have spotted you or may be fending off another deer. Read this situation quickly and decide whether or not to take the animal before it moves off.

A buck pawing a round patch of earth and stomping repeatedly to scratch, sniff and urinate on the ground is preparing a scrape. This buck's body language will let you know if you have time to shoot or not. If he is pawing quickly, urinating, and constantly looking in different directions, he is probably freshening up a scrape of a more aggressive buck and will not be at the site long. However, if he enters the scrape slowly, paws the earth with purpose, uses the overhanging branch, doesn't bother checking his surroundings often, and urinates infrequently, he is probably the buck who originally made the scrape and will spend considerable time at the location. This will give you more time to make a decision whether or not to harvest him.

The reason most hunters are familiar with the more common forms of body language, like tail flagging and hoof stomping, is because these are very common body language signals exhibited by deer. To learn about the more subtle forms of body language I mentioned in this chapter, and some that I didn't, spend more time observing deer during the off-season. One of the best places to observe body language is at a zoo or enclosure where there are several penned deer. Because of their proximity to one another, they use body language much more frequently. Observing certain forms of obvious and subtle signals of body language and then watching the reactions of the other deer will start to fine-tune your understanding of this nonverbal form of communication.

By learning to read, correctly decipher and then react to the body language signals we receive from people and animals, we will improve our odds of responding properly to any given situation at hand. For hunters, reading a deer's body language is another important hunting strategy you should plan on learning and using to your benefit. It's why I thought this book would not be complete without this chapter. It will increase your deer hunting success immensely.

This 12-point buck was taken after I watched the submissive body language of a smaller buck indicate that a buck higher in the pecking order was approaching.

133

This big bodied buck was taken deep in the Adirondack Mountains of New York. I am carefully looking him over to see what information I can find to use for a future hunt..

CHAPTER 11

DEAD DEER TALK

I have kept detailed records about my deer hunting for over thirty years. Every time I enter the woods I record pertinent information I feel will aid me in seeing and shooting a buck. In 1975, I developed my "Deer Diary Stat Cards" which list 80 different statistics related to deer hunting. Now, however, besides keeping my paper log book, I transfer this information to my computer's database each time I return from a scouting or hunting trip.

Categories include the usual information hunters should record like weather conditions, barometer levels, air temperature, wind direction, mast crop conditions and the like. However, I also believe it is equally important to record atypical information. For instance, I also record sky conditions, the amount of leaves on the trees, what direction the deer came from, what he was doing before I shot him and the conditions of the deer's range as well. When I shoot a buck I closely examine its entire body and enter all pertinent information about the buck into my records, too.

It's a little-known fact that "dead deer talk." What I mean is, if you spend some time examining your downed buck you can gather important information to pass onto friends still trying to score, use to take an additional buck (when and where legal), or use it the following deer season.

The first thing I do when I approach a harvested buck is closely examine its hide. The hide can tell you a lot about the buck. Once, after looking at a buck through my binoculars as he crossed a field, I noticed his hide was covered with briars, I figured out that the only place on the farm where he could have collected that many briars was in a swale known to be excessively thick with briars. Two days later, I took my second buck for that season (a big 8-pointer), as I posted near the swale. I shot the buck as he emerged from his bedding area. The briars from the first buck gave this buck's hiding location away.

I also look for fresh cuts, healed over scars, ripped ears, and bruised areas on the face. These clues can tell you about the social status of the buck. If a buck has ripped ears or other battle scars, I can bet that there is another buck of equal body and antler size within the area. You can pass this information on to family or friends or, if you hunt in a state that allows you to take more than one buck, you can use it yourself.

```
DATE _____              GAME ACTIVITY □ SLOW □ MOD □ ACTIVE
PLACE HUNTED _____              # OF GAME SEEN _____ SEX □ BUCK □ DOE □ FAWN
SPECIES HUNTED _____              # OF GAME SHOT _____ # OF SHOTS TAKEN _____
TIME 5AM 6 7 8 9 10 11 12 PM 1 2 3 4 5 6 7      IMMED KILL? □ YES □ NO  HAD TO TRAIL □ YES □ NO  HOW FAR? _____
AIR TEMP 0 5 10 15 20 25 30 35 40 45 50 55 60 65  LOCATED? □ YES □ NO
BAROMETER _ □ LOW □ MOD □ HIGH □ RISING □ STEADY □ FALLING   HOW FAR AWAY WAS GAME WHEN SHOT? _____
SKY □ CLEAR □ OVERCAST  MOON PHASE _ _ _____   WHERE WAS GAME HIT □ NECK □ SPINE □ HEART □ LUNGS □ BACK
WEATHER □ FOG □ DRIZZLE □ RAIN □ HAIL                           □ OTHER _____
□ FLURRIES □ SNOW □ OTHER ____ _____        DEER VITALS AGE ____ TYP # OF POINTS ____ NON-TYP # OF PTS _____
□ HEAVY □ STEADY □ INTERMITTENT                 STOMACH CONTENTS _____
WIND □ NONE □ LIGHT □ MOD □ HIGH □ GUSTY        COND OF HIDE _____ NOSE ___ ___ EARS _____ HOOFS _____ TEETH ____
HUMIDITY □ LOW □ MOD □ HIGH                     RACK COLOR _____ TARSAL GLAND COLOR _____
GROUND CONDITIONS □ DRY □ WET □ MUDDY □ DAMP □ FROSTED   WHAT WAS DEER DOING WHEN SHOT? _____
                □ FROZEN □ SNOW AMT _____  WHAT DIR DID DEER COME FROM _____ WHERE DO YOU THINK
LEAVES □ MOIST □ WET □ DAMP □ DRY □ V DRY □ FROSTED □ CRUNCHY   DEER WAS GOING _____
AMT OF LEAVES ON TREES OCT ____ % NOTE          BOW USED ____ ARROW SIZES ____ CAMMO ____ FACE CAMMO _____
AMT OF LEAVES ON TREES NOV ____ % NOTE _____  CAL OF RIFLE _____ GRAIN OF SHELL ___ _ GA ___ _ SLUG ____
HOW HUNTED □ GROUND STAND □ T STAND □ STILL HUNTING □ DRIVING   SCOPE _____ # OF HUNTERS IN YOUR PARTY _____
                □ OTHER _____              # OF HUNTERS SEEN IN WOODS _____
TERRAIN, DESCRIBE _____      HUNTED □ PRIVATE LAND □ PUBLIC LAND □ OTHER _____
NOISE FACTORS _____             NOTES, REMARKS & PRE SEASON INFO
CALLING METHOD □ HORN RATTLED □ DEER CALL □ DECOY □ OTHER   MAST CROP □ EXLT □ GOOD □ FAIR □ POOR □ NONE
SCENT SCREEN □ FOX □ SKUNK □ DEER URINE □ APPLE □ RUT □ OTHER   RANGE COND □ GOOD □ FAIR □ OVER BROWSED
        NOTES CONCERNING RUT & OTHER INFO       EST DEER PER SQ MI _____ BUCK P S M _____
                                                FAWN CROP □ GOOD □ BAD  YEARLING CROP □ GOOD □ BAD
                                                DEER KILL DUE TO CAR _ _ DOGS ____ LOST GAME ___ OTHER ____
                                                DATE OF 1st RUB SIGHTINGS _____ LOCATION _____
                                                SIZE OF TREE □ SM □ MED □ LG  REMARKS _____
                                                DATE OF 1st SCRAPE SIGHTINGS _____ LOCATION _____
                                                SIZE OF SCRAPE □ SM □ MED □ LG  SIGNS OF DOE IN ESTRUS _____
                                                SCRAPE BEING USED □ YES □ NO
                                                © 1986 PETER J. FIDUCCIA (REV.)
```

My Deer Diary Stat Card which I created in 1986. They have made the difference by helping me keep accurate records, instead of trying to remember what happened from season to season.

Several years ago, a friend, shot a buck that had a gray muzzle and its face and ears were covered with battle scars. It indicated to me that he was one of the more aggressive (dominant) bucks within the herd. I told him that a buck as badly beaten up as he was, was defending against other bucks similar in size. We continued to hunt that area knowing there could be additional big bucks. Within a week, we took a second larger buck from the same tree stand.

A dead buck's teeth can offer you more important clues. By figuring out the age of a deer, you can find out the "rack health" of the herd. If a buck has a 18-inch wide, 8-point rack, and is 2 1/2 years old, then the genetics, available browse, and food sources are more than adequate. Or, if the same age buck, however, was a spike or forked-horn, you may want to change hunting locations, or supplement the deer herd's food source.

I always look closely at a buck's hooves. If they are cracked, chipped, and have rough pads, then I am pretty well assured that he was a ridge-running buck bedding in rough terrain. If the hooves are shiny, soft and slightly longer than normal, I can bet the buck was feeding and bedding in the soft earth in swamps, agricultural farms or lowlands. I then plan the following year's strategies around this information.

Rack color also suggests where a buck spends most of his time. A bleached-out white rack usually indicates that a buck was living in an area with an excessive amount of sunlight. When scouting, and you happen to see a buck like this, don't look for his bedding area in the deep cedar swamps or crevices of dark evergreen ridges. Bucks who inhabit these type of areas traditionally have racks darker in color than normal. The exception to this rule comes from rubbing. When a buck rubs excessively, he removes the dark dried blood from the antlers no matter where he is living. However, most times, he won't rub long or hard enough to give the rack a high-polished, white, bleached-out look.

The most important indicator of where your buck was bedding and feeding comes from the contents of its stomach. This is where you separate the men from the boys. After shooting a deer, I open the stomach and carefully examine the contents. Look at the most digested and undigested foods. Knowing what the buck just finished eating and what he ate first, accurately determines his previous travel route prior to his death. I used this method of gathering information to help me put NY Yankees' third baseman, Wade Boggs, onto a big buck a few years ago. The year before that, I shot a buck with a stomach filled with whole kernel corn and semi-digested persimmon. Knowing a local farm usually has late-standing corn and also knowing where the only persimmon patch was across from the farm, I planned my strategy accordingly. When Boggs came to hunt, we posted between the only persimmon patch and the standing corn field. By 2:10 that afternoon, Boggs shot an enormous 10-point buck with a 20-inch inside spread weighing an unbelievable 255 pounds. This buck was unusually heavy for a New York state whitetail. Upon examining his stomach, we discovered undigested persimmons. . . he never made it to the corn.

By looking at the ears, hide, hooves, rack color, teeth and stomach contents of harvested deer, you can learn what routes deer are traveling, when they are traveling, where they are heading, how old they are, what social status rank they hold within the herd and much more. Remember, let the next buck you shoot "talk" to you.

Wade Boggs "listened to" a dead deer before bagging this NY beauty.

After looking this buck over, I found several healed over scars and fresh cuts.
These clues helped me to determine there was another buck of equal size in the area
I was hunting.

CHAPTER 12

HOW TO USE DEER CALLS EFFECTIVELY

The rhythmic sounds of the buck moving steadily through fallen leaves were only overshadowed by the noise of snapping branches as he trotted along the river bed. Now the big buck was in sight and I could plainly hear the guttural grunts he was making every few seconds. His big white rack glistened as he trotted toward my stand. He was moving so quickly that I thought he would trot right by me without offering me a good shot. I took out my grunt call and blew an extended, soft doe grunt. The buck skidded to a halt and glanced up at me as I pulled the trigger.

Thirty years ago, this chapter probably would not have caught your attention and for a very good reason -- you probably would not have believed deer calls worked. Using calls to attract deer back in the 60s was a well-kept secret used only by the old, savvy woodsmen who hunted the remote wilderness areas of the country. These old timers rarely talked about the effectiveness of using doe bleats. But, quietly and consistently, they used these rudimentary calls made of rubber bands and balsa wood to regularly attract whitetails.

It was just such an "old timer" who first introduced me to deer calls. During my second deer season, I was hunting in Childwold, NY (the Adirondack Mts.). I was sitting on a stand overlooking a swamp. Every so often, I heard a soft lamb-like sound. I honestly did not know what the sound was or what was making it. But, I did know that about every 15 minutes, the sound emanated a hundred yards or so from a dip below the ledge I was sitting on. Since this was only my second year of deer hunting, my patience level wasn't fine tuned. If I didn't see a deer within the first hour or two, I usually got up and skulked around hoping to jump a buck. To this day, I often smile when I thinkabout those "patience-less" days. It never seemed to fail, no sooner did I get up and start walking around then I would hear a gun shot ring out close by me. I must have unknowingly driven a lot of bucks to many hunters in those days.

In any event, by 7:30 that morning, my patience was gone and I was determined to go check out what was making this lamb-like noise. Just as I stood up to gather my gear, I heard the noise again. This time, I also heard a similar noise coming from the swamp. I thought to myself, "What the hell did I do? Did I unsuspectingly post on the border of lamb farm on the other side of the swamp?" Just then, a big doe emerged from the swamp and trotted toward the ledge below me. Never swerving, she was determined to reach the source of the noise. I watched as she stopped and then began pacing nervously back and forth. Then, the excitement started. Right behind her, from the swamp, ran two bucks. I started shaking and tried to decide which one to shoot, when a gun shot rang out. The bigger of the two bucks dropped in its tracks. I threw my .30-30 to my shoulder and tried to draw a bead on the second buck as it and the doe weaved and darted through the surrounding mature hardwoods. I never pulled the trigger. Naturally, I was pretty shocked at what had just happened.

As I sat there disgusted, I saw a hunter who was posted well below me, stand and approach the downed buck. I grabbed my gear and went down to talk to him. This old gentleman was the source of the doe blat I was hearing all that morning. He told me how he used doe blats for years to attract whitetails, especially from heavy cover like the swamp we were overlooking. He busted out into laughter with tears in his eyes, when I told him I thought I posted near a sheep farm. "Boy, there ain't a sheep or a farm between Childwold and Tupper Lake and they're 30 miles apart," he laughed as he held his belly.

While the old-timer field dressed the eight-point buck, I stood in there in amazement as he told story after story of how successful he had been over the years using a blat call. "Hell, boy, if you wanna kill bucks like this, learn to blow one of these here doe calls," he said. And the old gent placed an Olt deer call in my hand. "Your friends will think you're crazy for using it, " he said "but, I can betcha it'll work."

That was my introduction to deer calling. I bought an Olt call that afternoon in a tiny general store in Tupper Lake during a heavy snow fall. I blew it on almost every hunting trip that season without success! However, I didn't give up. The memory of that morning's hunt and the old gent's stories remained vivid within me, so I continued to use and practice the doe blat call.

By 1970, I was a much better deer caller, having learned to use a variety of calls other than the blat and even called in and shot a few bucks. I knew I was on to something and promised myself that, through trial and error, I would gain experience and confidence and become an accomplished caller.

Hunters have long benefitted from knowing how to use artificial calls to attract wildlife. A good example is elk hunters who have enjoyed the success of rattling, bugling or "mewing" bulls and cows for many years. Moose, duck, wild turkey, coyote and many other game animals have also been successfully "enticed-in" by sportsmen who made it their business to learn effective calling techniques to attract a variety of wildlife.

But deer hunters still are reluctant to try calls to attract whitetails. Unfortunately, these outdoorsmen are missing out on one of Mother Nature's natural seductions. By learning how, why, where, and when to use deer calls you will increase your success ratio.

All thirty species and subspecies of deer in the Americas are vocal animals. Whitetail, mule, and blacktail deer, for example, which cover a broad range on the continent, respond readily to calling. Biologists have confirmed and categorized thirteen different types of vocalizations made by whitetails.

Since I began deer hunting in 1965, I have taken 113 white-tailed bucks. Approximately half of these bucks were shot after I imitated deer sounds. Calling to deer has been one of the easiest methods I have ever used to trick white-tailed deer to my stand.

The secret to being a successful caller is the same as I have discussed in earlier chapters -- confidence. Knowing your call sounds authentic and believing in its effectiveness is critical to your success. Confidence can mean the difference between seeing and actually bagging game. A few years ago, I received a letter from a *Woods N' Water TV Show* viewer who also read many of my articles. An avid deer hunter, Chuck Jermyn, first decided to use deer calls after reading an article I wrote. In his letter, he told me he "was skeptical," as most novice callers are, and how in his first year of calling he "didn't harvest a deer." In his second season, however, after spending the summerand spring practicing, Jermyn called in several good bucks! By practicing, he gained confidence and it paid big dividends for him.

Practice is the name of the game when it comes to deer calling. A good caller carries several different types of calls and uses them throughout the year. Whenever you see deer, no matter what time of the year it is, call to them. Learn what type of calls make them curious, alarmed, relaxed or nervous. The best time to test the effectiveness of calls is in the spring and summer when deer are vocal and are not harassed by hunting pressure.

In the spring, does are vocal when they give birth to fawns. These vocalizations are crucial to the fawn's survival and include feeding, alarm, locating and other types of calls to help the fawn in its day-to-day survival.

You can effectively replicate several types of deer vocalizations. Snorts, blats, bleats, grunts, whistles, and barks can all be used to lure deer to your stand, just like rattling. The four calls that will bring you the most success, however, are also the easiest to learn: the alarm snort; the burp grunt (doe and buck); the loud blat; and the social bleat.

There are several keys to successful calling. First, an experienced deer caller learns to blow all calls softly. Occasionally, a louder, more aggressive call may be necessary. But, overall, louder aggressive sounding calls will scare away more deer (including big bucks) than they will attract. Although you have read and heard to the contrary, common sense applies here.

Many of you have told me repeatedly that while using grunt calls, you have had varied success. Sometimes they attract bucks and sometimes they don't. Invariably, the next question is, "Why?" There are many reasons why grunts and other calls work well sometimes and not others. Most times, however, negative response is generated after a grunt is blown too loudly and aggressively.

Let's take an average size eight-pointer walking up a trail with his nose held to the ground. Suddenly, he hears your loud, aggressive grunt. Basically, what you've just done is yelled at the top of your lungs, "HEY YOU!" You just scared the crap out of the poor buck. What happens next is automatic. Out of instinct, he glances in your direction and then realizes he made a critical mistake by attempting to make eye contact with a more aggressive animal. Immediately, he avoids a confrontation by looking away and continuing to walk without looking back. No matter how long or hard you grunt at a buck under these conditions, he will not respond. Why should he? Through your loud and aggressive call, you just announced that you're unquestionably the biggest, "baddest" buck in the woods. If he has any sense at all, even if he is a big buck, he'll avoid the fight and walk off. If, by now, you doubt that, go back and reread the chapter on rattling and fighting behavior. Make your calls softly and you'll be more successful.

The next most common reason for lack of success when calling is calling too much. When you're calling, you're no longer hunting the buck, he is hunting you. So, it's important that while you are trying to gain his attention by vocalizing, you don't want to talk so much that he pinpoints your location or becomes wary due to the unnatural frequency of your numerous calls. Limit the numberof calls you make to within common sense parameters.

Another reason for unsuccessful calling is calling to an animal that has responded to the call and is walking toward you. Once a buck responds and walks to you -- stop calling. Let his curiosity work for instead of against you. With that said, there are many cadences to each of the primary vocalizations. Learn and practice them and you will add another potent weapon to your deer hunting arsenal.

SNORT

Because the snort call represents, to most hunters, a deer fleeing, it is the most misunderstood and hardly ever used call. The snort vocalization has several meanings to deer. When you can decipher what each call means, you'll be very surprised at how effective each snort cadence is.

There are four cadences to the Primary Snort -- the Alarm Call, the Alarm Distress, the Social snort and the Aggressive snort. Each of these calls has a specific meaning and is used during certain situations. When you use a snort at the right time and under the correct set of circumstances, you can trick your quarry into thinking you are another deer. Use the wrong snort cadence under the wrong circumstances, however, and the deer you are snorting to will turn itself inside out trying to avoid you.

The snort can be a very effective attracting call when used properly.

ALARM SNORT

The alarm snort is frequently heard by most hunters. I could even tell you when and where you probably encountered a deer making this cadence of the alarm snort. Often, a hunter walking along a logging road or making his way through the woods to his stand jumps a deer. Because the deer does not wind the hunter first, it only reacts to the hunter's noise. I know you've heard this snort often. This deer, buck or doe, can be called back if you know what to do.

When you encounter a deer unexpectedly, the deer may respond by blowing a single snort, then run several yards, stop and blow a second single snort. "Whew . . . Whew." It is alarmed, but has not been able to pinpoint why. The deer is trying to locate and isolate the danger. By blowing back at the deer with an alarm/snort call, you will stimulate the deer's curiosity. Often, it decides to slowly make its way back toward the location where it first encountered the perceived danger.

When you jump a deer that blows the alarm snort, wait until the deer has blown the second snort. Then, place the call in your mouth and blow hard once, hesitate about two seconds, and blow the call again. Do not blow the call a third time until the deer snorts back. Once the deer answers you, respond to it with two more snorts. Keep doing this as long as you hear the deer approaching and snorting.

Several years ago, I snorted at a buck 57 times. Each time, the buck answered with a snort of his own. I was convinced I was calling to a wise old buck. As the tension mounted, I became more and more convinced that this was a really big buck. Finally, the buck emerged from the pines and I was surprised to see he was a small six point buck. I shot him anyway.

Years ago, my wife Kate shot her first buck while still hunting toward her tree stand. As she approached the stand, she saw a deer. She tried to position herself for a shot and she stepped on a branch. The deer heard the snap and blew an alarm snort. It ran off several yards, then blew a second snort. Kate blew back at the deer, and the buck answered. Each time the deer blew two snorts, Kate blew back two snorts. The buck, curious to see what had frightened it, kept coming closer to her with each series of alarm snorts. Finally, after several minutes of exchanging snorts to one another, the spike buck made its last move when it stepped out from behind the cedars and Kate dispatched him with one clean shot. Kate would have never had the opportunity to shoot that buck if she didn't know enough to call back to the snorting buck.

All variations of the snort work well. You will find, however, the alarm/snort to be the easiest snort to learn and use. However, the critical aspect when using a snort call is to not blow an alarm snort to a deer who is vocalizing an alarm-distress. You must know the different cadences of each call for them to be effective.

I often use the alarm snort when bow hunting. Intentionally, I walk through heavy cover with the wind in my face. Every few steps, I snap a twig or kick some leaves. I do this with the hopes of alarming a buck with the noise I am making. (Note: I have taken thirteen Pope & Young bucks. Half of them have been taken from the ground; and half of those have been taken while using this strategy.) Once I alarm a buck and he makes the alarm snort cadence of the primary snort, I know I have a better than average chance to call the buck back. I call this cadence of the primary snort, my "Too Late" call. As the buck and I exchange calls, he usually approaches without knowing I am hidden in heavy brush or pines and he continues to walk by me in search of "the other deer." I shot a few nice bucks at distances less than ten yards while using this tactic. The trick here is as the buck gets closer, you should blow the call more softly and in the opposite direction of the approaching deer. This makes the buck think the "other deer" is walking away and it often concentrates on nothing else other than trying to locate the "other deer."

ALARM DISTRESS

Another effective snort cadence is the alarm-distress call. THIS IS MY FAVORITE SNORT CADENCE. Here's how to use the Alarm-Distress call when hunting with companions. Locate thick cover like a cedar patch or a swamp and then post hunters along the networks of trails that are known deer escape routes. The trick here is to set hunters up on the outer fringes of the cover along escape routes. Don't be tempted to have them penetrate too deeply into the center of the cover. After all the standers are posted, wait a good half-hour for things to settle down. Then, walk into the middle of the thickest part of the cover without trying to be too quiet. When you have reached where you want to be -- take out interdigital scent and lay down several drops. Then, stomp your foot several times while blowing the alarm-distress cadence of the primary snort. The call sounds like this, "Whew -- whew -- whew -- whew, whew, whew, whew." Make the first three snorts loud and hesitate about a second between each sound. Then, make the next four snorts without any hesitation.

As you have read throughout this book, always try to create as natural a display as possible when calling or rattling. I know this is repetitive, but drilling it into your head is crucial to your success. Try to duplicate the complete illusion of what deer would do when they are vocalizing or fighting. Make an all-out effort to create all the sounds, smells (like using interdigital scent when blowing the alarm-distress) and motions (shaking brush or saplings) that deer make when they are vocalizing or fighting. By doing this, it helps to put the deer at ease when it responds. Inevitably, the deer thinks it is hearing, smelling and, sometimes, seeing another deer. Therefore, it responds more enthusiastically and with less caution.

The Alarm-Distress is also used when you are hunting alone. I have had the most success with this cadence of the snort when I use it hunting by myself. I use it to roust deer from cattails, ledges, brush piles, small woodlots, laurels and from standing agricultural fields. For instance, when hunting a farm with a field of standing corn, most hunters instinctively feel or, perhaps, even "know" there is a buck hiding within the standing crop. Here is how to convince the buck it's time to leave the security of his hideout. Pick a corner of the cornfield where the last two rows of corn meet. Find some cover. With the wind blowing toward you, put out extra amounts (several drops) of interdigital scent. Then, make the same scenario of calls and stomps I described above.

Often, only minutes after making the first call, you'll hear deer stalking through the corn looking for a safe exit point. Once they have found what they believe is a good escape route, they traditionally poke their heads out of the corn, glance back and forth (as if looking for traffic) and make a determined effort to the nearest cover. Usually, it is an adjoining woodlot. When the buck leaves the corn and carefully picks its way along the edges before going into the woodlot, is when you'll get your best shot. For me, carrying the snort call has created numerous hunting opportunities. Without it, many deer would still be safely hidden within the sanctuaries of cover I regularly come across while hunting.

THE SOCIAL SNORT

The social snort vocalization is from a reaction from a nervous deer. I am sure you have seen and heard a deer make this call. It is usually made by a deer nervously feeding at the edge of a field or in a woodlot. The deer puts its head down to feed, focuses its ears in a particular direction and then lifts its head up quickly, looking in the direction its ears were just pointed. Reluctantly, the deer lowers its head to begin feeding again, only to repeat the process. This nervous feeding and looking behavior goes on for several minutes before the deer decides to blow a non-aggressive, single snort. By blowing the snort, the deer tries to encourage whatever is making it nervous to reveal itself by either approaching the deer or at least **answering** it. Often, if it is another deer that the first deer was reacting to, it will answer the single snort with a single snort of its own. This "return" call immediately relaxes the first deer and it begins to feed more contently without lifting its head every few seconds. Often, the deer will feed in the direction of the other deer that answered it -- safety in numbers. If it doesn't hear a return social snort after making one, the deer usually stops feeding and retreats from the area.

When I see a deer acting like this, I know I can relax it and, sometimes, even attract it to me by using the social cadence of the primary snort. But, it's important to remember that the Social Snort only works on deer that are exhibiting the type of behavior described above. Never make the call until the deer has made a single quick snort **first.** Then, when it puts its head down to feed, make one, soft snort to the deer. Try to blow the call in the opposite direction of the deer. If the call is made correctly, the deer typically lifts its head, cups its ears toward you and then begins to feed again often heading in your direction. However, should the deer lift its head and become more nervous, you probably blew the call too loudly. Don't try to make another call until the deer starts to feed again.

I used the social snort last fall to attract a good eight-point buck while bow hunting in New Jersey. The buck was nervously feeding on acorns in a small woodlot that bordered an agricultural field. Every few seconds the buck perked up its ears and looked off behind him. Then, it put its nose into the leaves and resumed its search for more acorns. Before long, its ears started playing the radar game again. It lifted up its head, stared off into a thicket and walked off a short distance in the opposite direction of the bushes. I noticed it was getting more and more spooked each passing minute and that it was moving away from my stand. After watching his actions for a few minutes, I waited until the buck put its head down to feed again. I turned away from him and blew a single soft snort. The buck lifted its head, stared in my direction, and then began to feed again. Only this time, it moved purposefully and steadily toward me as it continued to feed. I didn't have to make another call. Within two minutes of making my first snort the buck was under my treestand. I released my arrow as the buck's nose was busily buried in the leaves looking for acorns. The buck never expected anything as the arrow found its mark. I don't think I would have had an opportunity to take a shot at that buck if I didn't try to relax it with a social snort. I think the buck would have eventually gotten so nervous from the original noise, it would have moved out of bow range and maybe even out of the area entirely, had I not relaxed it by making a social snort.

Over the years, carrying a snort call while deer hunting has helped me score on many deer -- some of which I know I would have never had an opportunity to harvest if I didn't use it. Most important, however, knowing when, how, why and where to use all cadences of the snort call has been most crucial to my success.

AGGRESSIVE SNORT

The fourth cadence of the primary snort is the aggressive snort. The aggressive snort is difficult to learn and could cause more problems unless you are a very experienced deer caller. Because it is complex to learn when and how to use, I won't attempt to touch base with it here; but, if we meet at a trade show, or at one of my seminars, ask me about this snort cadence and I will gladly demonstrate and explain it in detail to you.

BLATS AND BLEATS

Other primary calls include the blat and the bleat. Blats are made by all adult deer. Bleats are generally made by yearlings and fawns. Although, on occasion, a yearling musters up the vocal ability to make a blat. In any event, the two calls are distinctly different and should not be confused or you could get negative results. Remember, a bleat is much higher pitched than a blat.

FAWN DISTRESS BLEAT

Fawn bleats, used during the right time of year (usually the archery season), can be lethal. Fawns make several variations of a bleat. Fawns bleat when they're lost, hungry, hurt or in danger. For instance, a fawn separated from the group, lost, or is in danger bleats repeatedly for the doe. When the doe hears the distress call, it only takes her minutes to respond. Often, as she urgently responds to the call, the rest of the herd instinctively follows her. Frequently, this group includes a yearling buck. Occasionally, a mature buck may respond to the call knowing he will locate a doe near the source of the distress call.

A distress bleat must be blown aggressively. It sounds much like a rabbit in distress. "Baa-AAA ... Baa-AAA ... Baa-AAA." The pitch should be higher as you end the call. The more intensely you blow the call, the quicker a doe will respond. Blow the call in three successions only every half hour or so. By blowing it more frequently you will probably attract predators like coyote and fox rather than deer.

To imitate a hungry fawn, simply blow several very soft whiny bleats, "Baaaa . . . Baaaa . . ." every ten minutes or so. You must keep them non-aggressive to separate them from the alarm bleat. Many bucks have walked in to investigate this cadence of the bleat.

Although I am using a deer blat call here, this call is easy to make with your own voice.

ADULT BLAT

All adult and yearling deer make the loud blat. It is the most social call made in the deer woods. The blat is used by deer via different cadences to locate, warn, fend off, attract, and generally communicate with each other. It is meant to sound social and will arouse the curiosity of both bucks and does. This call -- "Baa-Baaaaaa . . . Baa-baaaaaa" -- should be blown gently. Stretch it out toa whine at the end of the call and do not blow the call often! Once every 30 to 45 minutes is enough. If a deer approaches, stop calling. By

152

eliminating the calling, you'll intrigue the deer to intensify its search for the source of the call.

Frank Brzozowski, an avid hunter, knows how well this call works. Frank, who hunted with me, never used a deer call while hunting. After seeing my success with deer calls, he decided to give calling a try on his next deer hunt. The following week, he left for a deer hunt in Alabama and brought a blat call with him. He attracted and shot an eight-point buck on that hunt using the blat.

"It took the buck only several minutes to respond," said Brzozowski. "I blew the call gently. Remembering I should wait a half-hour between calls, I put it away and began to watch the swamp. Several minutes later, I heard a twig snap and a low blat. I turned and saw the buck. Surprised that he answered me, I almost forgot to shoot. Luckily, I shot the buck before he could react to my presence."

One of my favorite calls from mid-December through late January is the estrus doe blat. Find an area that does use frequently. Make several long winy-sounding doe blats over a few hours. This time of year, an estrus doe walks through the woods emitting winy blats trying to attract bucks who have not yet picked up her estrus scent. The call can be made once every 15 minutes or so. Blow the call with reasonable volume (but, not too loud) creating a drawn-out winy blat. Like this <u>Baaaaaaaah</u> . . . <u>Baaaaaaaah</u>. You can repeat this call two to three times each hour. It's a terrific lateseason deer vocalization that has attracted big bucks for me over the years in many different states.

Because November through January can be cold, especially in the northern states, I protect the call from freezing by placing it inside the breast pocket of my shirt, underneath my jacket. In addition, knowing that deer move about much more during the midday hours late in the season, I either hunt all day or between 9:00 a.m.and 3:00 p.m. In either case, I dress in layers to protect myself from the elements to keep me comfortable enough to remain outdoors for a long time that naturally allows me to see more deer.

GRUNT

Along with the snort, the buck grunt is probably the most common vocalization hunters hear in the woods. Though it is not commonly known, both does and bucks grunt. Does grunt most of the year, while bucks grunt mostly during the rut. Grunting occurs throughout the year. You will have optimum success, however, when you imitate the grunt of a buck in rut or a doe in estrus. The best response to grunting comes between late October and mid-November, and again in mid-December. Grunting reaches its peak when both bucks and does are chasing each other or freshening scrapes during the peak rut.

For a grunt call to work effectively, it should be blown <u>gently</u>. If it is not, you'll scare off more bucks than you'll attract. Even trophy-sized bucks sometimes avoid a conflict when hot on the trail of a doe. Smaller bucks are definitely intimidated by deeper guttural grunts. Most hunters describe the grunts they have heard to sounds made by a domestic pig. Others describe it as sounding likea burp. Both are correct.

Other cadences or categories of grunts include the tending grunt, social grunt, submissive grunt, and trail grunt. Still, other grunts are combined with snorts and wheezes and are antagonistic to other deer, especially one buck to another. Deer combine these aggressive grunts with postural threats. Keep in mind, however, most sexual grunts are short, have a low pitch and intensity, and are repetitive only when the deer feels totally secure.

As most of us know, the grunt call is most effective during the rut. However, don't confuse actual mating with chasing. Once a buck is paired up with a doe, it's difficult, as it is with any male animal that you are trying to call away from a female, to make the buck respond. Yet, when bucks are chasing after does, grunting can lead to more action than you can ever imagine and, sometimes, handle.

FACTS ABOUT GRUNTING DURING THE PRE-RUT

The most overlooked stage, and least exploited, is the productive pre-rut stage. The false rut typically occurs in early October. Archers and firearm sportsmen who hunt during this most beautiful month of the year, confirm to seeing a yearly event where, straightaway, within a 24-hour period they find a mass of fresh scrapes throughout their hunting grounds. What happens to cause this obvious intense breeding change in bucks? The onset of the pre-rut.

Grunt calling tactics for the pre-rut are wide and varied. Bucks and does are sexually excited forthe first time in many months. They are enthusiastic to respond to anything that remotely suggests a sexual encounter. It is why false scrapes work so well during the pre-rut and why non-aggressive rattling techniques also get results.

One of the best grunt calls to make during the pre-rut is sometimes called a <u>trail grunt</u>. I have nicknamed it the <u>burp-o-matic</u> or <u>burp grunt</u>. It is a series (usually several in a row) of very soft, short, burp-like sounds made by a buck. Usually, his nose is held to the ground and he is zigzagging along searching out the scent of a doe. This scent doesn't necessarily have to be that of an estrus doe. Believe it or not, most bucks on these trails are chasing does who are about to enter estrus and are not in estrus, yet. It is why they are so excited. Bucks sense that if they can catch up with the doe, they can stay with her until she comes into estrus and will accept his amorous overtures.

The <u>burp grunt</u> sounds like this, "<u>Brp, brp, brp, brp, brp</u>." There are only a few silent seconds between each "brp." The key to this cadence is to keep it low. To judge what low means, you should blow it loud enough so a person could hear it 100 yards away (which really doesn't take much). Yet, not so loud that it sounds aggressive. I usually make the call every 30 minutes or so. If nothing responds, I repeat the sequence over and over again until I leave the woods. If something does respond, I immediately stop calling. Response does not only mean seeing a deer. A good caller learns to LISTEN as intently as he looks. Remember, almost 60 percent of any game hunters call, responds without the hunter ever knowing it was there. Keep a sharp lookout. More important, listen for response.

Last year, I was grunting for more than three hours and, to be frank, I became a little lackadaisical, from not seeing or hearing anything for quite some time. During the next grunting sequence, I heard what I thought were antlers rubbing against a tree. Because I wasn't paying attention like I should have been, I wasn't sure. The rubbing sound was close. It was just below the ledge I was grunting from. Trying to confirm what I heard, I stretched over the ledge to look and there, ten feet below and twenty yards in front of me, was a dandy buck standing by a sapling staring up at me. My heart sank as the buck whirled and ran off.

Sounds are as important as sights when calling deer. Listen for the snapping of a single twig, the rustling of a leaf, the sound of a buck's antlers being rubbed on a tree, the sound of urine hitting the forest floor and, to state the obvious, deer grunting back at you. These are all pertinent signs of response and should be treated accordingly.

Cup your hands over the end of the tube when blowing a grunt to add realistic tone variations to the call.

While hunting with my wife, Kate, and my son, Cody (who was four years old at the time), at Robert Bracken's Lazy Fork Ranch in Texas a few years ago, all three of us were crowded in a tower stand meant for one adult. I was grunting repeatedly every 20 or 30 minutes. Because we were crowded, it was difficult for us to turn and look out the back window of the blind. So, we watched the front and sides. About an hour had passed when Kate whispered, "Oh No! Cody, are you having an accident?" "No, Mom," the poor guy answered. Kate and I stared at each other for a split second and then simultaneously realized what we were hearing! We turned and looked out the back window, and there, directly under the stand, was a big 8-point buck urinating onto the sunbaked earth. The buck paced back and forth for several minutes, grunting and pawing where he had urinated before walking back into the sacawista grass. Again, here's a great example of how important it is to listen for a response.

Remember, and this is most crucial factor about calling, when a deer responds it is zeroing in directly on the location from where the sound is emanating -- that's YOU. All the deer's senses are focused on the noise. By continuing to call as the deer approaches, you almost guarantee that the deer will "make" you. And, he will either walk by like you weren't even there or he will bolt and run. Sometimes, he will "make" you from cover, some distance away and you will never even know he was there.

PRIMARY RUT

The primary rut encompasses most of the serious, aggressive behavior of deer during the breeding season. Therefore, I like to use two different cadences of the grunt during this period. The first is the grunt-snort-wheeze. The second is a variation of the burp-grunt I used during the pre-rut except the number of burps is reduced and prolonged.

GRUNT-SNORT WHEEZE

The grunt-snort-wheeze is an antagonistic, aggressive call. Of the grunt call cadences, it is the most difficult to master. This call is made by bucks of a higher position in the herd. The sound made by these bucks is meant to get the attention of subordinate bucks. It basically says, "Hey, you. Do you see this head gear? Are you ready and able to take me on? If not, beat it." That's exactly what most bucks will do when they hear this call made by a hunter -- they will leave the area. Interestingly, however, if there is an aggressive buck who holds a high position within the herd, he almost inevitably is motivated to respond. I use the grunt-snort-wheeze mostly with aggressive rattling and grunting tactics -- which I use infrequently.

Begin the call by making a long, guttural, deep grunt, "Eeeerrrrrp." Follow this with a short snort, "Whew." For the sake of clarity, although it has always been called a snort, it's more of a nostril-clearing sound, than a "certified" snort. Imagine it sounding as if you had a runny nose that was not full of mucus. Although you blew your nose hard, you would only hear a quick "Whew" sound rather than a long and voluminous mucus-clearing type noise. This is followed by a short wheezing sound. The wheezing can best be described as a short cough from deep within the lungs. However, keep it short. Cough as softly as you can while expelling all the air from your lungs. Combine these three sounds, to create the grunt-snort-wheeze. Don't become disappointed if you don't have a buck respond right away -- or at all. Again, this is a call designed to be used by trophy hunters.

The second cadence I use during the primary rut is the <u>Extended Burp Grunt</u>. Some call it the tending grunt. It is usually made by a buck with an estrus doe close at hand feeding or bedded down near him or, in some instances, has momentarily walked out of his sight. Every so often, the buck grunts to keep himself on the does' mind until she's actually ready to breed. He'll also make and extended burp grunt to warn off other bucks.

It is a highly effective call during the primary rut and is used from November 1 until late December. The trick to this call is that while it's a pitch higher than the pre-rut burp-grunt it is still not made loudly. Every 20 minutes or so, take the call and cup the end of the tube in your palm (the palm should be half-open and not tightly closed) and blow two or three short burps. They sound like this, "<u>Burp, burp, burp</u>." Each "burp" is slightly longer than the pre-rut "brp." When you get a response, whether is by sight or sound, IMMEDIATELY STOP CALLING. Deer are edgy after several weeks of hunting pressure and react more cautiously to everything, including other deer vocalizations. Often, they hesitate in the cover, listening and looking before showing up or coming out. So, let the deer's curiosity work for you instead of against you. Let his inquisitiveness build to a fever pitch, until he can't stand it anymore and brazenly walks out trying to locate the source of the grunt. You can make this call throughout the day. During firearms season, don't grunt during prime times (i.e., when a majority of other hunters are in the woods - dawn to 9:00 a.m. and 2:00 p.m. to dusk); instead, grunt between 10:00 a.m. and 2:00 p.m. and look for considerable success with this strategy.

LATE OR POST RUT

During the late rut, most of the immature (or latest born) does, and any other doe that was not successfully bred yet, comes into estrus. Many hunters have conveyed stories to me, that during the late rut, they have had much success with grunting. This doesn't surprise me. Grunting can even be effective into January and February. Some does are still experiencing estrus cycles in December, January and even into early February. The post-rut is a period overlooked by many hunters who are sure that the rut is long over and have already put away their grunt calls.

One sign to look for during this phase is a quick and dramatic increase in deer activity. Does coming into estrus during this period are BUCK MAGNETS because there are not many of them and they tend to have an intensity about their odor and body language. Curiously, they are as "bent" about finding bucks as the bucks are about finding them. They will trot along depositing estrus urine and make a series of soft, prolonged grunts, too. Although it's the same grunt they make beginning in October, does are more vocal with it during the post-rut. It's worthwhile to note here that this doe-grunt can be used in any of the above periods mentioned and is a highly effective grunt call for attracting bucks. This is especially true during slow periods of the rut when bucks are not enthusiastic about responding to the grunts of other bucks, but will respond quite readily to a doe grunt. Remember, does grunt all year and are the major users of a grunt called a Cohesive grunt, which I think is better stated as a Social Grunt. Does grunt to reprimand fawns, to call fawns and yearlings and to warn off young immature bucks. These non-sexual vocalizations can range from a squeal to a deep, guttural sound.

The post-rut doe grunt is a prolonged winy type grunt. The doe wants attention and she wants it fast. She walks through the woods making this guttural sound until she gets some attention. It sounds like this, "<u>Buuurrrrp</u>." She makes this sound without any continuity. Sometimes, two or three burps in a short period; or even several minutes will pass between her calls. In any event, it's an excellent call to imitate as long as you do not make it loudly.

The post-rut buck-grunt is an excited sound. It's a buck in a rush to find the season's final does in estrus. His intensity is dramatic. This is where many bucks create their undoing, as they ignore anything in their paths in order to get the brass ring. It is a time when all bucks have an equal opportunity to breed. They know it and react accordingly. Many larger, more aggressive bucks are physically worn to a frazzle by now. Younger bucks know they have a better chance of chasing off a buck that, until now, was more dominant during the other two phases of the rut.

When grunting during the post rut, you'll have more opportunities to see many more bucks than expected. This is the most forgiving period when it comes to grunting. If you are going to get away with making a mistake, it will usually be during this time frame as the bucks responding are in a frenzy. Sometimes, as the old saying goes, rules are meant to be broken. This is applicable here. Although I am a major proponent of calling and rattling softly, this is one time you can call a little more loudly and aggressively and get away with it. Sometimes, to get through to a buck passing by during the post rut, you have to elevate the volume of your call almost twice as loud as the soft calls you have been making all season. The post-rut buck-grunt is strikingly similar to the primary cadence, except it is made repeatedly and a bit more loudly. It goes this like, "Eeeerp, Eeeeerp, Eeeeerp" A few second pause and then, "Eeeerp, Eeeerp, Eeeerp." Again, a few seconds pause and three more "Erps." If you see a buck, stop calling and let him dictate what your next move is. If he moves away from you without ever looking, call again and stop when he reacts. If you don't see a buck, you can make the call every 15 minutes.

DOE GRUNT

A doe grunt is longer and sounds like, "Aaaaaahhhhhhhhh." The grunt of a buck on the trail of a doe in estrus sounds like a short burp, "Erp-Erp . . . Erp-Erp . . . Erp-Erp." If you hear and see abuck making this grunt, blow two short burp-grunts back. Usually, the buck lifts his head and walks straight toward what he believes is another buck on the trail of "his" doe. When you do not see or hear a buck, and want to attract one, extend the length of the call, "Eeeeerrrrp . . . Eeeeeerrrrrp." You'll know immediately if you are blowing the call wrong if it sounds like a duck call. You will find the grunt easy to use and one of the best calls for attracting bucks to your stand.

Leo Somma, from Long Island, New York, started using a grunt call during the '93 deer season. While bow hunting the first week of December -- the late rut -- in an area that receives a lot of pressure, Somma began using his grunt call at around 3:15 p.m. He blew two long burps, waited several minutes, and repeated the call. He was going to wait another several minutes and blow the call again -- when it dropped to the ground!

"I was just about to climb down from my tree stand to get the call," Somma told me, "when I heard a deer approaching. Within moments, a buck stopped 50 yards from my stand. He was on a well-used deer trail, apparently searching for the source of the call. He began rubbing his eyes and forehead on an overhanging branch. After several minutes, he went back exactly the way he came. In desperation, I tried to imitate a call by cupping my hand and calling to the buck. The buck didn't hear me and continued off. I have no doubt, had I not dropped my grunt, I would have had a shot at the buck."

Paul Butski is an expert wildlife caller. He has won several national turkey calling championships and now manufactures his own line of game calls. His favorite and most successful deer call is thegrunt. "Before I began using the grunt call, I knew bucks were slipping by me undetected. Now, since I've been using the grunt, bucks are coming in and looking for me," said Butski.

To help increase your success when grunting, create more of an illusion by combining your grunt with intermittent antler rattling. Also, shake a sapling or the branch of a tree a few times when you are grunting. These effects add to the realism of your grunting.

The most important advice I can give you about calling is to practice each call long BEFORE THE SEASON. Practice not only makes you a better caller, but it also enhances your confidence level tremendously. Remember the principle: Concentration + Positive Thinking X Confidence = Consistent Success. Being confident in your ability to imitate different deer sounds and knowing when to use an alarm-snort as opposed to a social snort, will put antlers on your wall and venison in your freezer. I'll close with this. When you think you've practiced your calling techniques enough, practice, practice and practice some more.

CHAPTER 13

RATTLING STRATEGIES THAT WORK ANYWHERE

RATTLING:
"The act of using a set of antlers to simulate a rack-meshing skirmish between two bucks."

Rattling has definitely captured the imagination of deer hunters across the country -- and especially throughout the Northeast over the last twenty years. I'll bet hunters have tried this one deer hunting method more than any other single hunting strategy over the last two decades. I started my writing career by penning an article called "Rattling Big Bucks of The Northeast" in 1983. This one feature article literally launched my outdoor communications profession.

The response to that rattling article was overwhelming. Everywhere I went, hunters asked me repeatedly, "Does rattling REALLY work in the Northeast?" I found it hard to understand why they couldn't believe and embrace the fact that deer, both bucks and does, respond to the clashing of antlers -- all across North America including the Northeast. After all, in the whitetail's world the sounds made by two bucks' antlers as they spar or fight are commonplace. The response to this noise is both basic and instinctive for bucks and does. It's Mother Nature's natural attraction. Rattling triggers an investigative response from deer and it is as just one more integral component of their breeding cycle.

Before getting into the details about how to rattle, etch these thoughts in your mind. Rattling is the most forgiving hunting tactic. Even if you make a few mistakes, you'll still rattle in bucks. As long as you forget everything you've ever been taught about traditional deer hunting methods, that is. You do not have to be quiet and sit motionless waiting for a deer to come by when you rattle. In fact, it's the exact opposite. Noise and movement are factors that help attract bucks to you. When you are rattling -- YOU'RE NOT HUNTING BUCKS ANYMORE, THEY'RE HUNTING YOU!

However, before I say anything else about rattling, I should qualify it with this: rattling works -- it really does. Not always, but often enough to make a difference in your buck hunting success ratio. It's not a cure-all magic buck hunting strategy. There will be times you'll just not believe how successful it is. There'll be other times you'll become frustrated with its seemingly ineffectiveness. All in all, it will aid you as a deer hunter and it will thrill you beyond your wildest dreams each time you rattle in a buck. Nothing related to deer hunting is more satisfying or exhilarating than rattling in a white-tailed buck. This, in itself, makes rattling worth while even if it doesn't work every time you try it.

Keep in mind, when you are rattling or calling, you are announcing to all interested bucks exactly where you are. As they respond to your rattling, they will focus all their senses (their ability to smell, see, and hear) on you! It doesn't take a buck long to pinpoint where the sounds are coming from. Because of this, you must take a few simple precautions when you rattle. If you do, you can have immediate success.

THE NATURE OF THE FIGHT

You may be tempted to browse over the next few pages -- you shouldn't. The reason I wrote about the behavioral and instinctive reasons why bucks fight is to arm you with important information other than basic deer hunting data about the subject. By understanding the natural instinctive behavioral traits of why bucks fight you will be a much better rattler and deer caller.

In order to understand why the sounds of meshing and grinding antlers attracts whitetails, hunters should fully understand the biological origins about the nature of FIGHTING. Animals fight for one of two reasons: to establish their dominance (a spot in the pecking order) within a specific social hierarchy or to establish their territorial rights over a certain piece of ground. Although white-tailed deer are neither TRULY territorial or dominant (despite what you have read about these subjects), they do, to a degree, adhere to these behavioral traits.

Deer are more hierarchical (which means they have no absolute fixed territories) than territorial. Some animals are purely territorial and defend a specific space, or turf, within a definite "scent or visually marked" area to the death. Still other species exist within hierarchies in their terrain and must deal with both types of aggression.

In my 32 years of hunting, videotaping and observing whitetails, I have never found them to be territorial -- **to the legitimate definition of the word.** Especially mature bucks. Documented research has confirmed that, when necessary, mature bucks travel many miles outside of their home ranges and so called "core areas" during the primary rut in search of does in estrus. In several papers on this subject, researchers have confirmed that tagged or radio collared bucks traveled as much as 30 or more miles in search of hot does. They also confirmed that it isn't uncommon for a buck to REGULARLY travel 5 to 10 miles during the rutting period in search of receptive does.

This means bucks who do this type of short or "long-distance" traveling from their home range enter into the so-called territory of other so-called dominant bucks. If territory and dominance were actually ruling traits of the whitetail, many bucks would die during fights over dominance or by defending territory. This simply does not happen!

Therefore, I strongly feel that these two words should be used carefully. The reason for this is to not get caught up in the web of promotional hype. Very few outdoor writers and some manufacturers create stories and product they think will market better by trying to make the hunting public believe that certain products and tactics will attract "the dominant buck" from within a herd. As if each herd has only one dominant animal who rules as a tyrant over all other bucks! If you let yourself be tricked by this marketing hype, you could wind up using wrong tactics based on erroneous information.

Webster's Dictionary defines dominant as "having the most control or influence; most overwhelming." Keep this definition in mind when you apply the word dominant and you're safe. It does not say "dominant over all others." In every herd of whitetails, there are several dominant bucks within that herd. There are many submissive bucks, too. You'll understand the importance of what I'm saying, further along in the chapter. It is also why I am about to explain, in detail, the **fight or flight** principle below. Read it carefully. Think about what I said above and what I'm about to say below and evaluate it with common sense. You'll realize a lot of the information you've heard about rattling, dominance, territory and aggressive hunting tactics is unadulterated horse poop.

Fights regularly occur within a resident buck's home range and also when transient bucks enter the home ranges of other bucks. These fights are rarely more than pushing and shoving matches. They are not designed to cause injury or death. Instead, Mother Nature uses a variety of ritualized signals and postures as her most efficient way of settling disputes within the same species. Animals of the same kind could not be programmed to fight to the death. If they were, it would not benefit the species as a whole and could cause its eventual extinction. If death occurs during a fight it's usually caused from the unintentional locking of antlers or from an accidental puncture wound of a point on a buck's antlers. Not because a resident buck instinctively reacted to a transient buck with over aggressive behavior and tried to establish dominance.

Territorial behavior is found in carnivores like the big five meat eaters of Africa (lions, hyenas, wild dogs, leopards and cheetahs), as well as wolves of North America. Most other animals are pressured to fight not to protect territory or to establish dominance, but to protect their "space" also referred to as their "defense zone." In the whitetail's world, most resident bucks simply ignore transient bucks' trespassing infractions as most of the transient bucks are **visibly** inferior in antler and body size. In addition, this ignoring behavior is further enhanced when submissive bucks display a yielding conduct. A submissive animal displays visible signals to a more aggressive animal that it does not want to be threatening. It will avoid eye contact, keep its head up high or turn its rump toward the more aggressive animal. With these forms of body language, the submissive animal clearly makes itself non-threatening. When this occurs, dominant or aggressive animals instinctively end any potential fighting behavior and the bucks go back to their normal non-aggressive conduct.

Bucks establish their place in the hierarchy in the late spring and early summer. This pecking order clearly shows each buck where he stands socially and physically among the other males within his immediate herd and, to some degree, bucks on the fringes of his home range. Therefore, there is no need for bucks to constantly fight to establish dominance during the rut. They already know their place within the male hierarchy. As the rut progresses and the more stronger, aggressive bucks become weakened from the constant stress of chasing and breeding does, this position in the pecking order changes. The so-called dominant buck, physically weakened and mentally drained from the rigors of the breeding season (if a buck can be mentally drained), is often displaced by another buck with similar or equal antler size but is more physically fit at that time.

I once videotaped a 10-point buck who was clearly the most aggressive buck within the herd, just by his sheer antler and body size. An eight-point buck chased him away from a doe. My only deduction, based on seeing this same scenario unfold numerous times since, is that the bigger buck was run off by a somewhat smaller buck, generally equal in body size, for no other reason than the smaller buck being more physically fit.

A classic example is when a young 20-year old, 6"1", 210 lb. boxer beats the 29-year old champ who is 6"4" and 230 lbs. Just because the champ is bigger and heavier and has more experience, doesn't always guarantee him a victory. Physical strength alone could help the younger boxer to dethrone his larger and more visually threatening opponent.

This is how body language helps to effectively diffuse actual aggressive physical confrontation between animals. Combat can be avoided through ambivalent posturing (which biologists refer to as displacement activity) and other forms of body language. For a species to continue to perpetuate and evolve successfully, Mother Nature installs this body language safety device when it comes to fighting. It prevents a lot of unnecessary injuries, death and wasted energy -- which is vital to the animal -- especially during courtship.

Along with body language, Mother Nature has also implanted some autonomic signals within the nervous system. Whenever an animal is aroused to the degree of the physical confrontation of ritualized combat, it undergoes several immediate but basic psychological changes. We are all familiar with the fight or flight axiom. To be a more effective deer hunter, especially a rattler or caller, you should clearly understand how it works.

When any mammal, including man, becomes aggressively stimulated, a full-fledged fight takes place from time to time. However, other than today's modern man who is so belligerent to his fellow man, in nature, serious fighting among wild animals occurs only as a last resort. Then, only when all other aggressive signaling and counter signaling has failed to resolve the dispute. A classic example of this is when two bucks of equal body and antler size confront each other. Once they have decided a hostile confrontation is necessary, their instinctive reaction is to immediately size up each other. Instead of running head long at each other, they use body posturing to warn off the other opponent. "Hey! Look me over good. Do you really want to brawl with me?" They use this size-me-up theory to try to avoid actual combat.

Then, psychological changes kick into gear. The animal wants to fight but receives other signals to flee. These contradictory signals are simply nature's way to **check and balance all aggressive behavior.** These are known as the sympathic and parasympathic systems. The sympathic signal simply prepares the animal's body for fierce fighting action. The parasympathic signal has the responsibility of counteracting the former. Basically, while one signal says to a particular animal, "I'm ready to rumble," the other says, "Maybe I'd better take it easy and relax and assess my opponent further." Even though a buck may emerge victorious from an out-and-out fight, the victory could be anti-climatic as he may also emerge with serious body injuries or a life-threatening drain of energy, making his victory bitter sweet at best. In the end, aggression drives an animal forward while fear restrains it. Any battle that can be settled with limited physical contact and replaced with elaborate threat rituals and posturing tremendously benefits the species and helps to further jettison it forward on the evolutionary ladder.

Therefore, if you want to include antler rattling in your "deer hunting bag of tricks," it is important to understand why bucks respond to rattling. This information I am sharing here will help make you a more intelligent and effective hunter. Remember one of the rules for effective hunting is to know your quarry as well as you know yourself -- maybe even better. If you follow this axiom, the more successful predator you will be. In the end, that's what man has evolved into and that's what you are as a deer hunter -- a predator.

Since our genesis as a thinking, upright, walking and speaking animal, we have evolved from the tree-dwelling, passive primate whose diet was strictly vegetarian to the ground-dwelling savanna primate who adapted scavenging and hunting into its lifestyle. These changes allowed it to continue to successfully evolve as a predatory species. For aeons, we continued along this hunting evolutionary path and eventually evolved from the solely predatory hunters of yesteryear to more of an opportunist omnivorous species. Then, we became farmers during the agricultural period of our evolution to, finally, the passive gatherer of today. Each time we enter a supermarket, we perform passive ritualistic gathering ceremonies. Therefore, the more you can know about your ancestral genetic pool as a predator, the more successful you will be as a hunter.

MY FIRST RATTLING EXPERIENCE

Antler rattling requires you to employ a few key factors for it to be a consistently successful hunting method. First, it necessitates that you believe that it works. It requires active participation in order for you to have any chance at all to CREATE THE ENTIRE ILLUSION. **It demands your confidence.** I began rattling in 1975. I wanted to research how rattling worked and then write about its effectiveness in an outdoor magazine. I packed my gear and headed to an area I hunted in Childwold, NY a small hamlet nestled between Tupper Lake and Cranberry Lake on Route 3 in the Adirondack Mts. I started hunting in the Childwold area several years earlier when International Paper Company opened, for the first time in over 100 years, a large tract of its lumbering land.

The first several years I hunted there, I saw many large Adirondack bucks shot by hunters. I thought surely this was the place to try rattling. My first experience was both comical and educational. I found a little knoll and began to rattle just as it became light. Not an hour after I began rattling, I heard the unmistakable crunching of leaves coming in my direction. Crunch -- crunch -- crunch. And there, to my surprise, was a big 6'6" Adirondack lumberjack-type man walking toward me while uttering a myriad of unpleasant profanities! When he got to within five yards of my nose, he stopped. In a very deep and threatening voice (which I can remember verbatim) said, "What the hell are you doing, stupid?!"

"I'm rattling," I said in a meek and embarrassed voice. "You're what?" he snapped back. Remember, in 1975 hardly anyone outside of Texas new about rattling, never mind used it as a hunting method. "I'm rattling," I once again said to him. I sheepishly showed him the small 4-pt. set of antlers tightly clutched in my hand, hoping he would consider them some sort of potential weapon to harm him if need be. "Well, I've got a bulletin for you, buddy. You hit those horns together again and I'm gonna stick them where they won't make any more noise!" Now, do you remember the fight or flight response I talked about earlier? I had no such response. All my instincts told me to run. Unfortunately, I was sure if I stood up this guy would see that I had urinated in my pants and would have beat me to death where I stood. So, instead, I guaranteed him I would put the antlers away and he would not have to be bothered by the noise again. He grumbled and said something to the effect, "Smart move" and left.

Interestingly, he walked off in a totally different direction from which he approached. I'm Italian and, therefore, I'm pretty headstrong. I interpreted his departure to a new direction as a signal of total disgust and that he was leaving the area. I waited for what I thought was an ample and safe amount of time and then mustered up the courage to start rattling again.

As luck would have it, not 15 minutes after my second sequence, I heard two shots, "BANG . . . . BANG!" Someone called out, "Hey Buddy! " (Now I was his buddy) "C'mere quick, you're not going to believe this."

I must admit I hesitated about going over to him. I had serious thoughts about the possibilities of not returning alive. But, the excitement in his voice sounded genuine and so over the knoll I went. To my sheer and utter amazement, there, not 75 yards from where I was rattling was a magnificent 8-point buck lying on the forest floor! Not 20 yards from the buck was the lumber jack yelling at the top of his lungs, "Buddy. You're not gonna believe this. You're just not gonna believe this. When you started that rattling stuff again, I decided to get up and come and pay you a visit. Just then, that buck broke out from the swamp and started to head right to you -- so I shot him!"

While disappointed that he shot the buck I rattled in, the dead buck did convince me I was on to a hunting strategy that was hot. I didn't rattle in another buck over the next couple of days, but I learned a valuable lesson. A lesson that may have even been better (well almost better) than shooting the buck. The lesson of having confidence that rattling works.

CONFIDENCE

From that day forward, I believed that rattling works. Every time I didn't get a response to my rattling efforts, all I had to do was think about that buck lying on the ground and I got a surge of new confidence about rattling. For the remainder of that deer season my success was very limited. Even when I rattled in a buck, I convinced myself, as you will, that I really didn't rattle him in. I made excuses for his presence like, "The buck was coming toward me anyway." Or, "Someone spooked the buck to me." In other words, even when you first have success with rattling, you won't let yourself believe it worked. All these excuses will be subliminally generated from a lack of confidence in yourself and the strategy you chose to use.

To compound this, you'll be your own worst enemy when it comes to rattling. I have seen it time and time again. Most hunters who give rattling a try eventually don't. The reason is simple -- they're just too embarrassed to be caught in the woods meshing and grinding antlers, rustling leaves, breaking branches and grunting! I guess all these antics make them feel foolish. That's really too bad. If you can get over the embarrassment about rattling, the rest (having a buck respond) is easy.

By the following deer season, I started "rattling in" bucks more consistently and believed I rattled them in. Once that happened, I was hooked. More important, now I was absolutely positive the tactic worked and I behaved like it did. Each time I rattled, I EXPECTED something to happen. I became an active, confident and believing participant. I knew I had to imitate all the sounds and sights caused by two fighting bucks to fool a buck into reacting. I had to stomp my feet to imitate the hooves of the fighting bucks, snap branches, rustle leaves, shake saplings and make subtle vocalizations all in an earnest effort to CREATE THE ENTIRE ILLUSION. As I said in Chapter 4, confidence is the most important factor to successful buck hunting. You can intensify that to the 10th power when it comes to rattling and calling.

HOW BUCK FIGHTS START

All battles between bucks begin with body posturing and ritual threat movements. Bucks approach each other slowly and display a series of body postures. Bucks will routinely head bow, paw the ground, arch their backs, lower their heads and rhythmically swing their bodies side to side. During a display of aggression they display either one or all of the above body movements. I have videotaped this behavior prior to a serious buck fight many times.

In order for you to be the best antler rattler you can be, you must psyche yourself up to assume the roles of both of the bucks who are about to battle with one another. If you've ever been to one of my lectures, you've heard me use this phrase over again as one of my key phrases to successful antler rattling and deer calling. You must **CREATE THE ENTIRE ILLUSION** for rattling to work on a consistent basis.

TONE IT DOWN

What I practiced and preached about rattling in 1984, however, is enormously different than what I recommend today. During my 22 years of trial-and-error, I discovered ways and reasons that helped me become a better rattler each season. I found out what worked and what didn't work. One of my most interesting discoveries over the last five years has been that **moderate rattling techniques work better to attract bucks than do aggressive rattling strategies.** This is quite contrary to what I advised hunters years ago.

Whether you are rattling or using deer calls, being over aggressive does not accomplish the kind of success that being less aggressive will. Although many hunters may tell you otherwise, take this to the Deer Hunting Bank. BE LESS AGGRESSIVE AND YOU WILL HAVE MORE SUCCESS. Many of the nation's top big game hunters agree with this advice. Judd Cooney, a long-time big game hunter, who resides in Colorado, is a strong advocate of less aggressive calling techniques. His calling and rattling articles and columns have sung the praises of less aggressive calling tactics. So has renowned deer hunter and wild game caller Paul Butski. Other professional hunters who agree to call or rattle less aggressively include Dick Idol, Barry and

Gene Wensel, and Paul Newsom.

Even though my aggressive tactics worked for me back in the early 80s -- I EVENTUALLY FOUND BY TONING DOWN MY RATTLING AND THE ASSOCIATED NOISES I MADE, MORE BUCKS RESPONDED AND ON A MORE REGULAR BASIS! Therefore, forget what I told you about rattling if you heard it from me more than five years ago. From here on, anything I say about rattling is under the theorem of what I now refer to as "controlled rattling." While you will still mesh and grind antlers, you will no longer bang them excessively hard. Likewise, while you will still rustle leaves, snap branches, thump your feet and the antlers on the ground, you will do all of this with much less aggression.

USING NATURAL OR SYNTHETIC ANTLERS

Certain types and sizes of antlers work better than others. If you choose to use natural antlers (I've used synthetic antlers for 10 years), they must be fresh. I know you've heard that you can use the same antlers year after year. If they dry out, some say you can soak them in water and it rejuvenates their sound and pitch. While this is true to some degree, it requires too much attention for me. Getting a fresh pair of natural antlers every two to three years isn't so difficult or expensive. More important, I don't want to see a big buck walking by, pull my antlers from my backpack only to realize I forgot to soak them, especially when I hear their dead pitch after grinding them together.

NATURAL ANTLERS MUST BE FRESH

If you are going to rattle with natural antlers, make the effort to use a fresh pair. Many times, hunters have told me they have used the same pair of antlers for years and they still rattle in bucks, even though the antlers are dead sounding. My response to them is that they'd be rattling in more bucks, more consistently, if the antlers they were using were fresh and not dead.

Let me explain why. When you begin to rattle with a dead set of antlers, the tone sounds the same to a buck that is 100 to 300 yards away. There isn't a buck in all of North America that is able to "figure out" whether or not a set of rattling antlers is fresh or dead -- not at these distances. Bucks simply just don't have that kind of brain power. So, they hear the antlers, and respond. As they get closer, however, the same buck instinctively picks up a difference in the tone of a dead set of antlers compared to a fresh set. He simply begins to get cautious. I can't afford to make any buck I'm hunting any more cautious than he already is. So, why make all the effort it takes to become a serious rattler only to lose the "edge" to the buck from using dead antlers. Believe me, if you want to be a more consistently successful rattler, use either a good-sounding medium-sized pair of **synthetic antlers** or use a fresh medium-sized **natural set of antlers** every year or two. By doing anything less, you spite no one else's nose, but your own. The decision lies with you.

Natural antlers are available from any taxidermist for a nominal fee. You don't even have to buy a matched set. They could be two lefts, two rights, or left and right from different bucks. **They key is however that they should be very close in size**. Bucks generally fight with bucks the same size. Notice I did not say a casual sparring or pushing session which is meant only to reinforce a pecking order. I'm referring to a serious fight or shoving match.

In south Texas, with friend Don Holley, I used synthetic antlers and a grunt call to bring in this monster 14-point buck.

WHAT SIZE ANTLERS WORK BEST?

The general size of the antlers, whether they are natural or synthetic, should represent and average size buck. I can best describe this as a set of antlers that would have a 10 to 14 inch spread and anywhere from 4 to 8 points. It is not necessary to use large or oversized antlers to rattle in big bucks. Here's where there is a lot of misinformation about rattling. You have read that in order to rattle in big dominant bucks (remember what I said about dominant bucks -- there is no such whitetail), you must use big, heavy antlers.

Here's where common sense comes into play when hunting whitetails. No matter how big the buck is, if he's responding to what he thinks is two other big aggressive bucks fighting, bucks that sound as if they are ranked high within the hierarchy, he is going to either avoid the fight totally or, at best, respond very cautiously. No man or beast wants to fight with the biggest, "baddest" boy in the neighborhood. It wouldn't make any sense. I have proven this to myself each time I rattled with large antlers over the last twenty years. **Therefore, this is tested theory.** Using big antlers will only cause you problems. You will be a lonely rattler and a frustrated hunter if you are determined to rattle with big antlers.

With that said, let me explain further. Most hunters across the United States and in parts of Canada are not hunting bucks with the body, antler size and buck numbers found in Texas, Montana, Alberta or Saskatchewan. In Texas, Montana, and other western states where whitetails are found, whitetails are generally ignored by mule deer hunters. Therefore, they get to mature into larger bodied and racked bucks. Many with racks scoring 140 and much higher. In Alberta and Saskatchewan, these bucks are not only physically larger, as they are the largest of the subspecies of whitetails, but they also have bigger antlers. Many bucks typically score in the 150s. Under these circumstances, you could use a larger set of antlers for rattling.

By using an average set of antlers **you will attract all size bucks.** Big bucks will respond, even the most aggressive ones within the herd. They know all they have to do is exhibit aggressive body posture to scare off the competition. Bucks of similar antler size respond instinctively realizing they have an opportunity to succeed. Smaller bucks are the teenagers of the buck hierarchy and haven't learned the lessons of life yet. They respond thinking there isn't anybody's ass they can't kick. These young ones are quickly taught otherwise.

One reason hunters give up on rattling is because they carry over-sized antlers into the woods. They soon learn how cumbersome they are to tote around all day. Inevitably, these guys wind up leaving the antlers in their vehicles. I can promise you, you won't rattle a single buck while hunting in the woods with your antlers back in the truck. A medium size set of antlers comfortably stores in a backpack and will be there when you want them.

Once you have a medium set of fresh, natural antlers the next step is to cut off the tips of the tines and remove the brow tines. I know you've heard, by some, that you should not do this because cutting the tines "alters" the sound or pitch, giving them less than a realistic tone. What nonsense. It won't. There are many bucks fighting with antlers that are broken and other bucks respond without hesitation.

You must cut the tips of the tines and brow tines, for no other purpose than to be able to create the entire illusion of two bucks fighting -- realistically and enthusiastically. If you are meshing and grinding and twisting antlers without taking off the brow tines and cutting off the tips of the tines, the only goal you will accomplish is maiming yourself. Once you have "ding"ed or cut your hand, especially on a frigid winter morning, I can guarantee (from past experience) you will give up rattling lickety split.

In the 1980s, before I cut off the tips and the brow tines, and before I started using synthetic antlers, I took off a thumb nail. I accidentally slammed the tip of one of the antlers under my nail and almost lifted it free from my thumb. It ruined the rest of my deer season. The next year, even after I cut off the tips and brow tines, I clearly remembered the pain from the year before. It took me awhile to get back into creating the entire illusion by meshing, grinding and twisting the antlers with real enthusiasm. I called it the "Sissy Syndrome." To avoid this, take my advice and cut off the tips of each point and brow tine. Then, take some fine sand paper and round off the edges. You won't regret it.

SYNTHETIC ANTLERS

You can make your rattling a lot easier by buying and using a quality set of medium size, authentic sounding, synthetic antlers. They are easy to use, convenient to pack, light, and they hold their tone (pitch) for years. The set I use was designed so when you hold them in your hands both antlers are pointed **away** from you -- a terrific idea to prevent the tips of the tines from hitting your hands. **NEVER** cut anything off a synthetic set of antlers. Cutting a synthetic set of antlers **WILL RUIN** their tone. I have used the set I bought nine years ago and they still retain their original tone.

A word of caution about synthetic antlers. There are some that sound realistic and there are some don't. Make sure they are not too big, feel comfortable in your hands, are easy to pack and sound good before you purchase them. Also, test several different brands before deciding to buy a set.

HOW TO RATTLE ANTLERS

In order for you to be good at rattling, you must imagine, in detail, what you're trying to re-create. You must understand the mechanics involved as far as the animals fighting behavior is concerned. I always try to CREATE THE ENTIRE ILLUSION of two bucks fighting when rattling. I mentally prepare and psyche myself by actually thinking that I am a buck about to battle with a buck of my equal. I try to imagine how the fight would start. To do this authentically, you must first determine if you're rattling during a time when most confrontations are serious pushing and shoving matches or whether you are rattling during the time when most confrontations are more aggressive. More about that later. As I said earlier, by duplicating the noises bucks make with their bodies and antlers during aggressive pushing and shoving matches, you'll have more success than if you try to simulate an all-out fight.

Bucks are not big horn sheep. They don't square off, put their heads down and run head long into each other. Keep this in mind as you begin to rattle. Whitetails follow specific and elaborate rituals prior to combat. Traditionally, combatants circle one another cautiously with their bodies arched and stiff as they prepare to either bluff off or enter into physical combat with one another.

Begin your rattling sequence by first putting out a small amount of buck urine scent near your stand -- usually about 20 to 30 yards away. Next, hold the antlers so the tines are facing in toward each hand. Then, gently, but firmly, tap the tips of the antlers back and forth and across each other a few times. Try to simulate two bucks posturing at each other in the hopes of one bluffing off the other. In almost virtually all of the whitetail buck fights I have ever videotaped, this "feeling out" process takes place before the fight develops any further.

After tapping the ends of the tines together several times, pause and then mesh the main portion or body (from the bases up) of the antlers gently but firmly together. Try to get the portion of antlers just above the bases (pedicils) to grind back and forth over each other. This is the section of antlers that usually has a lot of perlation (bumps) on them. Without breaking the antlers apart, continue to mesh and grind them together for about 20 to 30 seconds.

Not a single buck fight I have videotaped has ever lasted longer than 30 seconds. Pushing and shoving matches usually precede serious buck fights by two to three weeks. These shoving contests often last much longer than actual fights. Interestingly, the noise created by these shoving matches can be just as attractive to whitetails as the sounds created by down and out battles.

Then, when you are ready to separate the antlers rub the bases together hard to make a few more grinding sounds and then quickly pull the antlers apart. Intentionally try to drag or hit the tips of one antler across the tips of the other antler so that as many tines hit against each other as possible. This helps to re-create the sounds of antlers being pulled apart by two fighting bucks. Again, **ALWAYS TRY TO CREATE THE ENTIRE ILLUSION.** While you twist, mesh and grind the antlers, gently stomp your feet on the ground several times. In addition to stomping, step on leaves and small twigs while you're rattling. The stomping of your feet and the noises generated from stepping on leaves and twigs help to simulate the noises the hooves of two fighting bucks would make. On occasion, after breaking the antlers apart, make a couple of soft guttural grunts. However, this can be based on your mood and is not mandatory. Adding a grunt, before or after the rattling sequence, is up to you. If I had to guess, I would say that I include grunts before and/or after, 50 percent of the time.

SECOND SEQUENCE

Between each of your rattling sessions you must set the antlers down and carefully make a 360 degree turn. Look and listen for any sign that a buck is responding. Once you make your turn and you have carefully looked and listened and you are absolutely sure a buck has not responded, begin your second sequence.

I usually wait about 15 to 20 minutes between each rattling session. I want to be sure I don't see or hear anything that I might have missed before I begin rattling again. Once I am confident there isn't a buck lurking some-where close by (and one can never be absolutely certain about this) I start my next sequence. I do the same thing I did in the first session -- only this time I rattle a little longer and louder. Don't get crazy with it, simply intensify your rattling a little bit. Start by ticking the antlers together the same way as de-scribed above. Rattle for about 30 to 45 seconds and then rake the antlers apart. Again, intently look and listen until you're confident nothing has come in. Then, prepare for your next session.

THIRD SESSION

Before beginning your third session, however, wait a good 30 minutes -- sometimes a little longer. You want the woods to totally calm down. You also want to be sure nothing walks in from your previous sessions during this time. Once you are satisfied nothing has responded, start your third session. This time, rattle exactly as you did during the first session. If a buck doesn't respond after the third session, wait at least a half-hour and then rattle again.

Generally, on most occasions I don't leave the place I started rattling from. There are a few reasons for this. During the 20 years I have rattled, I have learned to rattle from the same location all day. As mentioned earlier, many times, after becoming frustrated that I didn't rattle anything in, I would get up to change locations. And often, only to see a buck run off. Because of this, I decided it was better to stay put than to play the shell game and move all over the woods.

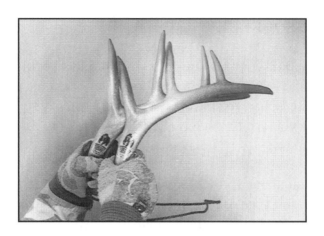

If you choose synthetic antlers, make sure they have a realistic tone, like these.

LOOK AND LISTEN

At the end of each rattling session, look all around the area slowly, thoroughly and methodically. Remember, most game hunters call in responds without the hunter ever knowing they were there. If we saw everything we called in, calling would probably be the only tactic hunters used. Part of the game of calling is that each animal responds differently. Some race in boldly, not afraid of showing themselves while others take every advantage of cover they can and never try to show themselves at all. And quite frankly, there are a myriad of other types of responses you'll have to deal with as well. In other words, as a rattler or caller, to be consistently successful, you must be capable of detecting the slightest indication (no matter how negligible the sign may be), that a buck has responded to your rattling.

As soon as you have finished a rattling session, put the antlers down and systematically make a slow 360 degree turn. As you are turning, LOOK, AND EQUALLY IMPORTANT, LISTEN for anything that might indicate a buck has responded. Many times I have rattled in a buck that "hung up" 30 or 50 yards from my stand. If I hadn't looked and listened carefully, I might have missed the fact that I had a buck respond.

Many hunters have expressed to me that they try **not** to make too much movement when they're looking around. That's too bad. Movement isn't a negative point to worry about when rattling. The incoming or responding buck or bucks **are actually looking for movement!** The undistinguishable motion a well-concealed hunter makes while looking around to see if a buck has responded can be all that's necessary to further motivate a buck to make the decision to continue in.

Deer can react like spiders to certain stimuli. They act and react to situations that instinctively stimulate a response. For instance, a spider sits in its web all day long without moving at all. As soon as an insect becomes entangled in the web, the spider feels the vibrations set off by the insect's struggle to free itself and it reacts instinctively by racing down the web to its entangled victim.

The same principle applies to bucks who are hesitant or hung up about your rattling efforts. After initially responding to the sounds of your rattling, they may stop 30 to 50 yards away and stand motionless, hidden in cover, waiting to see what develops. They need further motivation to arouse their interest. That interest may be generated simply by a slight movement. Bucks can immediately interpret the motion as the fighting bucks they are looking for!

For this reason, after I put the antlers down and begin to make my 360 degree turn, I intentionally shake a sapling tree and kick up a few leaves. The motion of the shaking sapling along with the noises I make with the leaves has often enticed a hung-up buck out of hiding and into the open.

Whatever you do, do not listen to the voices of doom who preach without any real knowledge of the subject that movement will hurt you when it comes to rattling. Controlled movement by a well-concealed hunter at the right time (you don't want to move around if you see a buck responding and it is looking and moving in your direction) will definitely benefit you by enticing hesitant bucks to react and help you locate bucks that are hidden in cover.

It's interesting to note here that although I just said you don't want to move around when a buck is coming toward you, you may want to try this. Even when a buck has focused its attention directly to me, and this is important, and is walking to me, I stretch out my arm to the furthest sapling and shake it back and forth. This one tactic has accounted for more bucks getting psyched up to change their approach from a walk to a run, than any other single technique.

While you're listening and looking around, **YOU MUST ALWAYS BE ALERT FOR THE SLIGHTEST INDICATION OF A RESPONSE** -- THIS IS CRUCIAL TO YOUR RATTLING SUCCESS. Many times, when you're done with your rattling sequence a buck may respond without you even realizing he is there! Therefore, it is important to look and listen carefully after each rattling session. This includes picking out an ear, leg or some other body part that is hidden motionless in the brush. Or, listening for vocalizations such as a low aggressive grunt, or hearing and seeing something as insignificant as a sapling waving out of sync with the other vegetation in the distance. Each of these signals could very well indicate a buck may have responded to your rattling efforts but has decided, for whatever reason, not to come all the way in.

Learn to move correctly and interpret the signs you see and hear while you are looking and listening. You will never be caught off guard. More important, you will discover many more hidden bucks that you may have not seen if you didn't move in a 360 degree circle and listen to what was happening around you.

RATTLING FROM GROUND BLINDS AND TREESTANDS

Rattling works better from the ground than from a treestand. In fact, while bow hunting, I have taken several Pope and Young class bucks rattling from the ground. Although I like to hunt from tree stands, it isn't always necessary when rattling or calling deer.

If I'm on the ground, I look for a large rock or a lot of brush to break up my form. Many times, when I'm rattling from the ground, I gather large branches and twigs and quickly erect a make-shift blind (about 4 feet high) to help conceal me. It also allows me to see approaching deer through the branches as I'm kneeling down while rattling.

If you decide to rattle from a tree, however, you must keep several points in mind. Always try to pick a tree that has a large straight trunk. You want the trunk to be wider than you. This will help to break up your outline.

You also want to pick a tree that has even more natural cover than normal to help break up not only your outline but the obvious movement that goes along with rattling. If you can, try to pick a tree that has a rough bark and lots of small dead twigs. Next, simulate the crunching of leaves and the breaking of branches by raking a single antler firmly up and down the rough loose bark of the tree. Snap small branches above or alongside of you and rake a single antler along a branch.

Here's a unique technique to try. To further enhance the illusion, fill a medium size ziplock bag a third of the way with fish tank gravel and place it in another larger ziplock bag. Put a small hole through both bags at the top and attach enough string so that it will comfortably tie around your ankle while reaching to the ground below. Then, as you're rattling, rhythmically move your ankle back and forth dragging the bag over leaves and twigs that are at the bottom of the stand. Again, you are helping to re-create the entire illusion of the sounds two bucks' hooves would make as they engaged in a pushing and shoving match or a fight. How far you take these extreme kinds of efforts is up to you. Let me make it clear while I have used the fish gravel tactic on occasion, I haven't made it a routine in my rattling scenarios.

TEAMING UP

Rattling works well from the ground or a treestand, even when you are rattling by yourself. **However, it really becomes a LETHAL TACTIC when you team up with a partner.** One hunter can rattle from a concealed location on the ground while the other hunter either takes a stand in a ground blind or in a treestand 25 to 35 yards away. When rattling works, the partners can switch positions within a day or so. I have had many people write to me explaining how effective this tactic really is. One complaint, however, is that the two partners have to decide early on when to switch positions.

I remember one such letter that came to me from a hunter outside of Buffalo, NY. The letter began by thanking me for the advice I had given them. However, the writer was clearly frustrated with his partner. It seemed the two decided to give rattling a try as a team. Sean agreed to rattle while his hunting buddy, Art, was the shooter. As soon as Sean "rattled in Art a buck" they agreed to switch positions. They must have been rattling at prime time because Sean rattled in a buck during his first sequence and Art decided not to shoot the buck even though it was standing broadside only 20 yards below his stand. A heated conversation took place and after all calmed down, Sean remained the rattler and Art the shooter. Again, Sean rattled in another buck. Again, for whatever reason, his partner passed up shooting. Of course, there was another argument. Somehow, Art convinced Sean that unless he shot the buck, it was still Sean's turn to rattle. The letter said Sean remained the rattler for two days. During this time, Art passed up five bucks!

"By time it was my turn to be the shooter," said Sean, "Art was mad as hell that he didn't take any of the bucks I rattled in for him. In his frustration, he mustered up quite a rattling session. Within minutes of hitting the antlers together the first time, a 4-point buck raced in and I shot him. Art immediately wanted me to rattle again for him. For some reason, I felt sorry for him and I did. But we never had another buck respond as closely as we did during the first three days. This year, our agreement is written in stone. Whoever rattles first, becomes the shooter as soon as a buck comes in and the other guy can get a shot. If he passes the shot, he loses his turn and becomes the rattler."

I had to laugh with these guys and not at them. I could just imagine how excited and impressed they were with rattling as a hunting tactic. The arguments must have been comical to witness. But, in all frankness, they probably weren't so funny for them. If you're going to rattle with a partner, make sure you have the ground rules laid out clearly and precisely and that you both agree to them prior to the hunt. Not only will you be more successful, but you will also remain friends.

PLAYING THE SHELL GAME / CHANGING LOCATION

Early on in my rattling career, I learned a real lesson. Many times, I became frustrated thinking I hadn't rattled in a buck. I would stand up to look around and, in some instances, even change locations. Many times when I stood up or moved, I would either see a tail or the entire buck as it broke from cover and raced off to safety. If I hadn't gotten up or moved, I would have never known these bucks were there. However, on the other hand, if I hadn't gotten up or moved, they may have eventually come in, too!

Moving around from one location to another to rattle is much less beneficial than staying in one place. Treat every rattling session as if a buck has responded, even if you don't see or hear it come in. Don't get discouraged in one spot and decide it would be better to try another location. By practicing this philosophy, you will never be caught off guard and more important, you will detect bucks you would have otherwise overlooked.

Common sense plays a big role here for a few reasons. One - bucks are like fish. You can see a trout or bass laying in a pool and make a hundred casts to the fish without enticing a strike. Then, just as you are ready to leave, you decide to make one last cast and the fish explodes from the cover and hits the lure. What you've just done is annoyed or aggravated the fish into striking. The same theory applies to bucks. A rattler can aggravate a buck into responding even when the buck has ignored his previous rattling efforts.

For instance, you may rattle in an area where a buck is bedded close by. For a variety of reasons, he doesn't respond to your rattling. He could be a submissive buck and is genuinely apprehensive about responding especially if you are rattling too aggressively. Or, he could be a buck that has been in physical combat during the night and simply doesn't respond because he is exhausted. Or, you could be rattling to a buck who isn't in the area yet. During one of your upcoming sessions, a buck could be either driven into your area, or, happens by on his own, and low and behold he decides to respond. Or, the worst scenario, he could be a buck with a doe and refuses to leave her or to reveal himself and the doe to two other potential competitors. Any of these scenarios can keep a buck from responding to your rattling. However, by being patient and rattling from the same stand, for whatever time you allot to rattling (generally I commit at least three hours), you can agitate a buck, who has ignored your previous rattling, into responding. Always keep this in mind especially when you are about to give up or change locations. In any event, the successful rattler develops extreme patience and a sixth sense about his surroundings. These attributes will enable you to rattle enthusiastically from the same location for longer periods of time. The more time you spend at rattling, the more success you will have.

WHERE TO RATTLE

If there was any one subject about rattling that has undergone more poppycock -- it's the subject of where to set up and rattle. I have read some real horse crap about this point. Some say you must rattle from atop a knoll because bucks won't respond coming down hill! Other articles have said the exact opposite. Yet, still others claim you must rattle from hollows in the ground to be most successful. When bucks want to respond to rattling, they won't care where they've got to go to get to the fight. Trust that statement and take it to the Deer Hunting Bank. Rattling is the most forgiving tactic a deer hunter will ever employ. Other than following a few basic rules, where you set up is the least of your concerns.

I'm not so much concerned about the terrain of the ground as I am about the deer activity in the area. In all of my hunting tactics, especially rattling and calling, I follow a simple principle. If you have ever read any of my deer hunting articles or have been at any of my seminars you have heard me mention what I am about to say, time and time again, "To consistently score on bucks, hunt does." That statement is a bit simplistic and requires some defining. The only time I concentrate on hunting bucks is in early October when they are still in bachelor herds, are secretive, concerned about gathering food, and are using different areas than the does. During these times, bucks travel off the main routes and consistently hang in thick cover. And it's in these places that I hunt them.

By late October, the pre-rut has started and until the next two phases of the primary and late rut are finished, bucks will be seeking out does. When this behavior starts, I look for places that are attractive to mature does. Eventually, these estrus does attract bucks. Hunting these social areas will provide buck opportunities for you.

I don't mean to make it sound all that easy, however. Remember that even though bucks get side tracked during the rut, and they become more visible, it doesn't mean you will catch them in the open acting foolishly all of the time. If you see a group of does standing in an open field, woodlot or in chest-high brush, concentrate on the fringes of the available cover to discover tending bucks. Many times, by studying the cover diligently, you will discover a buck or bucks accompanying the does.

WHAT PART OF THE SEASON IS BEST?

One of the questions I am asked about rattling is, "When is the best time to rattle?" If we're talking about time of year, I would have to say, as I mentioned earlier, the best time to rattle is from the last 10 days of Oct. through mid-November. Then, there will be a lull until about the first week or so of December when rattling is again effective for a few days.

The breakdown of the peaks and valleys of rattling response is obviously related to the entire rutting period. Just after the false rut, which occurs around October 10 through the 15, bucks begin to engage in daily semi-serious pushing, shoving and fighting matches. This is a good time to start rattling. Customarily, I begin to rattle around the 20th of October, but my success really starts to improve around the 25th through the 31st. And then, there is a short lull. Around November 3rd, the fighting behavior picks up again and builds in both frequency and intensity through the 15th. This is what I referred to earlier as the frenzy period of the rut when bucks are chasing does and are aggressive toward other bucks. I have had my best rattling success during the frenzy period of the primary rut. Following this is another lull as bucks are actually matched with does during the primary rut from mid-November until the end of the month. Then the post season rut comes into play. Around the 10th to the 15th of December, does that were not successfully bred, begin to come into estrus and attract a lot of bucks. Rattling works well from December 5th through the 10th as many of these bucks once again become aggressive toward each other.

TIME OF DAY

The best time to rattle is between 9:00 a.m. and 2:00 p.m. The reason for this is because deer are settled down and generally unpressured. They respond to calling and rattling better during this time period. I emphatically recommend to hunters who rattle, not to rattle before good light for a few reasons. First, bucks respond quicker in poor light because they are reacting to the sounds rather than what they interpret visually. Many times, bucks have remained totally motionless in poor light staring at me in an attempt to identify me as I approached my stand or when I got out of it in the evening. A half hour earlier, they would have turned themselves inside out at the mere sight of me.

By rattling before first light, you're inviting failure to your door. Yes, bucks will respond to your rattling at this time of day. Some will come rather close. But, unless you have enough legal light to shoot, you're going to have to let the buck pass. Worse yet, if a buck responds and gets close enough to see or wind you, he will send off a series of alarm-distress snort calls alerting all the deer in the immediate area to your presence. In addition, he'll stomp and snort as he leaves, depositing excess amounts of interdigital scent to act as a long-term chemical warning discouraging other bucks from using the area. Therefore, if you are fortunate enough to rattle in a buck later on, chances are he will smell the excess interdigital and retreat immediately.

When I'm hunting in heavily pressured areas like, New York, New Jersey, Pennsylvania, etc., I don't rattle at the crack of dawn. If I am hunting in remote areas like Alberta, Texas, Montana and the like, then I begin rattling at the crack of dawn as long as there is sufficient light to see bucks respond. Too often, in the more heavily pressured areas, I have rattled in a buck during this funky light and could not pick out exactly what type of rack he had or, in some instances, even exactly where he was standing! In these areas, you may only get one chance at rattling in a buck. I wouldn't want to lose the opportunity to get a shot at him because of poor light.

Rattling in poor light does nothing other than make problems. Avoid it -- unless you're rattling in remote places where the odds of having a half-dozen bucks or more respond to your rattling is likely. Then, perhaps you won't mind missing an opportunity to shoot a buck who comes in and gets away because you couldn't tell exactly where he was or, worse yet, just couldn't get a shot.

I have rattled in my biggest and greatest number of bucks between 10:30 am and 1:30 pm. The reason for this is very simple. Most hunters leave the woods by 9:30 am. You should apply this to all your hunting strategies. Deer immediately interpret this lack of pressure as an opportunity for them to move about. Not only do they feed or chase does, but they are also more inclined to respond to rattling or calling during this time.

With that said, let me emphasize that I am not preaching NOT TO RATTLE AT DUSK OR DAWN. These time periods are also good times to rattle. You must take into consideration the above factors and then decide if dusk or dawn rattling benefits you. If it does, do it. However, even if you rattle during early or late in the day, try the time periods I mentioned and you will soon discover mid-day hours provide optimum opportunities for rattling.

USING SCENT

To have a buck respond less cautiously, always try to control your human odor. Despite what you may have read or heard, it is virtually impossible to eliminate human odor. You can, however, reduce your human odor considerably by following a few important suggestions. Keep your clothing as free from foreign odor as you can. Shower often. I sometimes shower two times during a day's hunt: when I get up in the morning and when I come in for a break. Wash the bottom of your hunting boots every other day with a non-scented soap. Use deer scents to help mask your odor and attract whitetails.

Using buck urine when you're rattling will help to create the entire illusion.

Use a combination of scents when rattling. I use a premium apple scent to help mask my human odor and to calm deer I have attracted. My next favorite scent for rattling is buck urine. Bucks expect to smell other bucks' urine when they respond to a buck fight. It re-assures them that there really are other bucks close by. Tarsal gland scent is also excellent to use when rattling, as it, too, is a natural odor. So is a well-made premium estrus scent. Use all scents wisely; do not overuse them.

WEATHER

Rattling works in almost any type of weather other than extreme weather conditions. If I was pressed into pinpointing what type of weather I had the LEAST response, I would have to say during "blue bird" type days. You know the type of day I'm talking about. Sixty-five degrees, not a cloud in the sky, no wind, etc. While you can still rattle in bucks on days like this, it just doesn't yield the best response for rattling.

I have had good success on cool, cloudy days with a slight breeze. Foul weather yields the best rattling success. I have killed several big bucks when rattling in the rain. Days when there is a steady drizzle without wind are ideal, as are days with a light falling snow. There is never really a BAD day to rattle. It's like fishing. Any time you're rattling, it's better than going to work!

CONCEALMENT

Remember the most important aspect of rattling is to offer yourself the best concealment possible. Whether you are in a tree or on the ground, concealment is important to your rattling success. There is a lot of movement when rattling. If you're out in the open where your form is highly visible, a buck will pick you out and disappear long before you may or may not find out he was there. So, whatever place you rattle from, whether it's a treestand or on the ground, the number one factor is to rattle in an area that breaks up your outline with other vegetation, a blind, or rocks.

The second most important factor is to camouflage your face and hands. I don't care if you're rattling dressed all in blaze orange, as long as your face and hands are covered, your chances of success are as good as they can be. By not covering your face and hands (the two parts of your body that will be moving the most), you give the edge back to the buck. You can't afford to give a buck any more of an edge than he already has. ALWAYS cover your face and hands when you are hunting whitetails -- especially when rattling or calling.

If you don't believe how important covering your face and hands is, try this test. Pick out a spot in the woods, even an area where you are highly visible. Sit motionless on the ground without your face and hands covered. Almost all the wild game will spot your form as potential trouble (predator) and avoid you. Now, cover your face and hands and remain motionless in the same spot. You will discover that not only will 99% of the wildlife ignore you -- they will come closer to check you out!

Take this to the Deer Hunting Bank. If you want to improve your deer hunting success immediately and dramatically, cover your face and hands in a camo head net and gloves any time you go deer hunting. You won't regret using this advice. It is critical to your rattling and calling success because, as I've stated before, you are no longer hunting the buck, he is hunting you. He is focusing all his senses and attention exactly on what he perceives to be two bucks fighting -- YOU. Cover your face and hands.

What it boils down to is -- it doesn't matter what spot you pick to rattle from as long as you conceal yourself. If a buck wants to respond, he'll respond as long as you are camouflaged and take care of eliminating your human odor as best you can.

EXPECT ANYTHING

One of the most interesting aspects about rattling is there are no absolutes. Expect a buck to do anything. A buck may come in with the wind blowing right in his face and discover you. Instead of running, he'll stand defiantly in place as if to say, "What the hell are you doing here. Get out of the way I'm on my way to a fight!" Sometimes, he'll even try to face you down if he is frustrated enough.

This reminds me of an embarrassing but funny story. Several years ago, in an apple orchard in my home town, I built a large make-shift blind out of large twigs and branches at the edge of the orchard. I left an entrance from the orchard into the bind and cut three shooting lanes from the blind into the dense woods and swamp areas that the blind overlooked. The open orchard was behind me. The prevailing breeze blew regularly from the woods and swamp into the orchard. The deers' afternoon movement routine was to emerge from the swamp and woodlands and filter into the orchard behind my blind.

It was around 1:00 p.m. one November afternoon during the NYS bow season (Nov. 13th to be exact) and I decided to rattle from the blind. After settling in, I checked to see all my shooting lanes were clear. Immediately to the right of my blind was a very large pile of old apple tree trunks and branches. The pile was at least six feet high. I regarded it as additional concealment.

After making sure my lanes were open, I put out some scent to help reduce my odor. I picked up the antlers and started my first sequence. As sometimes happens when you rattle, I had no sooner finished the first session, when I heard the hooves of a deer running across the open apple orchard behind me! "Of course," I thought to myself, "he's coming in from an area I least expected a buck to respond." Which, to be frank, is not all that unusual when it comes to bucks responding to antler rattling. Bucks, on occasion, will approach from places you least expect. At any rate, before I could put the antlers down, the buck was standing on the opposite side of the pile of dead branches and twigs to the right of the blind.

At this point, I wasn't sure it was a buck as does will also respond to rattling. However, I strained my eyes to look past the mound of brush. I could see what I thought was a hell of a set of antlers. "Great," I thought to myself, "Now what do I do? He's too close to use a deer call." So, I decided to grab my antlers and while pointing them in the exact opposite direction of where the buck stood, I intended to tick the ends of the tines together as lightly as I could. Of course, Murphy's Law stepped in. As I grabbed the antlers, they accidentally swung into each other and made a louder noise than I intended.

What happened next, in reality, only took but a few seconds. In the "story telling," it may seem that the scenario played out much longer. Trust me - it didn't. As soon as the antlers clacked together, the buck's response was immediate. Without hesitation, he leapt over the brush pile (remember - it was at least six feet high and about eight feet wide) in a wild attempt to locate the "other combative bucks." Without any prior warning, there, above my head, in mid-air, was a mature buck who, through Newton's Law of Gravity, had no place to go but down next to me! I didn't even have time to grab my bow before the buck landed in the blind with me.

The embarrassing part comes now. I was scared. I thought the only safe thing I could do was to scream so the buck became aware of my presence so I could scare the crap out of him and have him jump back over the blind without goring my sorry butt. As he came down, I screamed, "Aaaaaaaaaaahhhhhhhhhhhh!" Not once, but a couple of times. As the buck landed, if he could talk, he would have screamed back at me, "Aaaaaaaaahhhhhhhhhh!" as he was as shocked and scared as I was. In his attempt to escape, he literally crashed through the brush pile he had just leapt over. I never picked up my bow during the entire ordeal!

You can never expect a buck to respond with any specific behavior. Nor can you try to guess, with any consistency, from what direction they will approach. For instance, if you are rattling and expect response from a certain direction, you may get a surprise if you are not paying attention to all directions. If a buck happens to be passing by behind you, hears the antlers, and decides to respond, even if it may not appear to be the best route in, he will.

You must be ready for anything to happen and from any direction. I have seen bucks respond to rattling and, with out question, identify the rattler. Instead of running off, they defiantly stood still, pawed the ground, and brazenly stared at the hunter. Other bucks have walked in, spotted the hunter and acted as if they ignored him as they calmly walked past the hunter in an attempt to locate the fighting bucks. All the while, they kept a close eye on the hunter as they pass within feet of him. Some bucks get downright aggressive, running in without regard to potential danger. Even when a buck like this sees a hunter, they are hesitant to leave and, instead, exhibit belligerent body language and behavior, only walking out when they feel THEY want to.

HOW TO GET STUBBORN BUCKS TO RESPOND TO HUNG-UP BUCKS

One of the problems you will have with rattling is the same age old dilemma any hunter who uses calls or antlers encounters. At times, the game you are calling to "hangs up" out of good shooting range. Although you have his attention, something stops or prevents him from continuing toward you. Most times, the reason a buck stops coming in is he has either seen your movement or, more likely, has picked up your scent. Although all his other senses are telling him he should be at this fight, his nose is saying, "Something doesn't smell right. You'd better stop and check this out." In either case, all is not lost. Remember, a buck responds to rattling can disregard signals of danger including human odor. Let me make it perfectly clear here - while a buck bent on responding to a buck fight, on occasion, may disregard human scent, it's not wise to NOT pay attention to human odor. Always try to rattle with the wind in your favor.

It is inevitable that bucks will hang up. However, it isn't a situation that is doomed to failure. There are several ways to motivate a buck that is hung up to come to you. You can either tickle or tick the antlers more gently, or as I will explain in the calling chapter, you can use a variety of deer calls, to help get the buck in. Whenever a buck hangs up, I try to fool him into thinking he has either mid-judged exactly where the fight is, or into thinking that the two bucks have moved off to another location. In either event, what I am trying to accomplish is to have the buck continue to check out the situation instead of losing interest and leaving.

Let's imagine the buck is standing 50 to 75 yards in front of you and refuses to come any further. As you're staring at the buck (whether you are in a tree or on the ground), pick up the antlers and gently, and briefly (3 to 5 seconds), tick the tips of the antler tines back and forth. Then, put the antlers down and get ready. What you have just accomplished is you have told the buck that he may have misjudged the spot of where the fight originated. Or, that the bucks have moved off and are about to start another fight.

Fifty-percent of the time, as soon as the buck hears the ticking of the antler tips, he stretches his neck upward and cups his ears toward the direction of the sound in an attempt to pinpoint the competitive bucks. Sometimes, the motivation generated by the sounds of the ticking antlers is so strong, the buck doesn't even bother stretching his neck or cupping his ears, he simply trots in for a closer look! This provides you with an opportunity to get a shot.

This tactic can be especially helpful to a gun hunter who may only need to get the buck to step out a few feet from behind a tree or heavy thick patch of brush. For an archer, it may be even more important and mean the difference between having a buck hung up about 50 yards out walk away or continue to walk in an additional 25 yards. In both cases, this ticking or tickling strategy may be all that's needed to turn a despairing situation into a successful one.

The reason you must look at the buck as you're "ticking" the antlers is to determine what direction he'll move next. If a buck walks off the way he came in after hearing the "ticking," the chances are you are about to lose this deer -- he's decided to go back from where he came. If this happens, you must do something other than "tick" to stop the buck from leaving -- and do it fast.

If a buck circles to the left or right, however, he is definitely interested in the "ticking" and is coming in! It may take a buck only a minute to get closer -- or as long as an hour. It all depends on the buck's personality. However, 98% of the bucks that I have seen exhibit this circling behavior have eventually come in to my stand! Just because you don't see the buck doesn't mean he's not close by. Pay meticulous attention when a buck has started to circle you. Scan the cover thoroughly and listen for sounds that may indicate an incoming buck. Don't ever give up on a buck that circles -- NEVER!

Here are a few other points to keep in mind about rattling. Hopefully, they will give you the confidence you will need to be a successful rattler. All antlered game instinctively respond to the sounds created by meshing and grinding antlers. It doesn't matter if it's a mule deer buck, a bull moose, a whitetail buck or a bull elk, all will respond to rattling. In 1986, I talked about how I could attract bull elk by rubbing a fairly large mule deer antler up and down a sapling. Along with the noise of the antler rubbing on the tree, the sight of the swaying sapling also aided the illusion. Back then, hardly a soul believed me. Today, several articles have appeared in national publications on how to rattle in bull elk.

All antlered game, including whitetails, respond to antler rattling. However, what is not preached often enough is that to complete the illusion, no matter if you're rattling for a bull elk or a whitetail, you must motivate all the animal's senses into believing what he's hearing is real. This means paying attention to wind direction, your scent, concealing yourself, and having confidence in what you're doing. More importantly, don't forget to add the other nuances that will definitely motivate the buck into responding. The snapping of branches, the rustling of leaves, the thumping of feet, the shaking of saplings, the use of buck urine, and including non-aggressive deer calls all help to CREATE THE ENTIRE ILLUSION to the buck you are trying to rattle in. These additional elements are critical and should not be overlooked.

Use them along with your rattling and the buck you are calling in will be much more likely to drop his guard than if you just meshed and ground your antlers together.

SAFETY

Finally, this chapter would not be complete without addressing safety. Hunters have told me that the only thing they rattled in was other hunters. While this may seem comical, it is also important to remember that if you can fool a buck into thinking he's responding to a buck fight, you can fool another hunter. Always be careful when you rattle, especially on public ground. When rattling on public ground, hang a blaze orange vest over your stand. Believe me, it won't stop a buck from coming in. But, it may alert another hunter to your presence. I never rattle from the ground without hanging a blaze orange strip of tape or a vest nearby to announce my presence.

Do not rattle on public land on opening day. Deer are pressured and don't react normally anyway. More important, with the excitement of opening day, you don't need to make yourself sound like to bucks fighting. Remember, when it comes to rattling, safety is the number one factor. No buck is worth getting shot over. Give rattling a try this season. I promise you won't regret it. It will be one of the best strategies you have to add to your deer hunting bag of tricks.

Rattling works throughout the United States -- even in the northeast!

CHAPTER 14

USING DECOYS TO BAG WHITETAILS

It was just getting light as I started tying the string from my natural deer tail decoy to my ankle. As I made the last knot, I could hear the crunching of leaves as several deer approached my stand from a nearby draw. I quickly tested the tail that was set up at the bottom of a small stand of thick evergreens (about 25 yards from my tree stand) which skirted along a small lot of oak trees. This spot seemed ideal because of the profuse amount of white acorns and the ample cover if offered.

The first deer to walk out of the draw and up the trail through the evergreens was a doe. Every few steps she stopped, looked around and sniffed the air current. For whatever reason, she acted as if something wasn't right. Behind her, I could see the bodies of several more deer -- one which had a decent set of antlers. "If the doe continues to walk up the trail, and the other deer follow her, I'll get a broadside shot at the buck without ever having to use my decoy," I thought to myself. I wasn't sure if that possibility made me happy or not. I really enjoyed using natural deer tails as decoys, especially since I had excellent success with them over the years. In any event, I was prepared to play out the scenario no matter which way it unfolded.

Just then, the doe caught sight of the deer tail as it laid motionlessly over a clump of tangles. Her cautious demeanor immediately turned semi-alert. I instantly knew what she was worrying about -- the lack of natural movement of my decoy. As she stared at the decoy tail I slowly, but deliberately, moved my ankle back and forth. This made the deer tail twitch gently side to side. The does reaction was immediate and predictable. She instantly relaxed. Her ears fell forward and as she watched the tail she moved up the trail angling toward the decoy. Within moments the rest of the deer, including the buck, followed her. After the buck passed my stand, I came to full draw. The buck and the other deer were entranced watching the doe as she approached within a couple of feet of the decoy tail. In doing so, she provided me the opportunity to take all the time I needed to make a good shot. The instant I released the arrow I knew the hunt was over.

I would not have had the opportunity to shoot at this buck, had it not been for the decoy tail. The way the doe behaved as she walked up the trail, I definitely think she would have either walked off in a different direction or turned around and went back the way she came, taking the rest of the deer with her.

Using a decoy on that particular hunt and under those particular circumstances made the difference. It's important to emphatically state, however, that using decoys is not the cure all answer to successful deer hunting. Sometimes, decoys work very well. Other times they just flat-out don't. As a hunter intending to use decoys you must accept those realities. However, it should also be stated, that along with my deer calls, a set of rattling antlers, knife, flashlight and other "must-carry" accessories, I always carry a natural deer tail in my backpack when I go deer hunting. You never know when the circumstances are just right to call, rattle, or use a decoy. It's better to be prepared than to be left flatfooted.

As a hunter who regularly hunts by breaking the traditional ways of hunting deer, using decoys just seemed a natural evolution of my deer hunting tactics. After all, I reasoned, the native American Indians used decoys quite successfully. We've all seen the western movie where an Indian brave drapes a deer hide (with head and antlers) over his body and cautiously approaches a deer to within a few yards. In researching the use of decoys, I discovered this scene wasn't conceived out of the wild imagination of a movie director. In fact, archive photos and journals strongly support the fact that native American Indians used decoys for hunting deer.

I have quietly used various hunting decoys for thirty years. Over the last ten years, however, I have also used full-sized deer decoys as well. In some instances, full-size decoys make deer nervous. Therefore, before deciding to use decoys to hunt whitetails, you should understand decoy takes understanding of decoy tactics, patience, knowledge of deer and their behavior (especially related to other deer) and, without question, you should have a lot of resourcefulness as a hunter.

While many outdoor journalists write stories about how rut-crazed bucks have charged and gored decoys, I have only seen this happen once. Then, the buck ran at the decoy and knocked it over rather than an all-out planned attack from a rut-crazed buck. In my experience, bucks charging decoys is not the norm, but rather the exception. Perhaps this type of aggressive behavior occurs with more regularity in areas with very low hunting pressure or in penned research facilities. Several times, both bucks and does were curious enough about a decoy to drop their natural apprehension and come in to investigate the decoy up close and personal. They have even stuck their noses under the hindquarters or licked the face of the decoy!

I often use an example witnessed by my wife, Kate. A couple of years ago, she used a small four-point buck decoy in a bedded position (Flambeau) and witnessed a mature doe cautiously approach the buck. As the doe reached the bedded decoy, she reared-up on her hind legs and struck the decoy's head with her hoof. When the buck failed to respond, she gave him a few additional kicks for insurance. She must have thought the buck was either dead or dizzy, because after kicking him several times, she decided he was no threat. The doe settled down and began to feed within yards of the decoy and never payed any further attention to him.

Bedded buck decoys can prompt a variety of responses from deer; be ready for anything to happen!

However, as I've said, not every reaction to a decoy is positive. I once set up a feeding doe deer decoy in a food plot, thinking it was a natural lure to attract bucks into the open. To my amazement, a mature eight-pointer stepped from the cover, spotted the decoy, and became unjustifiably anxious. The buck paced for several minutes, never took his eyes off the decoy and then finally snorted and ran. Occasionally, deer have reacted hesitantly and, in other instances, they have walked up to decoys I set up.

There are many different types of decoys from which to choose. Some are more convenient to use and carry than others. Most work equally well. Because I am primarily an attractor of whitetails (through various rattling and deer calling techniques) rather than a passive stalker or stander, I have been forced to become creative when rattling or calling.

I first thought about using a decoy to lure in deer that traditionally "hung-up" about 50 - 60 yards from my stand when I was calling to them. Years ago, there weren't any high-tech, lightweight decoys on the market. I decided it was time to get creative. I nailed a mounted doe head on a tree with a stuffed deer rump hung on the opposite side. For the record, I never tried this tactic anywhere else than on private property, where I was confident there were no other hunters. But, even then, I draped the head and hindquarters with red tape as I carried them in the woods. Although the combination of head and rump did attract some deer, they were just too clumsy to carry and use regularly. After a few trips afield, I opted to use one or the other instead.

This mounted doe head and mounted deer rump were my first "decoys".

The hind quarter decoy worked better for me. I think that was because when I had it mounted, the taxidermist elevated the tail. This gave the impression that the deer was either concerned about something or even in a state of estrus (at least in a buck's mind). However, it was inconvenient and embarrassing to use the rump regularly and I was concerned about my safety. Using something different was what I had to do if I wanted to continue to use decoys. That's when I began using a natural deer tail to attract deer. It was easy-to-carry, set up and a lot safer to use.

NATURAL TAIL DECOYS

Since then, I collect tails during hunting season. I clean the tail, comb it free of tangles, briars and other debris, spread it out between two pieces of cardboard, and place several rubber bands around the "tail sandwich." Then, I place it in the freezer to keep it fresh and to maintain its shape. Several weeks before hunting season rolls around, I take it from the freezer, cut a small hole in the hide at the base of the tail (large enough to pass a string through) and hang it outside to let it air out and soften up.

A natural tail tied to a branch 2 to 3 feet high is a great decoy.

Here are some ways to use a natural tail decoy. Whether you are a caller or a stander, a natural doe deer tail decoy can often make the difference between seeing and not seeing deer. In states where this is legal, hang the tail ten to twenty yards from your stand in semi-open cover (not too brushy, but not wide open either) at a natural height of a mature deer's rump (28 to 32 inches). If you are a believer in scent, as I am, **lightly** (and I mean LIGHTLY) sprinkle whatever scent is applicable on the tail (doe-in-estrus, tarsal, interdigital, or buck urine). Remember it is critical not to overuse scent. Too much scent will cause the deer to spook and leave -- bar nothing.

Also, be sure to have at least 30 yards of string attached to it. If you are hunting from the ground, tie the string around your shooting forearm. When hunting from a treestand, tie the string around your ankle. In either case, gently tug the string several times every half hour -- not enough to make the tail twitch erratically or high, but just enough to make it move gently side-to-side. If a deer happens to be passing or you call one in, the twitching tail often attracts the deer out of cover. In the worse case scenario, it will hold him still long enough to get a shot. Most important, it detracts the deer's attention from the hunter. When deer are passing your stand and look as if they aren't going to come close enough for a shot, make a soft blat and flick the tail quickly, two or three times. Deer, especially bucks, become interested enough to alter their direction and come directly toward what they think is another deer.

CLOTH DECOYS

I have also used camo cloth tail decoys as well -- although they don't work anywhere as well as the real tail decoy. Twelve years ago, I bought several of these cloth decoys depicting the deer's tail in several different positions. One has the tail extended to the side to imitate a hot doe. Another shows the tail hanging straight down imitating a relaxed animal. A third has the tail straight up in a flagging position to imitate either a spooked deer or a deer flagging to gain the attention of another deer. The problem with the cloth decoys is that they are affected by the slightest breeze and can get hung-up on brush. They don't move or look as natural as real tails do and they don't dissipate scent as effectively either. Camo cloth deer tail decoys remain, however, another decoy option.

FULL-SIZE REAL-LIFE DECOYS

Over the last several years, I have researched and used many different types of full-size deer decoys. I have set up full-size decoys in various positions and places in my food plot year round. These full-size decoys offer hunters many options as they are attractive to deer because of their life-size shape and appearance -- if used and setup properly.

Positioning is critical to successful full-size decoy use. First, and most important, set up the decoy where it is plainly seen by incoming deer, whether that's in a field or in the woods. Deer surprised by decoys often don't get over the initial startle and react negatively from that point forward. However, if the full-size decoy is placed in the open (not in heavy brush) and deer have time to see it from a distance, they react to it much more positively. Placing decoys in woodlots also offers you a better opportunity to conceal yourself.

Deer are naturally curious and will often eagerly investigate a decoy.

Obviously, it is most important to make sure the wind is in your favor. To further relax incoming deer you can use deer calls. The vocalizations the real deer hears make it feel that the decoy, although a bit corny-looking, is another deer. However, and this is very important, when using calls with decoys, you must **NOT MAKE AGGRESSIVE CALLS.** Make soft, infrequent vocalizations. Next, position the decoy so you have a good view in any direction. Shooting lanes are very important when using decoys. Deer, especially bucks, often circle a doe decoy several times (usually coming in from behind it) before eventually moving in. However, when setting up buck decoys, remember that bucks usually approach a decoy buck head-on. Therefore, you should set up a buck decoy with the deer's head facing you. This will give you a better shot as the buck approaches the decoy with his head facing away from you.

Always try to add some type of movement to the decoy. Because most full-size natural decoys don't move, here's a tip to be a little creative. On both the standing/feeding full-size decoy and the ready-doe full size decoy (a doe standing with hind legs slightly spread apart, giving a body language signal that she is ready to breed), attach (via a long thin screw) a natural deer tail with 30 to 40 yards of string. Use the string to gently tug at the tail to give a realistic tail movement to the full-size decoy. I have also used a single 6-inch wide strip of a white bed sheet attached to a full size decoy when using the string is not practical. The sheet moves nicely side-to-side even when there is hardly a breeze. It adds just the look you need for natural movement.

Here's another essential point. When using any type of decoy, mounted, natural, cloth, or full-size synthetic, never touch the decoy with your bare hands. Use lightweight rubber skinning gloves or surgeons' gloves to hang or set up your decoy.

Whenever using life-size decoys, look for a brand that is lightweight, easy and quick to put together, and comes with anchors. Decoys that cannot be secured will be problematic -- especially when deer get close enough to nuzzle, push, kick or smell them. An unanchored target will not stand up to this type of close investigation and any flimsy movement quickly alerts the deer that it's fake.

BE PREPARED TO SHOOT

Once you have assembled and anchored a decoy, set up in an area offering good cover and a clean shot. While some deer stay at a decoy investigating it for a long period, others come to a decoy quickly and leave as quickly as they came. Having a good clear shooting lane is important. This is especially true when using a buck decoy. Buck decoys often generate aggressive behavior from other bucks. Sometimes, a buck emerges from cover, intentionally bumps his body and, sometimes, his antlers into the other buck causing it to fall over if not securely anchored. When an unsecured buck decoy falls over, the natural buck either departs in panic, wondering what the heck happened or he walks out with his chest swollen thinking he's George Foreman. Again, having a good shooting lane is critical under these circumstances. Also keep in mind, it's probably a good idea to get your shot off before a buck reaches the decoy, especially if he's showing aggressive behavior. Once he gets to the decoy, the action will be quick, furious and even confusing.

OTHER STRATEGIES

As mentioned earlier, life-size decoys are available in several different positions. Standing at alert; standing with head-down and feeding; standing with head-up and feeding; lying down with headalert; lying down with head tucked. They are available in doe and buck models. I have had success with both buck and doe decoys in various positions. Of late, I have had considerable success with the ready-doe. However, different positions are warranted for different situations and time of year.

Always try to place the doe decoy with its head facing away from the area you think deer will approach. With buck decoys, as mentioned, position them with their heads facing you. From what I have seen, when a deer is hesitant as it approaches a decoy, it concentrates on the decoy's face. When they can't see the face, they approach a decoy much more willingly - and, sometimes, aggressively. This behavior, however, is not written in stone.

Some advice, whenever using a decoy, you must keep safety and the legalities of using decoys in mind. Even on private land, be careful about using a full-size, lifelike decoy during the firearms season. In my experience, deer in heavily hunted areas respond much less to full-size decoys because of hunting pressure, anyway. They do, however, react well to just the natural deer tail. Firearms season is when you might want to consider using a natural deer tail. Even during the archery season, it's a good idea to keep the decoy off to an entirely safe angle away from you. Being in the line of sight of the decoy (whether you are hunting from the ground or in a treestand) could be dangerous because of deflected arrows. Again, in setting up and using decoys, always keep safety in mind.

Tucked at the bottom of my bag of deer hunting tricks is a group of decoying tactics that are not only used to decoy whitetails to me, but are also used to decoy hunters away from my hunting area.

Keep in mind the information I share with you about decoying hunters away from your hunting location requires being somewhat devious. Your ethics, when using these strategies, can and will be questioned. My answer has always been to use the adage (with a slight adjustment), "All's fair when it comes to love and deer hunting."

Most hunters must contend with the very fact of having to hunt pressured deer on public ground. This excess pressure on deer and hunters is a two-sided coin. While it is true that excess hunting pressure creates some opportunities to shoot bucks as they are driven (intentionally or unintentionally) past you by other hunters -- most times excess pressure creates fewer opportunities to shoot a buck. Deer resolve themselves to using offbeat survival tactics and cagey hunters develop similar tactics not only to attract whitetails but also to confound the competition.

I developed some of these offbeat decoying tactics several years ago. They include using a scarecrow or human dummy, creating false rubs and scrapes, false tracks, and nylon stockings stuffed with human hair.

SCARECROWS

I first started using scarecrows about four years ago when I began to hunt near my home. When I first began hunting the land there were a lot of hunters. This excess pressure sent the deer into hiding within a week after the season began. As deer sightings by these other hunters became fewer, they expanded their search by indiscriminately walking around without regard to the time of day or other hunters.

The land, however, is steep and mountainous and most of the hunters stayed low and hunted just along the base of the mountain. Predictably, they would drive the swamps and thick cedar groves of cover in the low ground and send the deer scurrying up the mountainside. The mountain top's foliage on the south side is extremely thick. The deer, once spooked from the northwest side of the mountain below, try to reach this thick cover found on the south side by following very definite escape routes - most of which are right smack-dab in the middle of the mountain. In order to discourage these deer from going to the south side, I decided to set up a diversion.

I nailed together two 2 x 2s in the shape of a cross, stapled old hunting garments to it and used a cheap plastic pumpkin for a head. I made two of these decoys. One was nailed in a tree (out of reach of other hunters) so it wouldn't blow away. The other was placed on the ground (also nailed to a tree) along a deer trail within the sanctuary of the cover that the deer were heading. These decoys confused the deer into thinking hunters had discovered their bailiwick.

Many times, I watched deer trot up the mountain and, if they discovered the first decoy, they made an immediate detour. The new direction often took them close by my treestand. If deer that I couldn't see made it to the thick cover, some eventually bumped into the decoy planted there. These deer would come from behind my stand and drop back off to the middle of the mountain. Both detours put the deer within shooting distance of my stand.

As years passed, fewer sportsmen hunted this property. I no longer use human scarecrows as decoys, but these decoys served their purpose for the first year or two. These days, I use more traditional decoys.

There are, however, problems with using human scarecrows. You must build the decoys, dress them, buy a head, carry them into the woods and set them up. You must also check them several times during the season. When discovered by other hunters, they may or may not survive the encounter! I have had several human scarecrow decoys dismembered by hunters who were totally confounded by their presence. If you hunt private land, these scarecrow decoys can deter deer from certain trails and goat them into using others without having to worry about losing the decoys to curious hunters.

I also like to use scarecrow decoys in standing corn fields. Although I've only done this twice, both times I saw more deer than I would have otherwise. Sharpen the bottom of the decoy's 2 x 2 stick and shove it into the ground in the middle of the standing corn. Then, sprinkle it with cologne -- be careful not to get any on yourself. Deer sneaking into the corn throughout the day see or wind the decoy. By setting up with a good vantage point over looking the standing corn, you can get a shot at a buck as it tries to avoid the obvious danger (of the decoy).

Scarecrow decoys can be embarrassing to use, too. Two years ago, I set one up while bow hunting in a spot I call "The Bowl." I usually post on a ledge that is well concealed and overlooks a very narrow flat ten yards under me. Deer walk along a trail on the flat from either one of two directions. If they come in from my right, they usually drop off the flat to a ledge below before passing my stand. I decided to put a scarecrow decoy on the ledge below, so if a deer was about to drop off, he'd see it and, hopefully, turn back.

The first deer to come by from my right was a group of does. They headed right to the drop-off and, as they approached it, they turned and walked directly under me.

"Wow," I thought, "I can't wait until a buck passes." None did, however. After removing the dummy, I walked up the trail and back to my vehicle. There, I bumped into a couple of other hunters. No need to try and explain, let's just say the incident was embarrassing. Since then, I have never used a scarecrow decoy, other than on private ground where I know I won't meet anyone else.

If you can get over the inconvenience of making, carrying and setting up human scarecrow decoys and the possibility of being embarrassed when other hunters discover you using them, these decoys will deter deer from using certain areas and also increase your odds for success.

Human scarecrows can also get deer accustomed to human presence as well. Set one of these decoys up in a tree stand or on the ground, just after deer season ends. Although deer will react negatively to it at first and even avoid it, eventually, they will get used to it and realize it does not present a danger to them. After months of passing the decoy without incident, they learn to ignore it and confidently use the area despite its presence.

This is a great ambush tactic. The day before bow or firearms season begins, remove the decoy. Deer will assume the person sitting in the stand the next morning is the same non-threatening form they have become accustomed to over the last several months -- creating some excellent possibilities for you.

HUMAN HAIR

I learned this tactic a few years ago after reading an article in <u>Organic Gardener</u> magazine. The article mentioned a non-toxic method to keep animals, especially deer, from eating your garden vegetables. The article suggested hanging nylon stockings filled with human hair around the garden. Thus, another one of my unorthodox deer hunting ideas was born.

This tactic encourages deer to avoid one area and use another. Unlike the scarecrow, which is mostly a visual deterrent kind of decoy, the human hair decoy bag is strictly a scent decoy. It is simple to make and use. Go to any barber shop and collect some of the discarded hair clippings and place them into a nylon stocking. Caution here: don't let the barber do this for you. You collect the hair using surgeons' gloves. Also use the gloves to stuff the stocking and hang the sock in the woods. The hair's scent alarms deer walking along trails to alter their route. By setting up on alternate routes, you could get a shot at a good buck.

Through experience, I've learned that over a few days' period, the hair loses its odor and deer begin to ignore it. To keep the odor strong, you have to change the hair in the stocking every few days. Cumbersome, but fruitful.

FALSE RUBS

Here's where we get a bit devious. But, before I explain, let me tell you how false rubs work for bucks. Without getting into detail, a buck rubs a tree to make visual sign post for another buck to see. On occasion, large rubs play havoc with a smaller bucks psyche. They also effectively serve to agitate bucks with larger antlers who interpret them as an invasion into their turf by a competitive buck. By creating these aggressive false rubs, you can decoy smaller bucks into using other trails. Basically, this is the same principle as the decoy scarecrow. However, these large mock rubs are also highly effective ways to attract a big buck to your ambush site.

Seeing the big rub, mature bucks instinctively react by immediately checking it out. They approach and stop to smell it. For this reason, always use a forehead scent on the rub and a few drops of tarsal scent placed on the ground at the base of the sapling.

These rubs are easy to make. Find a suitable tree or sapling and take a rough-edged folding hand saw. Scrape the bark from the tree, gently but firmly. Begin this at about six to twelve inches from the base of the sapling to about 36 to 48 inches high. Intentionally leave some long strips of bark hanging from the tree and leave the fresh scrapings on the ground. Snap two or three branches above the rub, leaving some branches hanging in half, dangling down and others totally snapped off. All this helps to complete the illusion for the buck.

Many times, a buck either tears up the rub or creates one of his own close by. It's a terrific way to attract a buck walking along a trail out of range, especially during bow season. What makes these rubs attractive is the element of surprise. Bucks are extremely familiar with rubs in their own range. When a strange rub appears, especially a large one, it gets everyone's attention immediately, especially mature bucks. These false rubs only work for a day or two, however, and then you must move off to a new area and create fresh ones. Try to create them in areas where there are only one or two large rubs. They don't work as well in areas where there are many rubs already grouped together. Mock rubs also work better when made in thick cover bucks like to use.

I also use these mock rubs to trick other hunters. If I happen to discover a buck I want to hunt and I want to keep the hunting pressure down, I create rubs to attract other hunters. I make these rubs in areas that lead other hunters away from my area. I do this by creating a rub line, making anywhere from six to a dozen rubs that lead off into the opposite direction.

However, if you want to give this a try, don't make these rubs as large as the other rubs. Why? Two reasons. One, you don't want to unintentionally attract a large buck to this route. Two, you want the false rubs to be attractive to smaller bucks. They are made the same way as described earlier, except the rub is no longer than 12 to 18 inches. On this type of rub, don't break the branches. Although a small buck can certainly beat the pants off a sapling, try to keep these rubs docile, suggesting to other bucks they were made by a frustrated, submissive buck. Don't use any scent either.

Over the years, this tactic has worked magic diverting hunters away from hot spots I have discovered and into other areas. It's not as devious as it might seem, as these mock rub lines also serve to attract smaller bucks into these areas, too.

MOCK SCRAPES

Mock scrapes can be used just like mock rubs. The only difference is you are now creating a scrape and not a rub. Use a large heavy stick to clear out an area. With surgeons' gloves, try not to touch anything in or around the scrape area. To attract large mature bucks, make your scrape at least 4' x 4'. Again, try to CREATE THE ENTIRE ILLUSION by using a small amount of tarsal scent and a buck urine scent as well. I even go as far as placing a deer hoof print in the middle of the scrape (with a mounted deer foot). It's just another visual aid to complete the illusion.

Remember to break off one of the overhanging branches and let it hang in its broken state over the scrape. This mock scrape will attract bucks both visually and through their olfactory. I have found this to work best several days (Nov. 10 - 15) prior to the peak of the primary rut when bucks are in the frenzy period just before mating with does.

Obviously, these scrapes can also deter hunters from your area, just like the mock rub line. Again, make a scrape line leading away from your area. The size of these scrapes should be no larger than 2' x 2'. If you want to be a nice guy, place only a small amount of buck urine in them (not tarsal). This way, smaller bucks, by the sheer size and odor of the scrape will be attracted to them. You won't have to feel as guilty.

Try the traditional decoying tactics I talked about in the beginning of this chapter along with these three unusual decoying tactics. They will put you in the action this season. They will also help to reduce the hunting pressure in your area from competitive hunters. Remember, hunting pressure is the number one factor in determining whether or not you'll have a successful hunt. Trimming down this excess hunting pressure by using one of these unorthodox decoying tactics can't be all that bad -- can it? You decide.

CHAPTER 15

BACK YARD BUCKS

At this point, I haven't talked much about recommending that you should get off the beaten trail or chase bucks into the remote back country. The reason is twofold. One, I try to relate my strategies and advice to practical hunting techniques and the average hunter. Especially since the vast majority of you either can't find the time to hunt in remote back areas or don't have these areas where you hunt. Two, hunting in remote areas isn't all that necessary to score on big bucks. I am witness to the fact that a lot of big trophy bucks, some large enough to make the Boone & Crockett record books, are killed within sight of suburbia, somewhere in America each year. Even in states like Montana, Maine, and Missouri, big white-tailed bucks have learned to live, eat and mate within a stone's throw of civilization. No matter where you live, you have backyard bucks close by.

Bagging a big trophy buck is naturally every deer hunter's dream. I have listened to and read about many theories on what it takes to kill big bucks. It has been said in order to bag big trophy racked bucks, "a hunter must hunt in the most inaccessible and remote areas he can find, if he wants any chance at all at shooting a trophy." Nothing could be further from the truth. While a lot can be said for hunting trophy bucks in the back country, it doesn't mean it's the only way you can score on a record book buck.

During the thirty-two years I have hunted whitetails, I have taken some very large racked bucks (with scores in the 150s) all within twenty-five to 150 yards of civilization. Real civilization. Houses, highways, and even airports, areas most hunters would naturally <u>avoid</u>. Most hunters feel these areas do not provide the opportunity to take a good buck, never mind a trophy class animal. On several occasions over the years, I have taken some of my better bucks just outside of villagelimits. Remember, if you want to take bucks, especially big racked bucks, learn to be FLEXIBLE and INNO-VATIVE with your deer hunting tactics.

In the Northeast, in states like New Jersey, New York, and Pennsylvania and Connecticut, big racked bucks have learned to adjust their way of life in order to avoid hunting pressure. They have learned to become cotton tail rabbits and survive by leaving their usual lairs within their range hunting pressure increases. Consequently, some older and wiser bucks have learned to inhabit populated areas that lack hunting pressure during the hunting season. These bucks use back lawns, yards and shopping mall properties, when excess hunting pressure demands it. In these "avoided" areas, danger from hunting pressure for the wily trophy buck is nonexistent!

Years ago, I became "wise" to a buck that bedded down in heavy briars about sixty to seventy-five yards from a non-hunting friend's house. Each morning, the buck left an apple orchard across the street from my friend's place and bedded down behind his deck. From my tree stand in the apple orchard (a couple hundred yards from his house), I could hear his dog barking excitedly each morning around 7:45 a.m. The barking lasted for an hour or so and then abruptly stopped.

One day, I mentioned this to my friend. He replied very matter-of-factly, "I know. He's barking at a buck that passes through our yard each morning. He stops barking when the buck lays down out of his sight. He starts to bark again when the buck gets up and crosses the lawn as he leaves in the afternoon." That's all I needed to hear!

The next morning, with my friend's permission, I posted 25 yards behind his home. I could see thecars driving along the road in front of his house from my treestand, which was about fifty to 75 yards from the road. I watched his children get on the school bus and his wife leave for work, while I sat patiently waiting for the buck to show up. Then, it happened, his dog began to bark. It was 7:40 a.m., and there, as big as day, the buck casually walked across the yard. When he reached the end of the lawn, he walked off into the woods about 20 yards, paused, circled several times, and bedded down in tall cattails. He was 35 yards from the house, less than 30 yards from my tree stand, about 50 yards from the dog and about 75 yards from the main road! As I sat there, I was amazed at how relaxed this big buck was. He paid absolutely no attention to the dog, to the cars on the road, a jogger that went by or to the fact that he was so close to a house.

For over an hour he laid motionless in his bed. Finally, trying to get the buck to move, I blew an alarm snort call. I figured it would be a good plan to get the buck to stand up for me to get a cleaner shot at him. It worked! The buck stood up and as he was looking around to find what this other deer was so upset about, I drew my bow and sent the arrow toward its mark. By 9:30 that morning, I had a nice eight-point buck that field dressed over 180 lbs. had a gross antler score of 137 Pope & Young points!

Each morning, like clockwork, this buck waited for the school bus to pass by before he crossed the road!

You don't always have to "hike in" to score on big bucks. There are certain suburban areas across the country that, although they are next to heavily populated areas, still offer great hunting opportunities. A classic example of this is the southern area of New York state. While much of the state's deer hunting is in rural areas, a good percentage across the entire state is found right outside urban cities and towns. Westchester is only 10 to 15 minutes from midtown Manhattan. Yet, each year, bow hunters kill some of the state's largest bucks there.

In these suburban areas, deer, especially big bucks, survive along side of man, and attain one of the most important factors to achieve a trophy rack -- age. Hidden and left alone during hunting season, they mature into 4 1/2 to 6 1/2 year trophy class whitetail bucks by adapting to their habitat.

These bucks have "learned" to be flexible. They hide in areas hunters will not or cannot hunt. Here, these deer secretly go about their business of survival oblivious, to some degree, to the houses, strip malls, factories, half-acre swamps, small estates, and mini or gentlemen farms twenty-five to fifty acres in size that they call home during hunting season.

This isn't the only place you'll find big bucks in strange places. Even in areas where there is a lot of open hunting ground, deer often bed down in spots that are overlooked by most hunters. Big bucks are sensitive to hunting pressure. It doesn't take more than a few encounters with man in October to warn a big buck of what is about to take place -- predation. They quickly adapt to avoid it. If necessary, deer will bed down only yards off a major roadway to escape pressure. They have learned by quietly bedding close to the road, most hunters walk right past them and go deeper into the woods.

I shot this buck within 75 yards of the house behind me. Remember, in most states you need permission to hunt within 500 feet of a home.

One time I was hunting with my cousin, Leo Somma, at his home in South Hampton Bays in Long Island, New York. While driving back home for lunch, we saw a large buck bed down not more than ten yards off the road on opening day! Unfortunately, he was as safe as a bug in a rug because he was also bedded between two houses that were only yards apart from each other!

It is **not always necessary** to "get off the beaten trail" to bag big bucks. Learn to "accept" that sometimes the taking of a large racked buck means sacrificing the romanticism or ambience of a deer hunt.

Establish your hunting ethics. Your priorities. Is the taking of the quarry uppermost in your mind? Is the taking of larger racked bucks all that important? Or, is it acceptable for you to harvest any size buck as long as the aesthetic values of your hunt remain intact. That is, some hunters believe, and rightfully so, that not hearing traffic or seeing houses or coming up on other hunters is as important to the "hunt" as is the taking of a buck.

These hunters, year after year, hike deep into secluded or even remote pockets of woods to hunt deer unconcerned over the fact that they may indeed be "passing up" bucks bedded only yards off the highways or trails they walked in on. To these hunters, the aesthetic part of their hunt is their priority.

If you want to increase your chances of shooting a larger racked buck and be a more consistent hunter, especially in the Northeast, you MUST be more flexible and innovative than the above described deer hunter. Accept and learn to hunt very small patches of cover. **Apply this tactic even when it has nothing to do with hunting suburban bucks.** Even bucks that live in rural areas learn to hide from hunters by using scant areas of cover to conceal themselves during heavy hunting pressure. Many times, rural bucks seek out this type of cover only days into the season.

When I'm bow hunting on a friend's farm in New Jersey, I rarely see more than another archer or two, as my friend keeps the place well posted. Throughout the bow season, the bucks show no indication of being affected by hunting pressure. They enter the fields to feed long beforedusk. Come firearms season, however, they encounter many more hunters as my friend's entire family gun hunts. By the third day of the season, seeing a deer, never mind a buck, in the fields or woods of this farm, is all but over. They have moved off to less pressured areas.

Directly across the road there is a huge swamp that runs to the base of an extremely steep mountain. Both the swamp and the mountain are sur-rounded by open overgrown fields dotted with small pockets of cover. While everybody else huffs and puffs their way up the steep ledges of the mountain, or slushes through the swamp, I post in semi-open ground in small patches of thickets, cattails or 1/4 to 1/2 acre woodlots of second growth, only 30 to 50 yards from the road. I have scored consistently on good bucks by using this tactic on this farm. Again, hunting pressured bucks means treating bucks as if they were cotton tail rabbits. Expect a buck to be hiding in the slightest bit of cover. Soon, you will learn to check out these types of places as regularly as you would as if you were small game hunting. A word of caution here, never check a small patch of cover halfheartedly. I have seen friends check out these areas by kicking logs and shaking brush with their rifles hung over their shoulders or held lazily in their hands. I always feel sorry for them when they're left dumbfounded as a buck breaks from cover and darts to safety. Always check this type of cover with your gun or bow at the ready. And, more important, with your confidence in tact. If you expect a buck to be hiding there -- he will be.

Lastly, even after kicking or walking though a small stand of second growth, don't walk off and continue hunting. Instead, after you have gone through the cover, walk off ten or so yards to where you have a good vantage point and scan the area for a good 10 to 15 minutes. Big bucks can curl themselves up into small packages and have the uncanny ability to let hunters walk by within feet without getting nervous enough to run. They expect the danger to pass. When you stand and wait, however, even the wiliest buck's nerves begin to fray and he eventually gets nervous enough to jump up and try to escape.

Here's a tactic that will put you where the deer are by just paying a little attention to their sign. Find an area where deer bed between houses, etc., and then locate where they cross the road from the houses. Now, find where they enter the woods to feed on the other side of the road. Once you <u>KNOW</u> exactly where the deer enter one side of the road and exit on the other side, set up a ground or tree blind within sight of the road (check your local game laws first). Even though you won't have the aesthetics of your hunt, you will have action and, more important, the element of surprise. Bucks have learned <u>not</u> to expect danger this close to the road. Once inside the woods on the other side of the road, deer stop to regroup and offer hunters good shooting opportunities -- often, at close range racked bucks!

Let the first several deer pass by unmolested -- they are usually does and smaller bucks. The lead doe usually runs the group across the road. She then allows them time to regroup and then begins to move them on. Generally, only minutes later, the buck crosses the road and enters the woodlot behind the does. Interestingly enough, he often hangs-up only fifty or so yards from the road for several minutes. I have observed lots of bucks, especially big boys, "mill about" for thirty minutes before they decide to "move on."

Since most of the suburban bucks I've been talking about usually reside on very small patches of private land, it becomes critical for you to obtain permission long before the deer season begins. Start now, by introducing yourself to property owners, so that you may gain their confidence and trust. Let them know you are a safe, dedicated hunter. Assure them you'll be careful of pets, property and people. Guarantee them that you will be inconspicuous to the neighbors. Explain that you will treat their land as if it was your own. Promise them you will not make a pest of yourself and that you will hunt alone. Offer to provide them with a notarized hold harmless release. And, if they like game, offer to share your deer meat with them. Only then, will you greatly improve your chances of having their property available for you to hunt.

Unbelievable hunting opportunities can be realized when you are hunting deer that are extremely predictable. Living between and behind houses, in very small patches of cover, "makes" a buck follow very defined routes. They have few other choices. Varying from prescribed trails only brings them closer to encounters with the unknown. Therefore, come heck or high water, back yard bucks do not allow themselves the luxury of "roaming their range." They are the vulnerable, predictable trophies of suburbia! Cash in by learning to be flexible enough to hunt these overlooked trophies. Hunt big bucks, in small places!

CHAPTER 16

WEEKEND DEER HUNTER

It isn't unusual for today's deer hunters to be limited to just a few days of hunting time afield. Many, in fact, only get to spend opening day and, maybe, a weekend deer hunting. This isn't much time to accomplish the ultimate goal of seeing and bagging a buck. This lack of hunting time afield probably accounts for the fact that in most states across the country, especially the heavily hunted northeast where leisure-time is at its minimum, only one deer hunter out of ten fills his/her deer tag. Here's how to change the odds to your favor and maximize your limited hunting time afield.

The Weekend Deer Hunter starts out with several strikes against him. He more than likely doesn't have a place to hunt, whether public or private. Still others, if they do have a place to hunt, don't have enough time to scout. Yet others, who do take the time to scout, still don't use effective time-saving strategies and tactics specific for hunters with limited time.

The most effective strategy for Weekend Deer Hunters is to hunt private land. Deer that inhabit lands that are not over-hunted move throughout the day more frequently and less cautiously. Private ground is not as difficult to find as you might think. Every state has agricultural lands, gentlemen farms (50 acres or less), and small patches of ground bordering larger tracts that offer potential unpressured hunting opportunities. The key is to make contact with the owners of these lands **long before** deer season approaches. If you approach a land owner in June, July or August it will be much easier to obtain permission than if you ask permission just prior to or during the hunting season dressed in hunting attire. By obtaining permission to hunt these unpressured lands, scouting becomes less important as deer naturally use the property more freely. Therefore, it is to a Weekend Hunter's advantage to hunt on private land.

Obviously, hunting private land is not always possible. If this is your case, look for public ground that is less accessible to vehicles or ATVs or does not have groomed hiking trails. Traditionally, the masses of hunters stick close to roads or hunt back country that is somewhat accessible. By doing some homework, you can locate public land that does not attract hordes of hunters. Contact game departments in the state you are hunting and asking for a list of public hunting grounds -- especially the less "popular" tracts.

HUNT HI, HUNT LO

If you find yourself having to hunt the more heavily hunted public ground, use the other hunters to your advantage. For instance, if you're hunting an area where most hunters climb high, hunt low. Or, vice versa. Deer will wind or sense the intrusion and change their travel routines. Many times, sensing an invasion of the other hunters, deer turn around and head in the safe direction they just came from.

SCOUTING

Successful Weekend Deer Hunters, whether they are hunting public or private land, scout close to their hunt dates. Scouting weeks before your hunt, leaves you vulnerable to a change in food sources or changes in your quarry's routine. Weather changes could alter their food source and hunting pressure could change their travel routes. Not knowing what trails the deer use most frequently, what food sources they favor, where their prime bedding areas are located and, most important, what escape routes they use when pressured can result in seeing fewer deer or, perhaps, no deer at all.

Weekend Deer Hunters who, perhaps, have only a day to scout prior to their hunt, should concentrate their efforts on locating primary food sources. Knowing exactly what the deer are feeding on during your hunt immediately puts you in areas deer use to travel to and from their bedding and feeding grounds. Depending on the time of year you're hunting, these areas could include apple orchards, alfalfa, soybean and corn fields, or oak ridges (for the variety of acorns typically found in the hardwoods).

Novice hunter, Brian Monti, poses with his first buck and my son, Cody. Only able to hunt one weekend of the season, he successfully used some pre-season strategies that I passed along to him to score on his second day out!

Keep in mind weather plays an important role in locating an ACTIVE food source. For instance, deer may be feeding in apple orchards or alfalfa fields when the temperature drops considerably. Immediately, the deer forsake the apples and alfalfa (which are now frosted over and less palatable), and instinctively head for mast or corn crops. Mast (acorns) and corn raise a deer's body temperature and provide the necessary nutrition needed for the body to fend off the declining temperatures. Therefore, whenever there is a sudden drop in temperature, a Weekend Hunter should head for woodlots adjoining fields of standing or cut corn for morning or evening hunts. Where agricultural fields are not present, deer seek out acorns to raise their body temperatures. In thisinstance, deer are scattered throughout the hardwoods and not as concentrated on deer trails you should take a stand deeper in the hardwoods, especially in areas abundant with white oak.

As temperatures return to normal means, deer once again begin to feed on other favorite foods. They return to feed in apple orchards and grasses as they become more palatable or "tasty" to the deer during normal fall and winter weather conditions.

When your scouting time is short, don't fall into the typical trap of hunting only "buck sign" like rubs, scrapes, and thickets. Although this sign certainly indicates a buck has been in the area, it may be days or even weeks old, leaving you posted in an area that deer are not using. Even when you locate a fresh scrape, it may be wiser not to spend a lot of time hunting over it. Especially when you consider that most bucks wind-check their scrapes them from cover or during the safety of darkness. Obviously, the exception to this rule is actually "eye-balling" a buck using the area.

Once a food source is located, the next step is to find the travel routes that are used to and from the area. The **quickest and most productive** way to do this is to locate FRESH deer sign like droppings and tracks. The sign left by these two markings is indisputable. Fresh dung and fresh tracks translate into deer presently using that particular patch of woods or terrain. Hunting this fresh sign will put you where the deer are.

There are several unorthodox and traditional strategies that you can use to help attract deer, rather than wasting time waiting for a buck to meander by. When hunting time is limited, you can use scent (both food and attracting aromas), mock estrus trails, mock scrapes or different calling tactics. These techniques are covered in detail in the chapters on scent, calling, and scrape hunting.

QUICK CALLING

As I've said before, one of my favorite ways to hunt deer -- especially on lands that I haven't hunted before or where deer are not moving as willingly as they might -- is with deer calls. This tactic can be a part of the Weekend Hunter's emergency kit. As you've read, deer are extremely vocal animals. Using a call to deceive a wary old buck from cover works more readily than most hunters are willing to believe or admit. There are a variety of calls to use to help attract deer to your stand. Among the most effective cadences of the primary calls are the estrus grunt and blat, the alarm-distress snort, and locator blat. These particular calls are designed to attract deer by what they naturally represent -- vocally.

During the '95 season, I had only one afternoon to bow hunt a farm I regularly hunt in Hope, New Jersey. I didn't want to spend the entire time waiting for a buck to pass by my treestand. I decided to use a snort call to help me get the deer up and moving about. As covered in the calling chapter, the alarm-distress cadence of the snort is used by deer to warn other deer of **immediate danger**. You can use the alarm-distress cadence of the snort to intentionally spook deer from rhododendron, steep ledges, swamps, evergreen patches and standing corn fields. This is a great tactic when hunting time is limited! It is one of the rare instances (other than a deer drive) when a hunter actually uses his own human odor as well as a call to help him roust deer.

The other calls mentioned above can also aid you in seeing or attracting deer more quickly. The trick is to read the chapter on deer calls a few times so you learn and become confident in using the different calls.

Another strategy to help manage your hunting time is to lease or get permission to hunt a piece of private ground. Without a doubt, hunting on posted land greatly benefits the Weekend-type Hunter. Unfortunately, many hunters are bashful about trying to secure a piece of land. They shy away from asking permission because they don't want to be told, "No." If I've learned one thing about deer hunting, it is that when approached properly, most land owners (even if they say no the first couple of times) will, in the end, be receptive to giving permission to hunt their land.

You may not consider this a strategy. I guarantee you, however, it is one of the best hunting strategies you will learn. Mastering the ability to approach a landowner to provide you with permission to hunt his property is as important a tactic as any other strategy you'll read in this book. I approach each landowner with a clear idea of what I want to say and how I want to present my case to him.

Deer hunting with a limited amount of time on public or private land doesn't have to be frustrating or futile. By being creative and using unorthodox type hunting methods you will create deer hunting opportunities for yourself -- no matter how limited your deer hunting time is. Try the above suggestions this year and see if they don't work for you!

CHAPTER 17

SCORING & FIELD JUDGING ANTLERS

As the buck cautiously picked his way along the edge of the alfalfa field, I thought to myself, "This is the buck you're looking for. He should score high enough to make Pope & Young." As the buck walked under my stand I got ready to shoot. The buck put his head down to eat an acorn and it gave me the chance to draw my bow. I released the arrow before he ever picked up his head. As the arrow hit, the buck whirled, ran about 30 to 40 yards and fell. When I approached the buck, I quickly calculated the numbers and discovered, although his rack was big, his net score would be close, and maybe not enough, to make the 125 Pope & Young points needed to enter the books.

One of the most complicated aspects of deer hunting can be measuring (scoring) a set of buck antlers. Between the intimidating directions and the vast amount of misinformation about the subject, it's no wonder most hunters steer away from measuring antlers.

That's a shame. Measuring a set of antlers really isn't difficult at all, not as long as you keep in mind some basic guidelines. It is important to mention, however, if you are thinking about officially entering a set of antlers into the Pope & Young (archery Typical 125) or Boone & Crockett (firearm Typical 170) record books, **THE ANTLERS MUST BE SCORED BY AN OFFICIAL MEASURER.**

The following information is meant to give you the ability to **rough score** any set of deer antlers. Once you have learned the technique described below and have measured a few sets of antlers, you will probably become proficient enough to measure a set of antlers to within 10 to 15 points of an official score.

There are two ways to keep track of your measurements. Use a score sheet from one of the many organizations that maintain record books or simply use a piece of blank paper. The key is to break down the figures into the four groups of measurements that actually count in the final tally of calculations that you take.

Group or Column #1, called Spread Credit on all official score sheets, is for the inside spread of the main beams at their widest point.

Column #2 and #3, listed on the official score sheet as Left Antler and Right Antler, record the overall length of the Main Beams, listed as entry "F" on official score sheets, and the measurements of each individual tine on the left and right antlers. The individual tine lengths are called the "G" measurements. Each individual tine is assigned a "G" measurement. The "G" measurements begin with the brow tines which are referred to as the G-1s. The next tines after the brow tines are called the G-2s, next are the G-3s, G-4s and so on.

Column #4, which is referred to as "Difference" on the score sheet, is used to record the variation between each tine measurement. For instance, if the G-1s (which are the brow tines) score 4 1/8 and3 1/8 respectively, the entry in the "difference" column is 1. This column is often called the deduct or deduction column.

The other three measurements that are NOT used in the overall score total are the number of points on each antler, the tip-to-tip spread and the greatest outside spread of the antlers.

To achieve the most accurate total score, you must know where and how to take each measurement. To begin the process, whether you are measuring for your own satisfaction or to see if the antlers are large enough to be scored by an official scorer, you can make some **minor** mistakes and still have the overall score within the ball park. Keep in mind that most organizations require a "drying-out" period of sixty days before they allow an official measuring.

EQUIPMENT

The equipment needed to score a set of antlers is basic. A 1/4-inch flexible steel measuring tape which you will use to measure the antlers to the nearest 1/8 of an inch, a pencil, paper or a blank score sheet, and, if you have trouble with fractions, a calculator.

The process begins with the eight (or so) basic measurements you must make and where they are made.

#1 NUMBER OF POINTS (*This score is not added in*)
First, determine the number of points on the right antler, then the left. To be counted as a point, the point or tine must be at least one inch long. All points are measured from the tip of the point to the nearest point of the main beam. The main beam tip is counted as a point but not measured as a point. It is measured as the length of the main beam.

#2 TIP-TO-TIP SPREAD (*This score is not added in*)
Measure the width of the antlers from tip to tip. Simply stated, this means make a measurement between the tips of the main beams.

#3 GREATEST SPREAD (*This score is not added in*)
Now, measure the greatest outside distance or spread of the rack. This is done by measuring the outside distance between the two tines that are the farthest apart.

#4 INSIDE SPREAD
The inside spread of the main beams is measured at the widest point between the main beams. This number is used in the overall score. If the inside spread measurement is greater than the length of the longest main beam, then you have to use the longest main beam length as your measurement in this category.

#5 LENGTH OF ABNORMAL POINTS
Abnormal points are those non-typical in location or extra points beyond the normal pattern of points. They are measured in the usual way.

#6 LENGTH OF THE MAIN BEAM

Measure the length of the main beam from its lowest outside edge of the burr over the outside curve to the tip of the main beam. This measurement must be entered separately for both the right and left antlers.

My buck's right antler main beam measured 20 5/8 inches. Its left antler main beam measured 21 6/8 inches. There is a difference of 1 1/8 inches between the two. This difference (1 1/8) is a deduction.

#7 LENGTH OF INDIVIDUAL POINTS

Now measure each individual point on each main beam. Begin with the brow tines sometimes called the eye guard points. Every official organization refers to this point as the G-1. Each point up the main beam from the G-1 is referred to as G-2, G-3, G-4 and so on. **Remember, to be classified as a point, it must be at least one inch long.** The old wives' tale that a point is anything you can hang a ring off of does not hold true officially or unofficially when scoring a set of antlers or when counting the overall number of points on a set of antlers. To properly measure a point, measure it from the nearest edge of the main beam over the outer curve to the tip of the point.

Now, measure the length of each remaining point on each beam and enter or write down the individual lengths. Do not measure the end of the main beam as a point -- it is calculated in the overall length of the main beam.

#8 CIRCUMFERENCE OF MAIN BEAM

This measurement, referred on the score sheet as the "H" measurement is taken at four places along the antlers. What is important with these measurements is the location where they are made. The circumference measurement is made at the smallest place between two points. For example, the first measurement (H-1) is made at the smallest place between the burr of the antler and the first point.

The next "H" measurement is at the smallest place between the first and second points; and is called H-2. The remaining circumference measurements are H-3 and H-4. For the H-4 measurement, if there is no fourth point (or tine), then take the measurement halfway between the third point and the beam tip. There are no additional circumference measurements taken after H-4.

My cousin, Ralph Somma, once asked me to measure a symmetrical ten point buck he arrowed in New Jersey. I gave him a rough score of 129 Pope &Young points. Because Pope &Young only requires a minimum score of 125 -- it appeared the buck roughed out high enough to make the Pope and Young record books. Later that evening, Ralph called to say the buck "scored higher." When I asked why, he said his taxidermist said I missed the "H-5" measurement. There is no "H-5" measurement I explained to Ralph. "Not according to my taxidermist," he said. So it goes when it comes to measuring antlers -- there is a lot of misinformation out there. THERE IS NO "H-5" MEASUREMENT!

TOTALING YOUR SCORE

This is where the suspense is at its maximum! It is where you add and deduct all the measurements you have just taken. First, add the measurement of the column referred to as Spread Credit (the inside spread of the antlers) to the bottom of that column.

Next, add the left and right Antler columns to the bottom of the page. Then add the Difference column to the bottom of the page, too. Bring all the total figures from columns 1, 2 and 3 to the "Add Column" (found on the left-hand side of all official score sheets) and total them together. Then bring the figure from column #4 over. SUBTRACT COLUMN #4 from the total you got by adding columns 1, 2 and 3.

This figure is your subtotal rough score. Now, deduct from the gross number the length of abnormalpoints and all the "difference" measurements. This number is your NET or FINAL ROUGH score. The reason I say rough, is that until the rack is measured by an official scorer from Boone & Crockett or Pope &Young or any state record keeping organization, your score is not official and, therefore, only a rough final tally.

With a little practice, you, too, can learn how to score a set of antlers. After scoring a dozen or so with a tape, you'll soon find yourself looking a rack over and estimating its size close enough to what it eventually measures out to be. This is an added benefit because once you have learned how to estimate without a tape, you can begin judging antlers on live bucks and estimating whether they are large enough for you to shoot.

SAMPLE SCORE SHEET FOR
WHITE-TAILED DEER

Abnormal Points

			Right Antler	Left Antler
E. Total of lengths of abnormal points				
		Column 1	Column 2	Column3	Column 4

			Column 1	Column 2	Column3	Column 4
A. No. Points On Right Antler		No. of Points on Left Antler	Spread Credit	Right Antler	Left Antler	Difference
B. Tip to Tip Spread		C. Greatest Spread				
D. Inside spread of Main Beams		(Credit May Equal But not Exceed Longer Antler)				
F. Length of Main Beam						
G-1. Length of 1st point						
G-2. Length of 2nd point						
G-3. Length of 3rd point						
G-4. Length of 4th point, if present						
G-5. Length of 5th point, if present						
G-6. Length of 6th, point if present						
G-7. Length of 7th point, if present						
H-1. Circumference at smallest place between burr and 1st point						
H-2. Circumferenceat smallest place between 1st and 2nd points						
H-3. Circumference at smallest place between 2nd and 3rd points						
H-4. Circumference at smallest place between 3rd and 4th points						
TOTALS						

Enter total of Columns 1,2, and 3		Exact Locality Where Killed:	
Subtract Column 4		Date Killed:	By Whom Killed:
Subtotal		Owner:	
Subtract (E) total length of abnormal points		Guide Name: Address:	
FINAL SCORE		Remarks:	

Most state record book organizations use similar scoring system as the official Boone & Crockett scoring sheet.

MEASURING A BUCK ON THE HOOF

The buck stood absolutely motionless only 15 yards below my tree stand in thick brush. His head was turned at an angle that made it difficult to see both sides of his antlers. At this position, it was impossible for me to judge if his antlers were large enough for me to take him. I could clearly see one antler with six long points. The smallest, his brow tine (G1), was about four inches. I estimated the rest of his points (G2 through G5) to be about 9, 8, 6, and 6 inches, respectively. The total mass and length of the one beam looked good too; but, it was difficult to judge accurately as most of the main beam was covered by brush. I guessed the length of that beam to be between 20 and 24 inches. This was a "keeper" buck providing his other antler was symmetrical to the antler I was looking at.

Then, the buck's head whirled to check out a noise coming from behind him -- a young four-point buck. The intrusion by the young buck broke the stalemate and gave me an opportunity to see the other antler. Unfortunately, the only thing I could detect from looking at the back of the rack (one of the most difficult angles to accurately judge a buck's antlers), was that he had six antlers on his other beam and they were about the same size as the points on the other antler.

Most hunters would have shot the buck long before now. With six points on one antler, he was obviously a good deer. But I wasn't after just a good deer. I was specifically hunting for a buck that would score high enough to qualify for the Boone & Crockett firearms record book, which requires a minimum of 170 points for entry. Not an easy task to accomplish when you consider the odds. Only one hunter in 1.3 million kills a buck big enough to make the Boone & Crockett record books. Countless bucks come painfully close. So, it's critical to make sure you're looking at a Boone & Crockett buck before you pull the trigger.

Although I knew he had six evenly matched points on the other antler, I still had a few more things to figure out before taking the buck. I had to know the width of his antlers and the thickness of his beams.

Judging a buck in the field takes a little bit of skill and a lot of luck. First, your quarry has to stay in your view long enough for you to make several quick calculations. This means you have to know how to keep a deer from scenting or spotting you. Then, it's all a matter of priorities. Field judging deer doesn't necessarily have to be used only to determine whether a buck is big enough for Pope & Young or Boone & Crockett. It can be used simply to find out if the buck you are looking at is a record in your own mind and heart.

Trophy hunting is nothing more than setting your priorities before the hunt. For some, a trophy can mean taking a buck with a 16-inch wide rack and four good points to a side. A buck like this will score between 110 and 120 points, providing the other measurements, such as overall length and circumference of the main beams, are within certain parameters, too. A buck like this is not large enough to make any books, but it is good enough to make a lot of hunting companions envious.

There lies the age-old question of hunters who shoot bucks based on the size of their antlers, "Should I shoot?" Remember, no matter what size racked buck you are looking at, whether he's a 110 or a 170 plus, here's what to look for.

First you want a buck to have a symmetrical set of antlers. The more even both sides are, the higher it will score. Next, guess only the inside spread of his antlers. Typically, the average buck's ears, when held out to the side of his head in the alert position, measure between 16 and 18 inches, tip to tip. Next, look at the overall thickness of the antlers. If they are pencil thin, they will score less than if they were thicker. Finally, for a buck's antlers to go above 110 points, it must have at least four tines to each side of the antlers.

I like to be conservative when field judging. If I estimate a set of antlers' inside spread to be 20 inches, I bring it down to 18 to compensate for my excitement of the moment. I also do this with all other measurements as well. By figuring low, I eliminate the element of disappointment. Most times, the rack is slightly larger than I have estimated.

Wait until you can see the buck's antlers as he is facing you. Judging in any other position, especially if he is going away, makes judging the rack much more difficult. Then, as quickly as possible, estimate the width and thickness of the antlers. Finally, look over the points and add up the larger side. Providing the buck hasn't walked off by now, you can make an educated guess as to what he will score. THEREIN LIES THE REALITY OF FIELD JUDGING A BUCK'S ANTLERS. Most bucks will not give you the time to score their racks as I just described. So, if you are a trophy hunter, it pays to practice continually by estimating the score of a set of antlers from MOUNTED buck heads. This practice eventually will enable you to look at a buck in the field and, within seconds, determine the score of his antlers. This is especially true when you're hunting in areas with heavy hunting pressure.

Let's have some fun with judging some bucks. Here are a few in different positions and terrain. Most, by the mere size of their antlers, are keepers -- or are they? That depends if you are a serious Boone & Crockett trophy hunter, then each of these bucks needs careful scrutiny. If you're an archer looking for a Pope & Young record, these certainly look like keepers. Let's find out.

This buck, although not a trophy buck by any means, is quite typical of the size bucks many hunters see in the woods. Even if his rack was larger than it is, it would be difficult to score him for several reasons. Obviously, he's on the run and judging any buck's rack on the run is near impossible. Second, he's running away from you and judging a buck's antlers from the rear is difficult and inevitably leads to miscalculating the size of the antlers. Remember, when you're trying to score a buck's antlers, don't do so when they are walking away from you. Antlers will always give the illusion of being larger when they are walking away from you. Third, his ears are pointed back making it even more difficult to judge how wide the antlers are. It's easy to see, however, that he has no mass and very few points to worry about. In the heavily hunted portions of the Catskill mountains of New York, this buck would be a keeper. If you were looking for a buck to make the books, however, you'd have to let this one keep on running. You're looking at a buck with a rack that nets about 40 points!

Here's a perfect angle to judge a set of antlers. This buck is standing still in an open field with nothing behind him to obstruct his antlers, allowing you to look the rack over closely without distraction from branches or brush. It's easy to see by the position of his ears that his antlers are much wider than his ears, perhaps 20 to 24 inches. His brow tines (G-1s) while short, are symmetrical. One side has four points, while his other antler has five points. He's missing the G-2 on one side. You will have to deduct the entire length of that tine from the other side of his rack for the overall score. Remember higher scoring racks are those with very symmetrical racks. Unfortunately, the antlers don't have a lot of mass, which will hurt in the overall scoring of them. You're bow hunting -- do you shoot this buck or let him pass? This set of antlers requires careful scrutiny. A seasoned hunter who really knows how to score a rack would probably shoot this buck. He scores about 129 points -- too close to call unless you really know what you're looking at. If you're not looking to put one in the books, send that arrow on its way!

This buck is going to be difficult to score for several reasons. First and foremost, judging the tines on his rack is difficult because of the brush behind them. His ears are also laid back making it difficult to accurately judge the inside spread of the antlers. One side is held at a position that also makes it difficult to judge the length and number of tines on that beam. But, even a novice could easily determine that this is quite a rack. But, for the dedicated Boone & Crockett trophy hunter, shooting this buck could be a difficult decision. If the right beam holds five symmetrical tines, chances are this buck will score high enough to make the books. Everything else including overall mass, tine length, sweep (overall length) of the main beams and inside spread all look excellent. If you were looking for a Boone & Crockett points (170 net points) would you shoot this buck? I might have been fooled by this one because of the angle and the brush behind him. I would have been wrong. This buck happens to score 178 points

Here's another good angle. Be careful though. His ears are pointed more upward than outward, making his rack appear wider than it actually is. Another deceiving factor is that one antler clearly shows seven and perhaps

eight points! It's difficult to determine how many points are on the other antler, however. It appears to be no more than four. This buck, although a definite keeper for most of us, would have to be passed up by the B&C trophy hunter. The reason? He would lose a lot of scoring points for every tine that is missing on the opposite antler, dropping his overall score considerably. One of the first factors a trophy hunter looks for is a symmetrical rack. This buck probably scores in the high 140s or low 150s. Not high enough for entry into the Boone & Crockett record books, but a real keeper for Pope & Young.

Uh Oh! Here's a buck running away with this ears pointed in the wrong direction. At a quick glance, his rack may appear to be wider than it actually is. You can clearly see five points on one side, however, counting the points on the opposite side, from this angle, is difficult. He's not a buck to pass up if you're not trophy hunting. But, if you're looking for a buck to make the books, you would be forced to let this buck run away. It's just too difficult to judge his antlers accurately. If he has five equal points on both antlers, he may score 135 to 140. If he's missing his G-2, his score will quickly drop to 125 to 130. If you misjudge the width, there's further trouble. I'd let this buck pass. This is the most difficult of angles to judge a buck from.

Here's another buck that will be difficult to score since you only get to clearly see one side of his antlers. In addition, one of his ears is pinned back alongside of his head, making the judging of the width of his antlers harder. If you're a gambler, the odds are that he has five more tines on the other side - but are they symmetrical? And, what if he doesn't? If you're not hunting

for the books, it doesn't matter, shoot this buck. However, if putting a buck in the B&C record books is on your agenda, you would definitely have to wait until he steps out from the corn and presents a better look at the entire set of antlers. Judging by the mass, the width, the tine length, and the sweep of the main beam that clearly shows, I would guess this buck to score between 160 and 170 B&C points. A keeper as far as I'm concerned.

In most hunter's eyes, the following 8-point is a keeper. The position he's in greatly helps to estimate the size of his rack. With his ears held out, you can estimate his rack have an inside spread of about 20 inches. His brow tines (G-1s) are exceptionally long, which will add to his overall score. The rest of his tines have good length and his main beams are long. He lacks mass throughout his antlers, however. If you are looking for a buck to make the Pope & Young record books (which requires a minimum net score of 125) this buck looks good. What do you think? You may or may not be surprised

to know that this buck scores 137 points, which puts him into the archery record books. However, if you were looking for a Boone & Crockett size animal, he falls far short of the 170 net points needed.

Holy kicker points and double brow tines! Don't hesitate a second on this bruiser Batman! Shoot this buck instantly (on the next page). Even though he presents the perfect angles to judge his rack, any hunter, including a Boone & Crockett trophy hunter, would know this buck is a trophy of a lifetime. Judging by the position of his ears, he has a terrific inside spread, great mass, tremendous tine length and quite a sweep to his main beams. Even accounting for the deduction from all the kicker points and double brow tines, this buck is a dandy. And has a Boone & Crockett entry written all over him? For the record, this buck scored 195 B&C points - well above the minimum score needed for entry.

As the four-point buck slowly moved away from the 12-point buck I mentioned earlier, I was able to get several different views of the 12-pointer's

antlers as his head slowly followed in the direction of the four point. At that point, I estimated the buck to be between 155 and 165 points. I placed the crosshairs on his back and squeezed off my shot. When I finally put a tape to the antlers, the buck netted 156 7/8 Boone & Crockett points. Although it was on the low end of my estimate, I wasn't disappointed. I had guessed him correctly.

Judging a buck's antlers becomes easier with practice. Judge every buck you see in a magazine, on a wall, in the woods, and even shed antlers. Before long, you'll train your eye to estimate the size of a buck's antlers without much effort at all. Remember, field judging a buck's antlers not you to decide whether or not to shoot, but it also is a lot of fun.

In the end, however, a trophy buck is nothing more or less than you want it to be. If a buck passes your stand and his antlers send a surge of adrenalin through your body and you start to breathe fast, and perhaps even shake a bit, don't bother trying to measure his antlers -- *THAT BUCK'S FOR YOU!* only helps

CHAPTER 18

HOW OLD WAS HE & WHAT DID HE WEIGH?

Most hunters undergo a myriad of emotions after harvesting a buck. Unquestionably, the most exciting part of approaching a downed buck is the thrill of counting the points on his antlers. What almost invariably follows after the initial excitement has passed, are these two questions, "How old is my deer and what does it weigh?"

Unfortunately, there are many wives' tales about how to tell the age of a deer, especially a buck. Some hunters, no matter how experienced they are, are unaware of exactly how to correctly and accurately determine the age of a downed deer. Less experienced hunters believe they can age a buck by the number of tines on the antlers, by the color of the hair on the deer's muzzle (face), by the sway in its back, the droop of its belly or the gait of its walk. While these factors can suggest an approximate age of a deer, most often they are deceiving and misleading. Many wildlife biologists acknowledge, the only **reliable** and accurate way to age a deer is by examining the replacement and wear of its teeth.

Is it really important to age a deer? I think so and so do most seasoned deer hunting veterans. When you hunt the same property year after year, aging the deer gives you vital information like:
* the specific age classes of deer in the herd
* antler size in relation to the age of the bucks
* the yearly restocking rate of young animals
* the average life span
* the rate of decline of various age groups over a given period
* whether you should or should not have shot this particular animal

* information to form sound deer management practices for future hunting seasons and
* how to process and cook your venison.

All this information is important to both good deer management and for the general knowledge of the dedicated deer hunter.

Say for instance, that if, after aging a jaw, you discover that you consistently shoot 2 1/2 to 3 1/2 year old bucks that are only spikes, forked horns or very small six and eight-point racked bucks (with total antler widths of ten to twelve inches). It should become clearly apparent the bucks within this herd are not maturing with typical or desirable rack size. Therefore, you may decide it is time to change your hunting location. Or, if you own the property, you may decide to provide more supplements to the deer to improve their antler growth. There is either a genetic deficiency in the deer herd or a deficiency in food and minerals found on or within the land.

Moreover if you discover a majority of deer taken are only eighteen months old, this will tell you that the repopulation of the herd is occurring at a steady or growing rate. If most of the eighteen month old bucks taken are only six and eight pointers, you may want to leave these deer in the herd. Let them mature in order to grow larger sets of antlers and have a greater opportunity to pass on their genes.

In addition, by knowing the correct age of the deer you shot, you can also make important decisions when processing, preparing and cooking the meat. If you "thought" a deer was older than it really was, you could make the mistake of processing hamburger when you could be butchering steaks instead. Deciding to marinate could also be unnecessary once you realize the venison is tender enough not to require this overused method in venison preparation. While venison from older deer is usually stewed or made into chili, younger deer meat can be cooked more unusually. Therefore, by knowing the exact age of your deer, you can capitalize on the different methods of butchering, preparing and eating venison, too.

For the purpose of judging a deer's age through examination of its teeth, deer should be divided into two major categories: those under two years old and those over that age. To figure out what category a deer falls in, the decisive factor is the presence or absence of the deciduous teeth (baby teeth) and the stage at which these baby teeth have been replaced by adult permanent teeth.

The number of teeth in a deer's mouth occurs at specific ages. This predictable occurrence allows the aging process of an animal to be a matter of fact rather than a concoction of wives' tales. Learning how to properly age deer is relatively easy. It does take some understanding of tooth development, gum lines and enamel, and signs of tooth wear and tear. However, the descriptions of these indicators sound more scientific and difficult to learn than they actually are.

Deer are born with four teeth on their lower jaw. These four front teeth are called incisors. In about a week to two weeks, sixteen additional teeth erupt, giving the fawn a total of twenty deciduous (or milk) teeth. It now has eight front incisors and six premolar teeth on the bottom jaw and sixpremolars on the upper jaw. Deer do not have front teeth in their upper jaw.

At one year old, six more molars erupt on both the lower and upper jaws, giving the deer a full set of thirty-two teeth. As the deer ages, its teeth are worn down by a variety of factors -- all related to the texture as well as the type of food the deer eats. The darker material in the tooth is the dentine. As the hard enamel of the tooth is worn away, more of the dentine is visible. This amount of visible dentine is an important factor when aging deer.

A more accurate aging method involves examining the number of rings in a cross section of a tooth. Each winter, when a deer's blood-serum protein and phosphate levels are low, a layer of cementum is formed on the tooth. Consequently, a tooth has one layer for each winter the deer has lived through.

In my home state of New York, Dick Henry, Senior Wildlife Biologist for the NYS Department of Environmental Conservation (NYSDEC) agrees, "There are only two ways of accurately aging a deer. The first is by removing a tooth, cutting a cross-section and examining it under a microscope. The examination reveals rings in the tooth much like those of a tree. It is the most reliable way to age deer. However, because it is time-consuming, it is not a good method to use when aging large numbers of animals."

Andrew Burnett, Assistant Wildlife Biologist in the Bureau of Wildlife Management in New Jersey's Division of Fish Game and Wildlife, agrees with Henry. "We age deer in five groups: 6 months,1 1/2 years, 2 1/2 years, 3 1/2 years and 4 1/2 and older." After 4 1/2 years, biologists tend to classify them all in one class."

This is why biologists aging deer at game check stations rely heavily on a method known as tooth wear and replacement. The downside to the tooth wear and replacement method, however, is the process becomes more subjective and begins to get more difficult in determining the exact age after the animal has reached 4 1/2 to 5 1/2 years old. At this point, it requires a much more careful look at the wear and tear of the teeth than at the numbers of teeth.

When I first began hunting, I estimated the deer's age by its antlers. I quickly discovered how inaccurate this was after having the deer aged by DEC officials at deer check stations. That's when I made the decision to learn how to judge the age of a deer by examining its teeth myself. Now, whenever I shoot a buck, I still first try to guess how old he is by looking at his antlers. More often than not, this method definitely fools me. The only two reliable ways to accurately judge the age of a deer is to bisect a tooth or examine the teeth in its mouth via tooth wear and replacement -- period.

The tooth wear and replacement method can be deceiving at times. For instance, if deer live in an area like the Pine Barren regions of New Jersey, where there is a higher concentration of sand in the soil, tooth wear is quicker then normal. Here, an examination of the teeth from a 1 1/2 year old deer might look like the teeth of a 2 1/2 year old from the northern farmlands of New Jersey.

Other factors, found no matter where you hunt, that come into play when judging how old a deer is include information about the deer's variation of diet, possible misalignment of its jaw, and soil mineral content and texture. **However, most deer teeth generally go through a standard predictable aging process.** Apply this information to future hunts to improve your deer hunting strategies and help you to become a better and more informed deer hunter. A more informed deer hunter is a hunter who gains confidence in their abilities -- intensifying the C + PT x C = CS principle. That is Concentration

+ Positive Thinking x Confidence = Consistent Success.

The other part of the question we addressed at the beginning of this chapter is, "How much does my deer weighs?" By using a flexible cloth deer weight measuring tape, available at most sporting goods stores, you can quickly estimate the live weight, field dressed weight and the weight of edible lean meat from your deer. Place the tape around the chest of the deer, right behind the forelegs. If the deer has a chest measurement of 36 inches, for example, the live weight was about 145 pounds, field dressed weight of about 120 pounds and there will be about 65 pounds of edible lean meat. If you don't have a special deer weight tape measure handy, you could always take a piece of string and mark the chest circumference and estimate the weight when you return to camp.

By keeping an accurate and detailed log of the age and weight of all animals harvested on your hunting ground, in just a few short years, you will have an accurate indication of what type of antlers you can expect from the different age groups of the bucks within your herd. You will also be able to pattern the typical weights of the deer that inhabit the land. Wide variations from the average will tell you if the land is not able to support the population of deer or if environmental factors are changing the herd's pattern and size.

Since I learned the value of properly judging the age of a deer, I have become an absolute believer in aging all the bucks I kill. For the last twenty-five years I have never shot a buck without aging it. I feel this information is vital to my deer hunting skills. Start aging your bucks and does this season. If, for no other reason, than to correct your hunting companions when they guess the age of the deer harvested. Knowing how to accurately determine the age and weight of your deer will make your hunting more interesting -- and you'll be able to leave the guess work up to the others.

COMMON MISCONCEPTIONS ABOUT AGING DEER

As novice deer hunters we were subject to the facts and theories of our fathers and grandfathers as they passed on their knowledge and skills to us. Unfortunately, many of the "facts" they handed down, no matter how well intended, were riddled with misinformation. Below are some of the more popular misconceptions.

* **THIRD TOOTH** - This is a prevalent misconception. Trying to age a deer by the ridges (more precisely called crests) in the third tooth can be suggestive of the deer's age. However, it must be combined with evaluating the numbers of condition of all the other teeth to be accurate.

* **NUMBER OF TINES** - This is the most common mistake when trying to guess the age of a buck. While it is generally true that as a buck gets older, his rack will be larger, the number of points will not necessarily correspond with his age. With the right circumstances, a 2 1/2 year old buck could sport a 10-point a rack. While the same buck, when he is 7 1/2 years old and in his declining years, may have a set of antlers that have only four to six points with burrs and kickers.

* **MUZZLE HAIR COLOR** - While it is true that the older a buck gets, the more his muzzle turns grey, it is not uncommon for a younger deer to have a grey muzzle. All deer have white hair (which in low light can look grey) on their tail, bellies, chin and around their eyes and muzzle.

* **GAIT** - While a deer's gait can sometimes be indicative of its sex, it is not a good indicator of age. Judging a deer's age by the way it walks, or by the sway in its back or belly, is unreliable.

CHART #1
FIELD METHOD FOR WEIGHING YOUR DEER

Chest Circumference	Live Weight	Field Dressed Weight	Weight of Edible Meat
20"	49 lbs.	36 lbs.	23 lbs.
25	69	53	31
30	97	77	44
35	136	112	61
40	191	160	85
45	267	228	118

Note: (Source: Pennsylvania Game Commission)

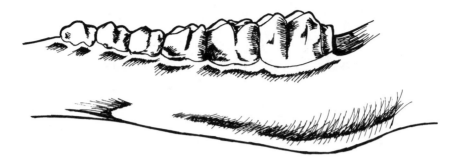

#1 - To tell whether a deer is either a yearling (1 1/2 year old) or 2 1/2 year old, carefully examine the upper **third** molar. This tooth, in yearlings, will be partially erupted through the gum line, but not all the way. The tooth will not show any signs of dentine. Dentine is a dark - almost black- accumulation of tissue forming the body of the tooth under the enamel making the crest of the tooth more visible.

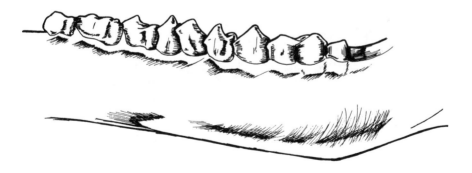

#2 - In 2 1/2 year olds, the upper third molar will be fully erupted and may, depending upon the deer's diet, already show signs of slight wear. The dentine is now visible but is well below the enamel of the crest.

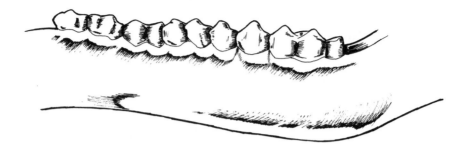

#3 - In 3 1/2 year olds, the first molar will show clear signs of wear regardless of the deer's diet. And, at this age, the sharp edges of the first molar have already begun to deteriorate from wear and are more blunt than the other molars behind it. The dentine of the first and second molar will be conspicuous and will be wider than the enamel on the teeth.

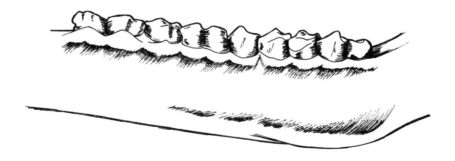

#4 - By the time a deer is 5 1/2 years old, **most teeth** will show signs of wear. They will have small ridges and the dentine will be broader than the enamel.

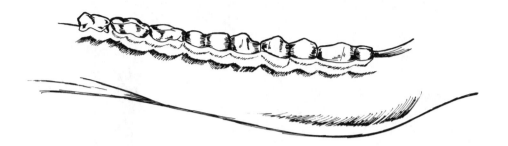

#5 - By 7 1/2 years old, all teeth show obvious signs of being worn down. Most teeth are in one way or another damaged, chipped, and sometimes broken. Most teeth have worn themselves to the point of being flat, except for the last two molars.

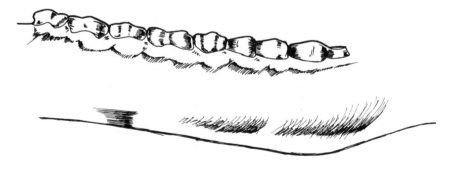

#6 - Deer 10 1/2 years old and older will have teeth worn down to or even below the gum line. The dentine is barely visible and some premolar may be missing. Even the last two molars are now clearly worn and almost flat to the gum line. The front incisors may be missing or worn to the gumline.

My wife and venison chef, Kate, and her favorite helper, our son, Cody.

Chapter 19

VENISON FOR THE TABLE

A deer book wouldn't be complete without including a chapter on cooking venison. Over the years, I have been fortunate enough to have had many guides, professional chefs, friends and hunting companions prepare for me some of the finest venison dishes any hunter could hope to eat. These scrumptious meals were delectable and left my mouth watering for more. However, none of these wild game dishes can match the imagination and taste of the venison recipes prepared by my hunting companion and wife, Kate. Here are six of my favorite dishes from Kate's Venison Recipe Collection. By the way, Kate will have her venison/big game cookbook on the market soon. I know you'll enjoy these recipes enough to order her new cookbook.

Remember, for any wild game to taste good, a hunter must consider these points. The best tasting venison begins by shooting deer that are young. However, since most of us want to shoot a buck, the key is to shoot bucks that are not stressed out. A deer shot while adrenalin is pumping through its system will be less palatable then a deer shot in a relaxed state. Also, field dress your game quickly and properly. Once your deer is back at camp or home, you'll enhance its flavor immensely by removing the hide as quickly as possible, thereby letting the carcass cool and dry out which avoids bacterial growth. The old wives tale of letting the deer hang for several days in order to age the meat, is nothing more than a misnomer. Hanging a deer outside without specifically controlled temperatures does nothing more than begin the rotten process. True aging of meat only occurs in a controlled environment of 38-42 degrees for several days. Therefore, you can guarantee yourself better tasting venison by quickly butchering your deer within 24-48 hours after removing the hide.

Improper butchering accounts a majority of foul tasting venison. To have better tasting venison, butcher the carcass with equipment that you can clean and wipe off the tallow, grizzle, blood, etc. frequently while butchering. Butcher on a non-porous butcher block which should be wiped down and cleaned several times. Next, and equally important, is to remove all the fat, sinew, and silver skin. This is crucial to good tasting venison. The last step to guarantee better tasting venison is to properly wrap each piece in plastic wrap, butcher paper and finally put into a zip lock bag with the air removed to prevent freezer burn - a major cause of poor tasting venison. By following these tips, I absolutely guarantee you will provide yourself with much better tasting venison that you have had before.

RACK OF VENISON WITH SWEET POTATO CASSEROLE
Prep time: 45 minutes
Cook time: about one hour

2 each	rack of venison ribs with about 8 ribs each
4 c.	white bread, cut into cubes
2 c.	heavy cream
4 Tbsp.	Dijon mustard
2 Tbsp.	Parsley, chopped
2 Tbsp.	chives, chopped
4 cloves	garlic, chopped
t. t.	salt & pepper

Preheat the oven to 350 degrees. Trim the top of the ribs free from meat where there is little meat. Also remove all the fat from the ribs as well. To protect the end of the ribs from burning, cover them with foil. Remember to remove the foil before serving. With a food processor, blend the cubes, cream, mustard, parsley, chives, garlic and salt & pepper until it is soft and can be patted onto the ribs. It should not be runny. Coat the ribs with the mixture. Do not cover the rib bones. Place the ribs into a baking dish and bake for about 30 to 40 minutes.

Because venison is such lean meat, it is important to remember that the coating must cover the meat side of the ribs to ensure that the heat does not dry out the meat. The coating will also impart a delicious seasoning to the meat as well.

Cut the ribs into portions and serve with pan gravy, sweet potato casserole, and green peas and pearl onions.

SWEET POTATO CASSEROLE

Prep time: 15 minutes
Cook time: 30 minutes
serves: 6

6 ea.	medium size cooked sweet potatoes
2 c.	thinly sliced apples, boiled for about 2 min.
3/4 c.	light brown sugar
t.t.	cinnamon
1/4 c	butter
1/2 c.	water

Preheat oven to 350 degrees. Butter the bottom and sides of a baking dish and alternate layers of potatoes and apples. In between each layer sprinkle brown sugar and cinnamon. Dot the top with butter and pour the water over the top as well. Cover and bake for 30 minutes. Serve warm.

VENISON AND BROCCOLI STIR FRY

Prep Time: 20 minutes
Cooking Time: 10 minutes
Serves Six: (or four very hungry hunters)

1/4 to 1/2 lb. venison (rump or loin meat preferably)
1/4 t. pepper
3 T. soy sauce
1 c. peanut or vegetable oil
1/2 c. beef broth or bouillon
1/2 lb. fresh broccoli in small flowerettes
1/2 c. thinly sliced celery
1/2 c. chives cut into 1-inch slices
1/4 c. thinly sliced waterchestnuts

259

Cut the venison into the thinnest strips possible. Be sure to cut across the grain -- otherwise the venison will be chewy. marinate the meat in 1 T. soy sauce, pepper to taste and 2 t. of oil.

Heat the remaining oil in a large skillet pr wok until it's warm. If the oil is too hot, the meat will clump together. drain and cook the venison for one minute. Remove the meat with a slotted spoon and set aside on a paper towel. Remove all but 2 T. of the oil and turn up the heat to medium-high until the oil almost smokes. Then add 1 t. soy sauce, the beef broth and broccoli and cook for about three minutes. Add the celery, chives, waterchestnuts and venison. Cook for about two minutes. Serve hot over a bed of wild or white rice. For a different flair, top the dish with minced raw onion, dried chinese noodles, and a tall glass of Oriental beer.

VENISON KABOBS

Cut the venison into 1-inch cubes. It is important to keep the size of the cubes as uniform as possible for even cooking. Trim off as much connective tissue and fat as possible. Mix together the marinade ingredients and pour over the venison cubes in a bowl. Gently toss the cubes so as to completely cover each cube with the marinade. Place the marinated venison in the refrigerator either overnight or, if you prepare the meat before heading to work, for the day. Cut the peppers and onions into 1-inch squares. Start with the mushrooms on the skewer, then alternate between peppers, onions and venison. End with a cherry tomato. While grilling the kabobs, baste them with the marinade. Turn the kabobs over once when they are half done. Serve with rice pilaf and freshly baked baguettes or fresh sesame bread sticks.

Prep time: 8 hours marinating
1/2 hour vegetable prep
Serves: 4

2 lbs.   Venison (one-inch cubes)

Marinade Ingredients
1 1/2 c.   Olive Oil
1/2 c.   Red Wine Vinegar
1/4 tsp.   Oregano

2 tbsp.	Parsley, chopped
4 cloves	Garlic, minced
t.t.	Salt and pepper

Kabob Ingredients

24	Whole large mushrooms
2	White or red onions
2	Green peppers
2	Yellow peppers
2	Red peppers
2	Cherry tomatoes

VENISON OMELETTE DELIGHT

Prep Time: 20 minutes
Cook Time: 20 minutes
Serves: four

1/2 c.	Olive oil
1 c.	Thinly sliced mushrooms
2 c.	thin, short strips of venison
12	scallions (green onions), chopped
2	minced slices of ginger root
2	celery, thinly sliced
2 c.	bean sprouts (drained)
12	eggs, well, beaten

Heat one tablespoon of oil in a skillet and saute the mushrooms until they are clear. Wipe out the skillet, heat 1 tbsp. oil over medium high heat and stir fry the venison strips (lightly seasoned with salt and pepper). Remove from heat and set aside.

Wipe the pan and add 2 to 3 tbsp. oil and stir-fry the scallions, ginger-root and celery until they are clear and crisp. Remove from heat and combine with mushrooms, venison and eggs. Heat 1 tbsp. oil and drop in the mixture to make small omelettes, golden brown on both sides. Additional side dishes can include soy sauce, chinese noodles and hot, steamed white rice. For those who enjoy spicy meals, Tabasco and hot chinese mustard will also go well with this meal.

CHRISTMAS VENISON ROAST WITH BABY MUSHROOMS

Prep time: 40 minutes
Cooking time: 1 hour
Serves: 6 to 8

4-5 lb.	Venison Roast
1	Lemon
3/4 lb.	fresh spinach (washed with stems removed)
1/4 lb.	Fresh baby mushrooms (washed)
1/2 lb.	swiss cheese, grated
5 strips	bacon, cooked & crumbled
t.t.	Salt and pepper
1/2 c.	shallots, minced
1 qt.	brown sauce
1 1/2 c.	red wine
1/4 lb.	butter

First prepare the stuffing. In a large sauce pan, heat about 3/4 stick of butter over medium heat. Add 1/4 c. shallots. When they become clear, add the spinach and mushrooms and cook for about 3 minutes. Add the grated cheese, season to taste and constantly stir for about 2 minutes. All ingredients should be thoroughly mixed. Place the stuffing in the refrigerator to cool.

Preheat the oven to 350 degrees. The best way to maintain an even thickness of the meat is to butterfly the roast. Once it is laid out, season the meat with salt, pepper and lemon juice. Place the stuffing on the venison, toll and tie. Melt 1/2-stick butter in a saute pan over medium-high heat. Please the roast in the saute pan to quickly brown all four sides. Remove it from the saute pan and place it in a roasting dish. Roast it in the oven for about 1 to 1 1/4 hours. The ideal method to check if the roast is done is by using a meat thermometer. It should read between 125 to 130 degrees.

Once the roast is done, remove it from the oven and prepare the sauce. In a saucepan, heat 1/4 stick of butter and remaining shallots. Cook for about 2 minutes and then add red wine and brown sauce. Stir and simmer for about 15 minutes. Season to taste. Pass the sauce through a strainer before serving.

COWBOY STYLE VENISON STEAK

Prep time: 10 minutes
Cook time: 5 minutes
Serves: Four

6 ea.	1-inch thick cut steaks with all the fat trimmed
6 ea.	large red onions, peeled and sliced 1/4" thick
3/4 c.	melted butter (clarified butter is better)
2 tsp.	chopped fresh thyme
t.t.	salt and pepper
3/4 c.	barbecue sauce

Heat the grill to a medium-high setting. Please the onions on a baking sheet. Pour butter over the onions and then sprinkle with thyme and salt and pepper. Cook under a broiler very slowly for about 20 minutes. Baste them with butter every 5 minutes or so. If you use clarified butter, it will not burn as easily as regular melted butter. The onions are done when they are golden brown. Season the steaks with salt and pepper and place on the grill until they are medium rare - about 3 to 4 minutes on each side. Do not overcook, since they will become tough and chewy. Serve immediately with the onions on top of the steaks and on the side. Pour a bit of barbecue sauce over the onions on top of the steaks. This is a tasty meal that can be served with a fresh Caesar salad, garlic bread and a cool, red wine, a Zinfandel or a big, lush Pinot Noir.

Photo Credits

All photos are by the author except for those credited below.

Ted Rose - 2, 14, 21, 22, 37, 42, 56, 71, 72, 92, 103, 105, 109, 110, 124, 162, 228, 238, 239, 240, 241, 242, 244, 245.

Pete Rickard, Inc. - 54, 114, 115, 120, 121, 189

FeatherFlex - 201, 203

Leonard Rue - 197

Primos - 54

Corcoran Shoe Co. - 63

E.L.K. - 180

Gail Sampson - 61

Chris Ramirez - 152, 156

Laura Clinton - 138

To ask Peter Fiduccia any deer hunting questions, you can email him at **peter@fiduccia.com** or visit his web site **www.deerdoctor.com.**

For a free newsletter from *Going Wild in Kate's Kitchen* or to get a free monthly wild game recipe, visit **www.cookinginkateskitchen.com.**